Rethinking the MBA

Rethinking the MBA

Business Education at a Crossroads

Srikant M. Datar
David A. Garvin
Patrick G. Cullen

Harvard Business Press
Boston, Massachusetts

ISBN: 978-1-4221-3164-0

Library-of-Congress cataloging information forthcoming

The paper used in this publication meets the requirements of the American National
Standard for Permanence of Paper for Publications and Documents in Libraries and
Archives Z39.48-1992.

To Swati, Lynn, Marion, and Shayda

Contents

Acknowledgments

We benefited from the support and assistance of a large number of people in developing and writing this book and would like to take this opportunity to offer our thanks.

Our first debt is to the many deans, faculty, administrators, executives, and students who kindly consented to interviews, provided us with data, sponsored our case studies, and otherwise helped us generate the raw material that lies at the heart of our analysis. This book simply would not have been possible without their assistance and goodwill, and we are deeply grateful for the time, thoughtfulness, and attention that they devoted to our never-ending questions and requests.

We are also grateful to our Harvard Business School colleagues, who contributed in a multitude of ways. John Quelch and Robert Kaplan launched us on the project by suggesting the idea of a colloquium on the future of MBA education, convincing us to assume the assignment, and then helping us to design a format and approach. Our dean, Jay Light, was an enthusiastic champion; he graciously provided the resources necessary for the project, as well as unwavering support during the three years that we were hard at work. Over one hundred of our faculty participated in the colloquium we held in May 2008 to discuss our preliminary findings. Many also took the extra time to offer, in writing, a rich set of suggestions for possible curriculum changes. A number of our colleagues also provided extremely helpful feedback during informal discussions, lunches, and hallway conversations.

Our research team was absolutely outstanding. Michael Thomas was responsible for assembling the aggregate statistics and trend data of chapter 2, Patricia Hernandez was responsible for the curriculum analysis of chapter 3, and Carin Knoop and James Weber wrote all of the original case studies that appear, in modified form, as chapters 7 through 12. We met often with the members of this group, both individually and collectively, and were repeatedly impressed by their creativity, scholarly standards, and dedication to the project. They not only contributed much of the data and supporting analysis that underlie our arguments, but also helped us develop several key ideas.

During the process of writing, we had many helpers as well. Colleen Kaftan carefully and sensitively edited the original case studies so that they fit seamlessly into part II of the book. Jeff Kehoe, our editor at Harvard Business Press, provided wise counsel throughout the writing process, steering us toward stronger, more compelling arguments and story lines. The four anonymous reviewers of the draft manuscript provided us with thought-provoking suggestions, criticisms, and questions that significantly improved the final version.

Our assistants, Alexandra Gural and Andrea Truax, kept us on course from beginning to end. They made appointments, managed our increasingly complex calendars, coordinated interviews and group meetings, kept us on task, and helped us produce the polished, final version of the manuscript. Without their guidance and gentle direction, we would never have completed this project.

As is customary, we save our deepest thanks for our families. Srikant thanks his wife, Swati; David thanks his wife, Lynn; and Patrick thanks his mother, Marion, and his partner, Shayda. All four provided us with continual support—much needed during a three-year project—as well as countless suggestions and ideas. They were invaluable sounding boards, as well as thoughtful critics. Most important, they kept us grounded during the long process of developing and writing this book by helping us maintain a healthy perspective. Many times their love and encouragement kept us going. For these reasons, we dedicate this book to them.

Introduction

A Degree in Transition

I N 2008, Harvard Business School (HBS) celebrated its 100th anniversary. It was an occasion for celebrating past achievements, but also an opportunity to reflect on the challenges facing all business schools in a rapidly changing environment. MBA programs, in particular, were the subject of growing scrutiny as they wrestled with questions of how to prepare students for increasingly complex organizations and careers. These new demands would require MBA programs to take a broader view of their graduates' responsibilities to multiple stakeholders, and to provide their students with a deeper understanding of such phenomena as globalization, leadership, and innovation, as well as the ability to think critically, decide wisely, communicate clearly, and implement effectively.

In this context of escalating demands on MBA programs, we began our research for a colloquium on the future of MBA education. Our efforts started modestly. Initially, our focus was internal, with the spotlight on our own institution and its strengths and weaknesses. As our dean, Jay Light, wryly put it, "It was our view that you need to think critically about what you are doing every 100 years or so, whether you need to or not."[1] Our research objective was to generate sufficient raw material for a two-day event that would allow our faculty to reflect on the school's history and consider its positioning for the future. But that effort quickly expanded as we began to gather data on industry trends and spoke with deans and faculty at other schools. "Thank goodness you're doing this," they said. "All of us need to take a hard look at where business education is headed."

With that prompting, we broadened our scope. We realized that the timing was auspicious, and that many in the larger business school community were ready for a deeper, collective reflection on our enterprise. The seminal reports on business education by the Carnegie Corporation and the Ford Foundation were at that time nearly fifty years old, having been published in 1959; Porter and McKibbin's comprehensive follow-on study, published in 1988, was dated as well.[2] In the meantime, public criticism of graduate business education had sharply escalated, as had calls for reform. A number of schools had already responded vigorously, launching significant, highly publicized changes in their MBA programs. Major reviews were under way at countless other institutions.

We therefore began collecting data with a larger goal in mind: documenting both the forces reshaping business education and schools' responses to them, in order to prompt a dialogue about the future of the MBA degree. The time and resources available to us forced us to focus our efforts on a subset of schools. For the most part, we studied leading MBA programs in the United States and Europe, supplemented by information on a small number of business schools in Asia and Latin America and a few non–business school institutions teaching management and leadership. We focused on leading schools because changes at top-ranked institutions are frequently indicative of broader trends. In fact, when we shared our findings with administrators and faculty from a wide range of MBA programs across the globe, they strongly affirmed our observations and recommendations. Some had already begun implementing the changes we describe. Nevertheless, an important caveat to this study is that our conclusions about rethinking the MBA are based in large part on data from, and events and changes at, the subset of institutions that we examined.

In the process of completing our project, we received an unprecedented level of cooperation from deans, faculty, administrators, students, executives, oversight councils, and accrediting organizations—in short, from virtually every group involved in and concerned about the future of MBA education. On March 6 and 7, 2008, we convened a collection of deans, faculty, and executives at Harvard Business School to discuss our preliminary findings. It was a sobering meeting, and one that prompted considerable debate about the long-term health of the enterprise. On May 16 and 17, 2008, we held a similar two-day meeting with our own faculty, who responded with equally lively debates.

It is in the spirit of those debates that we decided to write this book. Our goal is to prompt the same degree of reflection and discussion that we encountered at our two colloquia, while also pointing the way forward. Prospective readers, however, may well ask, "Why do we need *another* look at the future of business education?" There has, after all, been an outpouring of articles and books on the subject in recent years, and many of them have been deeply thoughtful. Most studies have questioned the relevance, value, and purpose of the MBA degree; a few have proposed dramatic changes. We have found these studies to be invaluable, and they inform our views and are referenced throughout our book. But we also found them lacking in important respects. Most have been either sweeping critiques or historical reviews, with limited data on current programs and limited sampling of the perspectives and needs of diverse constituencies. For the most part, they have been critiques from within—by academics, for academics—often at the level of philosophy and first principles.

Our approach is different. It is heavily empirical and relies on several unique sources of primary data. First, we conducted extensive interviews with business school deans and business executives. We interviewed thirty deans, primarily from highly ranked business schools in the United States and Europe. All interviews lasted at least an hour, and many were considerably longer. We also spoke informally with many other deans and associate deans from business schools across the globe. We interviewed an equal number of current or former business executives, largely senior members of their organizations with some responsibility for or familiarity with MBA recruiting. They were selected from four broad sectors to reflect a diversity of views: financial services, consulting, multinational corporations, and high technology. In all cases, we used detailed semistructured interviews, aimed broadly at identifying respondents' perceptions of the value added by the MBA degree as well as current weaknesses, deficiencies, or unmet needs. We also probed for their assessments of the reforms already under way at different schools. In addition, we benefited from informal discussions with several hundred executives, both individually and in groups.

Second, we collected detailed industry data in search of unnoticed or emerging trends in graduate business education.[3] Here, we focused on changes over the last decade in applications, enrollments, tuition and fees, faculty hiring, and other critical variables, often broken out by school rankings. We received extraordinary assistance in this process from the Association to Advance Collegiate Schools of Business International (AACSB), the Graduate Management Admissions Council (GMAC), and the Graduate Business Administrators Group (GBAG), who aided us in assembling, compiling, and interpreting the critical data.

Third, we developed composite portraits of the curricula at eleven leading MBA programs. We selected these programs as representative of a broad cross section of MBA program content, architecture, and pedagogy. The data, which were assembled from school Web sites and publications and then validated through conversations and correspondence with school administrators, faculty, and deans, present a fine-grained picture of the offerings of each school. They help us answer a question that has arisen repeatedly over time: Just how similar or different are business school programs? Most analyses to date have focused on only a small subset of variables, such as the number and type of required courses; our data, by contrast, range from the macro to the micro, covering the overall architecture of programs and structure of curricula, the sequence and range of first- and second-year required and elective course offerings, pedagogical approaches, and the content and topics featured in individual courses.

Fourth, we identified a range of exemplary course offerings that were responsive to the opportunities and needs cited by deans and executives. These courses were all innovative in some respect. Several featured novel subject matter, others employed nontraditional pedagogies, and still others introduced radically new ways of looking at long-established subjects. In each case, we examined the course syllabi and then spoke directly with teaching faculty to understand precisely how the courses were designed and delivered. The resulting portraits are highly granular and can be viewed as templates for others to follow.

Finally, we developed six case studies that capture, in sharp relief, the themes we uncovered in our interviews. Each case features a single institution—the University of Chicago Booth School of Business, INSEAD, the Center for Creative Leadership, Harvard Business School, Yale School of Management, and Stanford Graduate School of Business—and each shows, in a distinctive and well-developed form, how a leading MBA or executive program has responded to one or more of the distinctive forces affecting the industry as a whole. INSEAD, for example, shows an institution responding to the demand for students with a more global perspective, whereas Yale shows a program in full-fledged pursuit of integration and a multidisciplinary perspective. Each case also illustrates the accompanying process of change or development that the institution followed as it altered its curriculum and responded to new pressures and needs. In writing these cases, we had the full cooperation of deans, administrators, and faculty. In every case, we made site visits and conducted extensive interviews, including focus groups with students to ensure that their voices were heard and their experiences accurately represented.

Together, these data present an unusually detailed picture of the current state of MBA education. Although our focus is on top-ranked institutions, we believe that they are bellwethers for the industry and are representative of larger trends. The data show an industry facing important challenges and institutions wrestling with basic questions of purpose, positioning, and program design. They also show an industry that has already begun the slow, painful process of adopting new approaches in order to maintain its relevance in a rapidly changing business environment. However, they come with an important caveat. All of our initial data were collected before the global economic crisis. How, if at all, does the crisis change our findings and conclusions? To find out, in the spring of 2009 we reinterviewed several deans, updated our six case studies, spoke with numerous executives, alumni, faculty members, and students, and collected additional post-crisis data. Our goal was to understand what business leaders might learn from the crisis, how business might change in its wake, and how our conclusions about the future of MBA education might have to be altered or modified to accord with the new reality.

On the one hand, the economic downturn has provided some schools with a temporary respite from the forces buffeting graduate business education. Because MBA programs are often viewed by young people, especially those with few other career options, as a safe harbor for weathering economic storms, business school applications have historically been countercyclical. This crisis is no exception. In its aftermath, applications at the higher-ranked schools rose, although typically in a far more muted fashion than during past recessions, as did the number of takers of the Graduate Management Admissions Test, a likely indicator of future increases in applicants.[4] Midranked schools, meanwhile, have been busy promoting their superior job placements with regional employers and their specializations in energy, brand management, supply chain management, and human resources as ways of beefing up their applicant pools and class sizes.[5] These advantages, we believe, albeit real and possibly significant in the short run, are likely to be temporary because most of the other forces unleashed by the economic crisis add to the already long list of concerns and unmet needs cited repeatedly by critics, the trends already under way, and the curricular changes that have been steadily gathering momentum.

Consider, for example, one of the long-standing selling points of leading business schools—the access they provide to lucrative, highly selective careers. As chapter 2 notes, students have long gone to business schools to gain entry to high-paying jobs in investment banking, private equity, and hedge funds. Even before the crisis, our interviewees reported, companies in these fields were starting to shift their hiring away from MBAs. As a result of the economic meltdown, access to these fields has dropped even more dramatically. Many jobs have simply disappeared. According to one estimate, in the eighteen-month period ending December 2008, 240,000 people were laid off on Wall Street.[6] Compensation has fallen as well; in some cases, it is now capped by law. To respond to this shrinkage in the financial sector, business schools will have to alter their orientations and direction. They will have to attract a new set of recruiters, develop graduates with a different set of skills, and offer a different mix of courses. All are likely to lead to adjustments in business school curricula much like those described in chapters 5 and 6 of this book.

Meanwhile, part-time and executive MBA programs, which fueled much of the growth in business school enrollments in recent years, are currently facing increasing pressure. For many students in these programs, the economic proposition looks less attractive as corporations reduce their support. Business schools are finding that this growth engine—which chapter 2 notes has sustained many programs, especially those in the middle tier, for much of the last decade—is beginning to sputter.[7] To attract and retain students, business schools will need to consider changes in curricula that enhance the value of MBA training in ways that are responsive to the criticisms and concerns described in chapter 4.

Increasingly, we believe, business schools are at a crossroads and will have to take a hard look at their value propositions. This was true before the economic crisis, but is even truer in its aftermath. The world has changed, and with it the security that used to come almost automatically with an MBA degree. As a recent report observed, "On the nation's B-school campuses, hope used to spring eternal. No more."[8] High-paying jobs are no longer guaranteed to graduates, and the opportunity costs of two years of training—especially for those who still hold jobs and are not looking to change fields—loom ever larger. To remain relevant, business schools will have to rethink many of their most cherished assumptions. They will have to reexamine their curricula and move in new directions.

The core of our conclusion is that business schools need to do two things if they are to develop effective leaders and entrepreneurs, as opposed to individuals trained primarily in analysis: reassess the facts, frameworks, and theories that they teach (the "knowing" component), while at the same time rebalancing their curricula so that more attention is paid to developing the skills, capabilities, and techniques that lie at the heart of the practice of management (the "doing" component) and the values, attitudes, and beliefs that form managers' worldviews and professional identities (the "being" component). We believe that shifts in MBA enrollments, changes in recruiting patterns, and a rising chorus of concerns from deans, faculty, executives, students, and the public at large make this rebalancing necessary.

In the years since the Ford Foundation and Carnegie Corporation reports, business schools have introduced greater rigor and disciplinary thinking into their programs. Although this has been a welcome improvement, it came at a cost. Business schools often failed to emphasize the limitations of the theories they taught, the extent of the challenges and complexities of applying these theories in practice, the associated skills and attitudes required for thoughtful, effective application, and the critical lenses and judgment needed to evaluate specific contexts accurately and draw correct conclusions. Rebalancing MBA education toward doing and being aims to reduce the impediments to informed action that result from these deficiencies in skills, attitudes, and beliefs.

Innovative thinking provides an example. "Knowing" about brainstorming, experimentation, and other creativity techniques does not prepare MBA students to "do" innovative thinking in the workplace. The latter requires sustained practice with, and immersion in, innovation processes—how to obtain customer insights, how to stimulate out-of-the-box thinking, and how to test and craft creative solutions. Similarly, "being" skills are important to managers as they work with and through others to achieve their organizations' goals. To inspire and influence others over sustained periods requires careful reflection and introspection about one's strengths and weaknesses, values and attitudes, and the impact of one's actions on others. Without "doing" skills, knowledge is of little value. Without "being" skills, it is often hard to act ethically or professionally.

Looking across MBA programs, we identify eight unmet needs, many of them related to doing and being. Each presents an opportunity for MBA programs to innovate and change. These needs are as follows:

- *Gaining a global perspective:* Identifying, analyzing, and practicing how best to manage when faced with economic, institutional, and cultural differences across countries

- *Developing leadership skills:* Understanding the responsibilities of leadership; developing alternative approaches to inspiring, influencing, and guiding others; learning such skills as conducting a performance review and giving critical feedback; and recognizing the impact of one's actions and behaviors on others

- *Honing integration skills:* Thinking about issues from diverse, shifting angles to frame problems holistically; learning to make decisions based on multiple, often conflicting, functional perspectives; and building judgment and intuition into messy, unstructured situations

- *Recognizing organizational realities and implementing effectively:* Influencing others and getting things done in the context of hidden agendas, unwritten rules, political coalitions, and competing points of view

- *Acting creatively and innovatively:* Finding and framing problems; collecting, synthesizing, and distilling large volumes of ambiguous data; engaging in generative and lateral thinking; and constantly experimenting and learning

- *Thinking critically and communicating clearly:* Developing and articulating logical, coherent, and persuasive arguments; marshalling supporting evidence; and distinguishing fact from opinion

- *Understanding the role, responsibilities, and purpose of business:* Balancing financial and nonfinancial objectives while simultaneously juggling the demands of diverse constituencies such as shareholders, employees, customers, regulators, and society

- *Understanding the limits of models and markets:* Asking tough questions about risk by questioning underlying assumptions and emerging patterns; seeking to understand what might go wrong; learning about the sources of errors that lead to flawed decision making and the organizational safeguards that reduce their occurrence; and understanding the tension between regulatory activities aimed at preventing social harm and market-based incentives designed to encourage innovation and efficiency

To make progress in these areas, business schools will need to continue to experiment with, and commit more broadly to, new pedagogies. Many of these techniques involve hands-on exercises and experiential learning. Some schools are using reflective exercises, supported by individual coaches, to develop leadership skills and build a sense of purpose and identity. Other schools are teaching innovative, integrative, or critical thinking in small groups. Field experiences and action-learning pedagogies are helping students gain a global perspective, learn about the challenges of implementation, and see the gaps and difficulties of applying knowledge to practice.

Pursuing these opportunities is not without challenges. They range from securing faculty with skills that span theory and application to broadening the research methods and research domains of business school scholars to addressing the higher costs of curricula that rely heavily on small-group experiences and action learning. Although these challenges are significant, we believe that they are not insurmountable, and offer a number of suggestions for how they might best be overcome by individual and collective action.

That, in brief, is the premise of *Rethinking the MBA*. To make our argument, we have divided the book into two parts. Part I describes the larger environment in which business schools operate today. This section of the book is thematic and synthetic, focused on the broad forces reshaping institutions and their behavior. Among the topics we address are the shifts in supply and demand that are redefining the MBA marketplace, the current portfolio of programs and course offerings, the criticisms and concerns raised repeatedly by both insiders and outsiders, and the curriculum innovations and programmatic changes that have begun to emerge in response. Part II addresses many of these same issues, but in a more granular, particularized form. That section of the book contains our six case studies, each one a portrait of an individual institution that has adapted in a particularly powerful or exemplary way to the forces we describe in the first part of the book. The case studies show that programs facing a similar set of pressures have chosen different directions and paths, tailoring their approaches to their own distinctive traditions and values. We conclude the book with a chapter that draws larger lessons and presents a set of prescriptions and proposals for graduate business education based on our own interpretations of the trends and changes we have observed.

Ultimately, this is a hopeful, positive story. Business schools have long been flexible, resilient institutions, and we believe that they are already demonstrating their capacity to respond to today's challenges.

The global economic crisis has intensified the pressure to change, even as the resulting shortage of resources has made change more difficult. Despite these difficulties—or perhaps, more accurately, because of them—we believe that business schools have already begun to reassert their relevance.

Part One

The State of MBA Education

To understand the challenges facing graduate business education, one must first understand the underlying forces of supply and demand. The MBA degree may be a highly distinctive product, but it is not immune to the forces of the marketplace. Part I examines these forces at both the macro and micro level. In the process, it provides a comprehensive, fine-grained portrait of the changes buffeting MBA programs today.

Chapter 2 begins by taking a high-level "view from the balcony." It focuses on three broad trends reshaping graduate business education: (1) the move away from two-year, full-time, in-resident programs and the associated shift toward a more diverse set of offerings, including one-year MBAs, part-time MBAs, executive MBAs, and a host of specialized master's degrees; (2) the increased questioning by employers of the value added by the MBA degree; and (3) the resulting bypassing of the degree by both students and employers, with undergraduates increasingly hired directly by firms, promoted internally, and then staying on the job rather than leaving for an MBA because of the traction they have already gained in their careers. In combination, these forces have led to a hollowing out of the MBA marketplace. Chapter 2 presents data showing substantial declines in the number of students attending two-year, full-time MBA programs at midranked schools.

Chapter 3 puts business school curricula under the microscope. It presents a detailed examination of the MBA programs at eleven leading business schools. Unlike most previous studies, it is both broad and deep, with comparisons of programs on four dimensions: content, pedagogy, architecture, and purpose. Whereas previous studies have concluded that MBA programs are very much alike, our findings convey more of a mixed picture, with considerable commonality in basic, required core courses but striking differences in program structure, the portfolio of course offerings, the flexibility afforded students, and overarching purpose and emphasis. These differences, chapter 3 notes, lead to markedly different student experiences and allow schools to claim that their programs are varied and differentiated. However, most of the differences fail to address the most common criticisms of MBA programs—that they are overly analytical, do not fully address important business needs, and underemphasize essential topics and skills.

Chapter 4 examines these criticisms in detail, while also noting a set of opportunities and unmet needs. It does so by drawing on two sources: published critiques of MBA programs, written largely by academics, and our own interviews with deans and executives. The chapter begins with a brief historical overview, tracing the creation and rise of MBA programs, their delicate positioning within universities, the sharp critiques by the Ford Foundation and Carnegie Corporation, the subsequent changes in content and focus that made programs more scholarly and rigorous, and the rising chorus of concerns that has come in the wake of these changes. Among them are declining student engagement and an overly analytical curriculum. The chapter then describes eight broad needs for the future identified by our interviewees: (1) a global perspective, (2) leadership development, (3) integration, (4) an understanding of organizational realities, (5) creativity and innovative thinking, (6) oral and written communication, (7) the role and purpose of business, and (8) understanding the limits of markets and models. Each was identified by both deans and executives as a topic essential to effective business leadership that was not sufficiently well taught by graduate business programs today. These needs are not all new; several have been identified in past studies. Our contribution lies in the level of detail, nuance, and fleshing out of the required changes, and in the rich supporting quotations and examples provided by our interviewees. Chapter 4 provides a focused set of suggestions for improving business education, often in the voices of those most intimately involved in educating and hiring today's business school graduates.

Chapters 5 and 6 present a range of programmatic and curricular responses to the needs identified in chapter 4, with supporting details provided in the case studies of part II. The two chapters are distinguished by both subject matter and level of analysis. Chapter 5 describes how business schools have tackled the challenges of a global perspective, leadership development and ethics, and integration, whereas chapter 6 describes how schools have responded to the challenges of understanding organizational realities, fostering creative thinking, strengthening oral and written communication, contemplating the role and purpose of business, and understanding the limits of markets and models. In general, schools have been far more responsive to the first three needs. As a result, a range of alternative responses already exists; some approaches are relatively simple and easy to implement, others are more complex and demanding, and still others require deep and sustained levels of commitment and expense. For each need, chapter 5 describes the costs and benefits of the full spectrum of approaches and presents illustrative examples from several MBA programs.

The responses described in chapter 6, by contrast, are less widely established. In many cases, schools are still feeling their way. Experiential learning, for example, is frequently viewed as the best way of teaching students about organizational realities, but few schools have fully mastered this approach. Efforts in the area are still evolving; most remain works in progress. Schools are similarly wrestling with how best to teach creative thinking, oral and written communication, the role and purpose of business, and understanding the limits of markets and models. Frequently, the most effective responses we were able to identify were singular efforts—individual courses or projects—rather than integrated, programmatic offerings. For this reason, chapter 6 describes in detail a small number of cutting-edge courses in each area of need, rather than presenting a range of possible responses. Each example is intended to serve as a stimulus for fresh thinking rather than as the one best way forward, in hopes that schools will improvise and expand on these approaches to develop distinctive solutions of their own.

The Changing
MBA Marketplace

A T FIRST GLANCE, the marketplace for graduate management training looks strikingly healthy. Applications and enrollments continue to rise, tuition and fees continue their steady march upward, and the number of programs continues to expand. At the same time, however, there are a number of disturbing signs suggesting that the MBA degree—especially in its traditional full-time, two-year form—is at a crossroads.

The Golden Passport

First, the good news. For many years, a wide range of indicators have been positive. In the United States, graduate management training has long been regarded as a "golden passport" for many jobs, the ticket of entry to prestigious, high-profile positions. Whether the job is CEO of a large, multinational corporation, head of a high-tech venture capital fund, or a powerful government job such as secretary of the Treasury or mayor of New York City, the MBA has frequently been the degree of choice. In fields such as investment banking and strategy consulting, it has long been virtually a requirement for entry, the primary means of gaining admission to an otherwise inaccessible field. Applications and enrollments have followed suit. In the United States, the number of students receiving one of the many different types of master's degrees in business grew more than sixfold in the last three decades, rising steadily from 21,561 in 1969–1970 to 150,211 in 2006–2007.[1]

Moreover, interest in these degrees has become increasingly global, especially in rising nations such as India and China. Seventy-four new graduate management programs were introduced worldwide in 1997. A decade later, 641 new graduate management programs were introduced in the first half of the year alone. Of these, 113 were North American, and the other 528—over 80 percent of the total—were international.[2] Although it is difficult to get precise numbers on the enrollment of international students in American graduate management programs today, there is no question that demand has been on the rise. The percentage of international students who took the Graduate Management Admissions Test (GMAT) and sent their scores to top U.S. business schools—a reasonable proxy for demand, because there is no evidence suggesting that students have increased the number of schools to which they apply—rose dramatically in recent years. In 1998, 24 percent of GMAT score senders were international; of that total, 5 percent were from India and 5 percent from China. By 2007, 42 percent of GMAT score senders had become international, with 21 percent from India and 8 percent from China (figure 2-1). In 2009, however, in part because of the financial crisis and difficulties in obtaining student loans and in part because of an increase in high-quality MBA programs in other countries, the number of international students enrolled in U.S. MBA programs declined for the first time in several years.[3] Time will tell whether this is a one-year deviation or the beginning of a long-term secular decline.

Tuition and fees have risen commensurately. Mean total costs (tuition and fees) at top U.S. MBA programs nearly doubled from 2000 to 2006 for public school in-state residents and rose approximately 75 percent for out-of-state attendees. During the same period and starting from a much higher base, mean total costs at private or independent schools rose approximately 50 percent (figure 2-2). Although the effective price is usually lower because of grants and financial aid, these figures do suggest a thriving enterprise facing an expanding market and steady increases in demand.

FIGURE 2-1

Country of citizenship of GMAT takers sending scores to top U.S. MBA schools

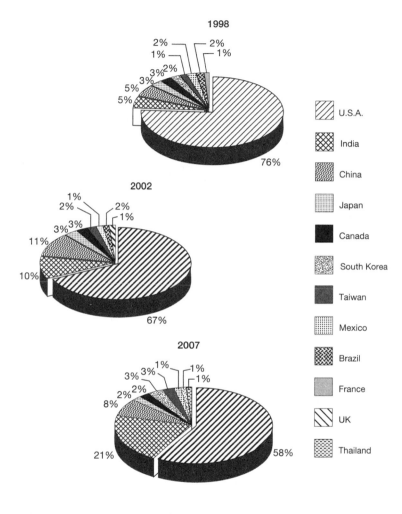

Source: Graduate Management Admissions Council.

The Rise of Substitutes

The figures, however, mask significant changes that lie just below the surface. In particular, the traditional MBA degree—two years of full-time, in-residence training—is losing its place as the dominant model

FIGURE 2-2

Mean total student tuition and fees at the top twenty U.S. MBA schools: 2000 to 2006

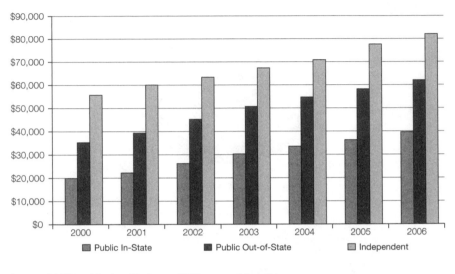

Source: AACSB and *BusinessWeek* annual MBA program information.

of graduate business education. Twenty years ago, if one spoke of "graduate training in business," one was speaking almost by definition of the two-year MBA degree. Yet today, substitutes abound. They include one-year MBA programs, one-year specialized master's programs, part-time MBA programs, executive MBA programs, online MBA programs, and corporate training and development programs. (The appendix to this chapter provides a list of the wide range of master's degrees offered by a sample of leading U.S. business schools.) The traditional two-year program now accounts for only 40 percent of the MBA degrees conferred by AACSB-accredited business schools.[4]

In Europe, the one-year MBA degree has already become the dominant form of MBA training.[5] As table 2-1 indicates, of the 31 leading European business schools ranked among the top 100 schools globally in surveys by the *Financial Times* and the *Economist*'s Intelligence Unit, over two-thirds—22 schools—offer degrees in twelve months. Four programs are even shorter. Only IESE and London Business School

TABLE 2-1

European MBA Programs

1. Audencia Nantes School of Management (France): 12 months
2. Bradford School of Management (UK)/TiasNimbas (Netherlands)/Tilburg University (Germany): 12 months
3. Cass Business School, City University (UK): 12 months
4. Cranfield School of Management (UK): 12 months
5. Escuela de Alta Dirección y Administración (EADA) (Spain): 11 months
6. Esade Business School (Spain): 12, 15, or 18 months
7. EM Lyon Business School (France): 12 months
8. HEC School of Management (France): 16 months
9. IESE Business School, University of Navarra (Spain): 21 months
10. IMD (Switzerland): 11 months
11. Imperial College Business School (UK): 12 months
12. INSEAD (France and Singapore): 10 months
13. Instituto de Empresa (IE) Business School (Spain): 13 months
14. International University of Monaco (Monaco): 10 months
15. Judge Business School, University of Cambridge (UK): 12 months
16. Lancaster University Management School (UK): 12 months
17. Leeds University Business School (UK): 12 months
18. London Business School (UK): 15–21 months
19. Manchester Business School (UK): 18 months
20. Mannheim Business School (Germany): 12 months
21. Nottingham University Business School (UK): 12 months
22. Nyenrode Business Universiteit (Netherlands): 12–15 months
23. Rotterdam School of Management, Erasmus University (Netherlands): 12 months
24. Said Business School, University of Oxford (UK): 12 months
25. SDA Bocconi School of Management (Italy): 12 months
26. University College Dublin: Smurfit School of Business (Ireland): 12 months
27. University of Bath School of Management (UK): 12 months
28. University of Edinburgh Business School (UK): 12 months
29. University of Strathclyde Business School (UK): 12 months
30. Vlerick Leuven Gent Management School (Belgium): 12 months
31. Warwick Business School (UK): 12 months

Note: All listings are full-time MBA programs that were ranked among the top 100 globally in 2008 by either the Financial Times's Global MBA rankings or the Economist's Intelligence Unit rankings. They are listed alphabetically rather than by ranking because not all schools appear in both surveys. Data on program lengths were taken from the Web sites of each school, accessed December 1, 2008.

continue to expect two full-time years from most of their students. Because many of the one-year programs admit students with deeper, more extensive business backgrounds and experiences, many employers and recruiters view students graduating from European one-year and two-year programs as more similar than different.

In part, the reasons for differences in program length in Europe and the United States are historical and idiosyncratic. Many graduate business programs in Europe were originally established outside traditional universities or in countries such as the United Kingdom, Ireland, Spain, and the Netherlands where master's degrees were frequently one year in length. They therefore did not face the same pressure to offer two-year programs as their U.S. counterparts, which were struggling to establish academic legitimacy and strove to offer master's programs that fit the two-year norm that has long prevailed in arts and sciences departments. But even in the United States, a small number of graduate business programs today offer a shorter, accelerated option. Northwestern, Cornell, and Emory have one-year MBAs for students who have already taken the core required courses prior to enrollment (meaning that most have been undergraduate business majors), and Dartmouth offers a one-year MBA for graduates of science PhD programs. Carnegie Mellon offers an MBA in sixteen months, and Rochester offers one in eighteen months.

Meanwhile, more specialized one-year master's degrees have proliferated, especially in finance and financial engineering.[6] In 2007–2008, there were 103 MS in finance programs worldwide; 66 were in the United States. Business schools at the University of Maryland, New York University (NYU), Massachusetts Institute of Technology (MIT), Pepperdine, and Purdue offer the degree, as do many U.K. business schools, including Cambridge, Cass, Cranfield, Imperial College, London Business School, and London School of Economics. Although the number of these programs will probably decline in the aftermath of the economic crisis, the surviving programs are likely to retain their appeal to both experienced finance professionals who want to accelerate their progress up the ranks and physicists, mathematicians, and computer scientists who want to change fields and gain access to finance jobs. This phenomenon is hardly limited to finance; it has spread to a large number of other business functions as well. In

2007–2008, there were 188 programs worldwide offering an MS in management, 286 offering an MS in accounting, and 1,819 offering a full-time master's degree in some other business-related field.[7] In 2009, Manchester Business School, for example, offered twenty-six different specialized one-year master's degrees, including Corporate Communications and Reputation Management, Information Systems: e-Business Technology, Human Resource Management and Industrial Relations, and Operations, Project and Supply Chain Management.

At the thirty-six U.S. business schools in our study, students are increasingly obtaining MBA degrees through part-time and executive MBA programs. They favor such programs because of their convenience and lower opportunity costs: they can be taken locally while still holding a full-time job. Schools have been supportive because, as the dean of one high-ranking traditional program put it, they serve as "an alternative delivery model."[8] The range of part-time offerings is vast, ranging from weekend programs such as those at Chicago Booth, to morning programs such as those at Pepperdine University, to online programs, which may (e.g., the University of Virginia) or may not (e.g., George Washington University) include an on-campus component. At almost all schools, however, the acceptance rates for these programs are considerably higher than the acceptance rates for their full-time MBA programs. Part-time programs at leading business schools in major cities have admission rates close to 40 percent, whereas many other part-time programs have admission rates near 80 percent. At the most selective programs, median GMAT scores for part-time and full-time MBA programs are similar, whereas at less selective schools scores for part-time programs are approximately fifty points lower.[9]

Executive MBA programs, aimed at midcareer professionals with a decade or more of work experience, have proliferated, and for similar reasons. The patterns of acceptance rates and median GMAT scores (when required) at executive MBA programs are fairly similar to the patterns of acceptance rates and scores at part-time programs. At the leading business schools, one dean reported, "We get better students with our executive MBA. They are more of the movers and the shakers, more knowledgeable and also more experienced." Executive MBA programs require periodic weekends or weeks in residence to attend classes, and run for sixteen to twenty-four months.[10]

A Hollowing Out of the Market

What is the combined impact of these trends? To understand them better, we analyzed data on the top thirty-six U.S. business schools. We focused only on U.S. schools because that allowed us to draw on comprehensive statistics collected annually by the AACSB. We limited ourselves to the top thirty-six programs in order to access publicly available rankings data (we determined a school's rank by averaging the annual rankings over several years provided by *Business Week*, the *Financial Times*, *U.S. News and World Report*, and the *Wall Street Journal*). The results appear in figures 2-3 through 2-6.

A look at the combined data shows a mature, slowly growing industry (figure 2-3). Overall, between 2000 and 2008, enrollments at the top thirty-six U.S. MBA programs grew from 37,282 students to 41,259 students, an increase of 10.7 percent. Most of the increase came, as

FIGURE 2-3

Total enrollment at the top thirty-six U.S. MBA schools: 2000 to 2008

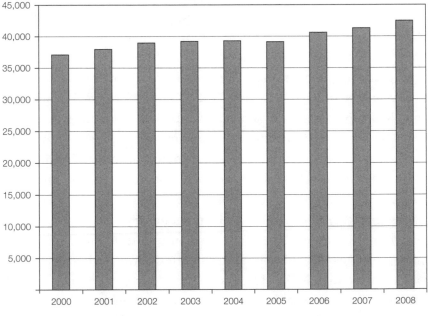

Source: AACSB, *BusinessWeek*, *U.S. News and World Report*, and Deans' offices of business schools.

FIGURE 2-4

Enrollment at the top twenty U.S. MBA schools by program type: 2000 to 2008

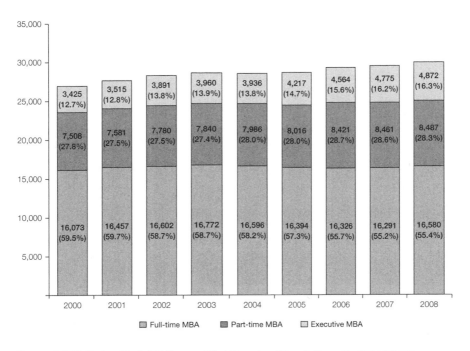

Source: AACSB, *BusinessWeek*, *U.S. News and World Report*, and Deans' offices of business schools.

mentioned earlier, from growth in part-time and executive MBA programs. However, a comparison of the higher- and lower-ranked schools shows two distinctly different pictures. At the top twenty schools (figure 2-4), full-time MBA enrollments remained reasonably steady over the period, whereas part-time and executive MBA enrollments rose. Full-time enrollments were 16,073 students in 2000 and 16,580 students in 2008; they fluctuated in a relatively narrow range during those nine years. Meanwhile, part-time and executive MBA enrollments rose by a slightly larger amount both absolutely and proportionally: from 10,933 students (40.5 percent of the total) in 2000 to 13,359 students (44.6 percent of the total) in 2008.

At the lower-ranking schools (numbers 21 through 36), the picture was considerably different (figure 2-5). Their full-time MBA program enrollments fell sharply, from 5,527 students in 2000 to 4,642 students

FIGURE 2-5

Enrollment at the next-highest sixteen U.S. MBA schools by program type: 2000 to 2008

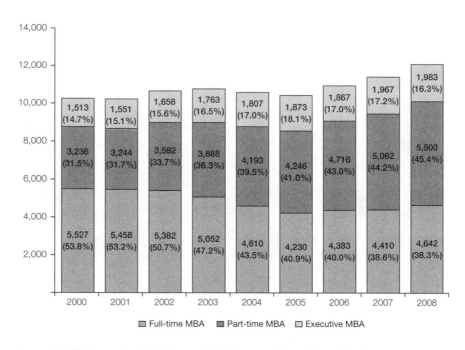

Full-time MBA   Part-time MBA   Executive MBA

Source: AACSB, *BusinessWeek, U.S. News and World Report*, and Deans' offices of business schools.

in 2008. Nor was this decline limited to a few schools; as figure 2-6 illustrates, the declines were virtually across the board and even included some of the higher-ranking schools.[11] In several cases, schools lost one or more full sections of students. These declines were accompanied, in many cases, by a greater proportion of applicants being offered a place in the full-time MBA program. As one dean put it, "Good, often proud, schools are having trouble building a class."[12]

Yet during this same period, part-time and executive MBA enrollments at these schools showed substantial gains, rising from 4,749 students (46.2 percent of the total) in 2000 to 7,483 students (61.7 percent of the total) in 2008. How did these schools meet the rise in demand? Not by hiring new tenure-track faculty or by growing the faculty across the board, as did the higher-ranking schools, but instead by drawing heavily on nontenured adjuncts and professors of practice. Between

FIGURE 2-6

Percentage change in U.S. full-time MBA enrollment by program rank: 2000 to 2008

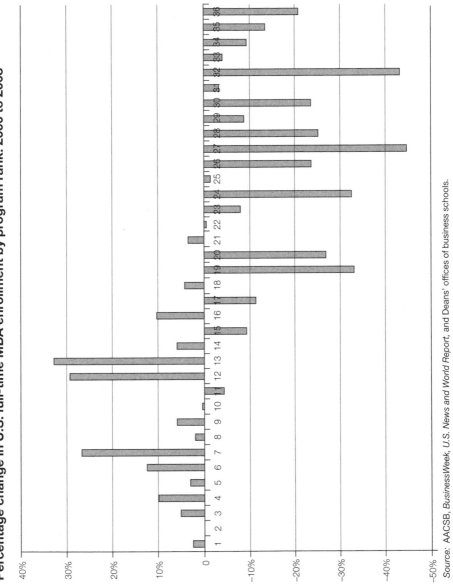

Source: AACSB, *BusinessWeek, U.S. News and World Report*, and Deans' offices of business schools.

2000 and 2006, the period for which we have data, the number of assistant professors at these schools fell from 381 to 367, and the number of associate professors fell from 363 to 346. The number of full professors grew modestly, from 499 to 520, but the number of instructors grew dramatically, from 138 to 189, an increase of over 37 percent.

Figure 2-7 presents the percentage change in full-time MBA program enrollments from 2004 to 2008 for leading European schools, ranked by averaging the annual rankings over several years published by the *Economist*. Although data for European schools are more limited, the patterns are similar to those observed for U.S. schools, showing significant declines in enrollment for most schools ranked from 16 to 31 and even for some schools in the top fifteen. Asia and Latin America, as growing developing markets, show markedly different trends. Although our data are partial and incomplete, they show business schools in these regions exhibiting strong increases in full-time MBA enrollments.

These figures suggest a hollowing out of the full-time MBA marketplace. At the highest-ranking schools, full-time MBA enrollments have remained steady, while part-time and executive MBA enrollments have risen slightly. But at the lower-ranked schools, students have already voted with their feet. Part-time and executive MBA programs are favored over full-time programs, even when classes are taught increasingly by instructors rather than tenure-track faculty. The shift toward part-time and executive MBAs, we believe, is a mixed blessing. Our field work suggests that, in many cases, it has been a response to declining full-time enrollments. Although in the short run the shift protects schools economically, in the long run it is unlikely to be sustainable, especially if full-time enrollments fall much further. In part, this is because the growth in part-time and executive MBA students had been strongly aided by employers subsidizing students for the costs of attending these programs when the economy was growing. Subsidies have fallen substantially in the wake of the downturn. Moreover, part-time and executive MBA programs differ from full-time programs in several other important respects. Part-time and executive MBA students, who continue to work and often expect to remain employed by their present employer, face much lower opportunity costs and very different value propositions than full-time students, who are gearing up for new jobs and potentially very different careers. Beyond

FIGURE 2-7

Percentage change in European full-time MBA enrollment by program rank: 2004 to 2008

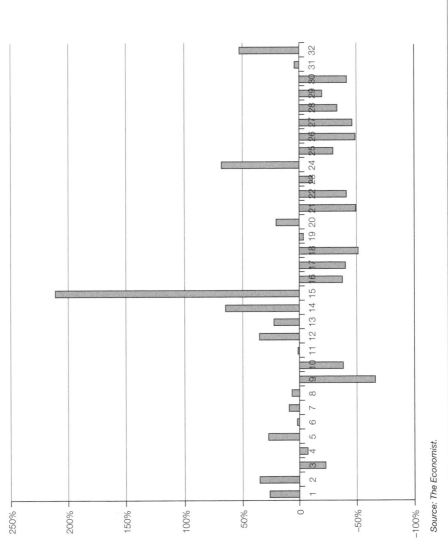

Source: The Economist.

a certain size, many institutions are likely to resist the continued rise of part-time and executive MBA enrollments because of a concern that programs have become too dependent on the vicissitudes of the economy and on a student body that can commit less time to academic work. In addition, part-time programs have student bodies that are usually much less diverse than those enrolled in full-time programs.

The question, of course, is whether the decline in full-time MBA enrollments will continue to be limited to lower-ranking schools. There are conflicting schools of thought. Some believe that the decline at the lower-ranking schools is cyclical, driven largely by a strong economy that discourages talented and successful individuals from leaving their jobs to study for an MBA. In this view, the demand for full-time MBAs will pick up as the economy slows. Our data suggest otherwise. Full-time enrollments at these schools fell during the last economic slowdown of 2001 to 2003 and did not pick up notably in 2008.

Others see the decline in full-time enrollments as a more secular trend. Lower-ranking schools might be bellwethers of the industry, serving as leading indicators and predictors of changes that will soon affect all institutions. According to this view, even the top schools will soon have to rethink their offerings if they are not to suffer the same fate. Still others respond with a quite different interpretation, seeing the data as evidence of a flight to quality. According to this view, the market may have bifurcated, with different forces affecting lower- and higher-ranking schools. In this scenario, the top schools will be protected from the forces now buffeting lower-ranking schools because of their national and global brand reputations, their superior faculty and quality of instruction, and their distinctive added value. Is there any way to determine which of these alternative futures is more likely?

Voices from the Field: How Deans and Recruiters View the MBA Degree

Immediately after graduation, a significant majority of the graduates of the leading two-year, full-time MBA programs take jobs in financial services and consulting, driven in part by financial rewards that make it very difficult for companies in other sectors to compete for graduates.

The numbers—at least before the recent financial crisis—have remained consistently high. In 2006, for example, 52 percent of Chicago Booth graduates took jobs in financial services and 22 percent took jobs in consulting; 42 percent of Harvard graduates took jobs in financial services and 22 percent took jobs in consulting; and 46 percent of Yale graduates took jobs in financial services and 15 percent took jobs in consulting.[13] The boom in jobs in financial services and consulting during the last ten years made obtaining a prestigious MBA degree—long viewed as essential to gaining entry to these careers—a very attractive option. Even if one had previously worked in the industry, an MBA from a high-ranking school was, for many years, a de facto requirement for climbing the ladder.

The deans we interviewed from higher-ranking schools were clear on the value that they believed accrued to those armed with an MBA: it ensured access to these (as well as other) attractive, otherwise inaccessible careers. In their eyes—as well as those of many students—the full-time MBA is increasingly aimed at "career switchers." For those wishing to change fields—to enter investment banking, private equity, hedge funds, or strategy consulting from a prior position in industry, government, or the nonprofit world—the MBA has long been viewed as absolutely essential. One dean, for example, noted that nearly 80 percent of students at his prior institution had switched careers upon graduation.

The problem for the higher-ranking business schools is that there are a number of forces at work that threaten to undermine or reduce the opportunities for employment in financial services and consulting. Post-crisis, many lucrative jobs in financial services, and to a lesser extent in consulting, have simply disappeared. Each day brings new reports of hedge fund closings and the scaling back of private equity investments. Not surprisingly, the enormously high compensation packages in these fields are shrinking as well, making jobs in these sectors far less attractive. These changes threaten one of the key selling points of the top U.S. business schools. A further challenge comes from the fact that companies in these industries have increasingly been promoting from within.[14] In part, this is because technical work, such as sales and trading, now contributes a large share of the firm's profits relative to activities such as investment banking. Consequently, many companies are actively discouraging their best young people from leaving lower-level positions for business school, arguing that their odds of success are actually better if they stay at the firm. This theme can be heard, with minor variations, from executives at two financial services firms:

> Previously the Wall Street tradition was to send Analysts for the MBA. That's no longer the case. We do not want to show these people the door because they are valuable to us. Now, a third of the Analyst class is offered full-time Associate positions without doing an MBA. For technical work, the training an Analyst gets from a Wall Street firm is better than the training they would receive at business school.

> With the exception of investment banking and investment management, the firm is, by and large, not hiring MBAs, even though we are much bigger. Instead, we hire undergraduates from elite institutions, who rise up the ladder. They are paid more, faster, to induce them to stay.

The same point was made by a senior partner in a consulting firm, who, when asked pointedly if he would advise a highly successful junior person with several years at the firm who was intent on a career in consulting whether an MBA would be valuable for his future, answered, "Definitely not."

At the same time, financial services and consulting firms are increasingly substituting non-MBAs for MBAs. The numbers are small but growing. Before the crisis, a managing director at one large investment bank noted that his firm still hired 300 to 400 MBAs per year but only about fifty technical experts with PhDs or comparable degrees, even though it set out each year to hire twice as many. These latter individuals are viewed as essential because the fields of finance and strategy have become increasingly analytical and because leading financial services firms are, as one experienced financial executive put it, "increasingly dominated by traders, who believe business school is a waste of time." According to a senior manager at a leading investment bank:

> The investment banking industry needs to recruit more technically competent people than it did in the past because our

products, and the industry as a whole, are more complex. The requirements are higher than even the most quantitative MBA programs can deliver. As a result, we are aggressively pursuing PhDs in business, finance, mathematics, physics, and operations. The common thread is that all are people who are highly analytical and can translate complex situations into mathematical models. The percentage of MBAs that we hire will go down in the next ten years.

A director of a leading consulting firm made much the same point:

We now hire a very large number of non-MBAs into our Associate roles. In fact, our incoming mix is 50 percent MBA and 50 percent non-MBA. The non-MBAs mostly come from medical schools, medical school residency programs, law schools, and a variety of PhD programs in economics, applied math, physics, life sciences, and computer science. The non-MBA portion of the mix is growing, and we are actively seeking to expand into these sources.

In the past, deans and business school faculty had a ready response to questions about the value of the MBA degree: graduate business training was a way of getting ahead of the pack and igniting one's career. MBAs, the argument ran, were a breed apart and were more likely to be placed on the fast track. They might not be the best technicians, but their breadth of training and skills would win out over the long haul. Although this may still be true in some fields, it appears to be less true in others. At least before the crisis, for those in financial services wishing to accelerate their careers (i.e., who hoped to stay in the same function or area and get promoted more rapidly or frequently at the same company), the two-year, full-time MBA was no longer viewed as necessary. Both the head of a leading hedge fund and a senior executive at a leading investment bank made much the same point:

Something has changed in the last few years. We've always hired young people from elite colleges and universities and started them as Analysts. For many years we found that after six or seven years with us and one or more promotions, they would hit a wall—we had to send them to business school to get the grounding and perspective necessary to make it to the upper rungs of the firm. But recently, we've found that our young people have been able to make the jump without leaving for an MBA. Those two years of training just aren't needed.

You are three times as likely to become a Managing Director at our firm if you are an Associate who came up through the ranks than if you are an Associate hired after an MBA.

Whether the financial crisis will alter these views about obtaining an MBA is still unclear.

Taken together, the threats identified throughout this chapter suggest challenges for all MBA programs, including the most highly ranked programs. Enrollments are under pressure, and questions are being raised about the value-added of the degree, especially the two-year, full-time version, when compared with alternatives. To learn more about the opportunities for strengthening the traditional MBA degree, we examined the structure and content of the programs at eleven leading schools (chapter 3) and spoke at length with deans and executives about their perceptions of program deficiencies and how they might be improved (chapter 4).

Appendix: Master's Degrees at a Sample of Leading U.S. Business Schools

(Schools are ordered by increasing number of master's programs offered; within categories they are listed alphabetically by school name)

Harvard Business School

Full-time MBA: 2 years

Tuck School of Business, Dartmouth

Full-time MBA: 2 years

Darden School of Business, University of Virginia

Full-time MBA: 2 years

MBA for Executives: 23 months, with a third of the core curriculum delivered online; in residence once a month on Friday and Saturday

Stanford Graduate School of Business

Full-time MBA: 2 years

Sloan Master's Program: 10 months, full-time, leading to a MSc for midcareer executives

The Wharton School of the University of Pennsylvania

Full-time MBA: 2 years

Executive MBA: part-time (24 months), two locations: Philadelphia and San Francisco

Yale School of Management

Full-time MBA: 2 years

Leadership in Healthcare MBA for Executives: offered jointly with Yale's School of Medicine and School of Public health: 22 months

Carlson School of Management, University of Minnesota

Full-time MBA: 2 years

Part-time MBA: 2 to 7 years

Executive MBA: 21 months

Fisher College of Business, Ohio State University

Full-time MBA: 2 years

MBA for working professionals: 2 to 5 years

Executive MBA: 18 months

Tepper School of Business, Carnegie Mellon University

Full-time MBA: either 2 years or 16 months (take classes during summer rather than an internship)

Part-time MBA: usually 3 years

Distance learning MBA: usually 3 years

The University of Chicago Booth School of Business

Full-time MBA: 2 years

Evening and weekend MBA: part-time, 2.5 to 5 years

Executive MBA: 20 months, offered in Chicago, London, and Singapore

Wisconsin School of Business

Full-time MBA: 2 years

Evening MBA: 3 years

Executive MBA: 2 years

College of Management, Georgia Institute of Technology

Full-time MBA: 2 years

Evening MBA: 2 to 6 years

Executive MBA in Management of Technology: 19 months

Global Executive MBA: 17 months

Columbia Graduate School of Business

Full-time MBA: 2 years

Executive MBA:

New York-based EMBA: 20 months

Global EMBA (with London Business School): 20 months

Berkeley-Columbia EMBA: 19 months

Goizueta Business School, Emory University

Full-time MBA: (a) 2 years; (b) 1 year, with an undergraduate degree in business or economics or prior coursework in statistics, financial accounting, corporate finance, and microeconomics

Evening MBA: 24 to 33 months

Executive MBA: 16 months

Haas School of Business, University of California at Berkeley

Full-time MBA: 2 years

Evening and weekend MBA: part-time, 3 years

Berkeley–Columbia Executive MBA: 19 months

Master's in Financial Engineering: 1 year

Johnson School of Management, Cornell University

Full-time MBA: 2 years

Accelerated MBA: 1 year, requires an advanced degree, leadership potential, and strong quantitative skills

Executive MBA: 22 months, classes on alternate weekends in New York area

Cornell–Queen's University (Canada) Executive MBA: 17 months, earn two degrees

Kelley School of Business, Indiana University

Full-time MBA: 2 years

Online MBA: 2 to 5 years

MSc in Information Systems: 2 to 3 semesters, full-time

MSc in Accounting: 1 year, full-time

Kellogg School of Management, Northwestern University

Full-time MBA: (a) 2 years, (b) 1 year for students who have either an undergraduate degree in business or have taken the core courses

Part-time MBA: 2.5 to 5 years

Executive MBA: 2 years (for midcareer executives)

Stern School of Business, New York University

Full-time MBA: 2 years

Part-time MBA: evening and weekend-only options, 2 to 6 years

Executive MBA: 22 months

Trium Global EMBA (Stern, LSE, HEC School of Management): 16 months

Anderson School of Management, University of California at Los Angeles

Full-time MBA: 2 years

Fully Employed MBA: 33 months

Executive MBA: 22 months

UCLA–National University of Singapore Business School Global Executive MBA: residential sessions in L.A. and Singapore

Master of Financial Engineering: 1 year

Fuqua School of Business, Duke University

Full-time MBA: 2 years

Executive MBA:

MBA Cross-Continent: 16 months

MBA Global Executive: 18 months

MBA Weekend Executive: 20 months

Goethe Executive MBA (dual degree with Frankfurt University's Goethe Business School): 22 months

Kenan-Flagler Business School, University of North Carolina

Full-time MBA: 2 years

Weekend MBA: 20 months

Evening MBA: 24 months

Global MBA: 21 months

Master of Accounting: 1 year, full-time

McDonough School of Business, Georgetown University

Full-time MBA: 2 years

Evening MBA: 3 years

International Executive MBA: 18 months

Georgetown-ESADE Executive MBA: 16 months, in six 11-day modules

Executive Master's in Leadership: part-time, 13 months

Olin Business School, Washington University

Full-time MBA: 2 years

Professional MBA: 3-year evening program

Executive MBA: St. Louis and Shanghai, 18-month weekend program

MSc in Finance: 1 year

Master of Accountancy: 1 or 2 years

Ross School of Business, University of Michigan

Full-time MBA: 2 years

Evening MBA: 3 to 4 years

Executive MBA: 20 months, in residence once per month on Fridays and Saturdays.

Global MBA: 16 months, for corporate sponsored executives only

Master of Accountancy, Master of Supply Chain Management: both 1-year programs

Sloan School of Management, Massachusetts Institute of Technology

Full-time MBA: 2 years

Sloan Fellows Program in Innovation & Global Leadership: 1 year

Leaders for Manufacturing: 2 years, MBA or MS, with School of Engineering

Systems Design and Management: 13 to 24 months, MS, with School of Engineering

Biomedical Enterprise: 3 years, MBA or MS, with Harvard–MIT Division of Health Sciences and Technology

McCombs School of Business, University of Texas

Full-time MBA: 2 years

Evening MBA: 33 months, part-time, classes on Monday and Tuesday evenings

Texas MBA at Houston: 2 years, part-time, classes on alternate weekends

Texas MBA at Dallas: 2 years, part-time, classes on alternate weekends

Texas Executive MBA: 2-year program for midcareer professionals

Texas Executive MBA at Mexico City (with Tecnologice de Monterrey): 2 years

Texas Master of Public Accounting: 12 to 18 months, full-time

Marshall School of Business, University of Southern California

Full-time MBA: 2 years

MBA for Professionals and Managers: 33 months, evening program

Executive MBA: 2 years

EMBA in Shanghai: conducted at Shanghai Jiatong University, 21 months

IBEAR MBA: intensive 12-month, full-time program in international management

Master of Accounting: 1 year, full-time

Master of Business Taxation: 1 year full-time, or 2 years part-time

Master of Medical Management: 12 months, part-time

MSc in Business Administration: full-time or part-time, for students who already have an MBA and want to go deeper: 1 to 5 years

Simon Graduate School of Business, University of Rochester

Full-time MBA: 21 months, or accelerated program in 18 months

Part-time MBA: average 3 years

Executive MBA: 2 years

Master of Science degrees, full-time (9 to 11 months) or part-time (15 months to 3 years), in nine areas:

Accountancy

Information Systems Management

Finance

General Management

Marketing

Manufacturing Management

Medical Management

Service Management

Technology Transfer and Commercialization

A Close Look at the Curriculum

CURRICULUM IS NO more than an assemblage of classes and materials that collectively constitute an educational program. It plays two distinct roles, serving as both "a rule book of regulations and requirements" and "an expression of what . . . [an institution] . . . believes education means."[1] Curricula are normally divided into required and elective components. Of special importance is "the common core, taken by all students [because it] . . . provides a base of shared knowledge, a series of points of reference, and builds esprit de corps."[2]

There are, not surprisingly, myriad variations and a large number of design choices. The most basic decisions involve *content*: which disciplines and subject areas to cover, which courses and classes to require, and which concepts, theories, techniques, and modes of thinking to feature. An associated set of decisions concerns *pedagogy*: which teaching approaches to favor when conveying material or developing skills, and what methods to use for evaluating students' mastery and academic understanding. At the next level come decisions about *architecture*: how to divide up required and elective portions of the curriculum, how to structure and sequence classes, what types of concentrations and specializations to allow, and the extent and composition of joint or combined degrees. Finally, at the highest level come decisions about *purpose*: what broad goals and educational ends the curriculum is expected to serve.

Standardization or Differentiation?

In some settings, such as elementary and secondary education, these decisions are largely dictated or defined by overseeing bodies and accrediting institutions. The result is a high degree of consistency in curricula across institutions, at least within broad geographical areas. In bachelor's, master's, and doctoral programs, by contrast, many of the critical elements of the curriculum are subject to discretion and local tailoring, with limited efforts to impose standardization or uniformity. Even so, powerful forces favor convergence. Institutions tend to mimic the leaders in their fields, accrediting groups impose standards, and societal pressures and educational trends frequently push curricula in common directions. The shifting stance of colleges on required courses provides a telling example. In 1890, the required curriculum at the average American college amounted to 80 percent of all courses. By 1940, as students became more diverse, the number of course offerings increased, and possible fields of study mushroomed, that share had declined to 40 percent.[3]

MBA programs are subject to the same forces. Particularly in the years following publication of the Ford Foundation and Carnegie Corporation studies, schools tried to upgrade their course content by embracing the model curricula described in the reports. The pressures for conformance were strong. Both studies were highly directive: they identified the particular set of courses that should be offered and even indicated the number of hours that should be devoted to each.[4] The result, according to a careful analysis of business schools published in 1988, was the emergence of "a cookie-cutter mentality . . . [and] . . . a distressing tendency for schools to avoid the risk of being different."[5]

The question, of course, is whether such consistency is still to be found today, and if so, to what extent. The last two decades have been periods of extraordinary growth in business education, with schools competing intensively for students and faculty. Competition normally increases the amount of differentiation in product and service offerings. Articles in the popular press cite "the wave of recent MBA redesigns" and the rise of "B-schools with a niche."[6] At the same time, the forces favoring imitation, driven largely by business school rankings (discussed in the following chapter), have increased. According to one scholar, the result is a collection of virtually identical MBA programs, based on a "dominant design" with few significant variations.[7] Two deans offered similar assessments:

> There is a great interest in what everyone else is doing, driven by the rankings. The result is commoditization and mass production of graduates around a core curriculum that is indistinguishable across schools.

———

> When our alumni do not believe that there is any difference between the top MBA programs and see them all as finishing schools, there is a differentiation problem.

Prior Assessments of MBA Curricula

Prior studies offer conflicting evidence on these points. A 1999 study of MBA programs at twenty-five leading U.S. schools sorted programs into groups according to the core courses and concentrations that they offered.[8] Using statistical methods, the authors identified six distinct groups or clusters of schools, and further noted that each of the five leading programs belonged to a different cluster, suggesting considerable variation and no single route to superior performance. However, a closer examination of the study's data on core courses shows a striking degree of similarity. Six courses—finance, financial accounting, marketing management, microeconomics, operations management, and organizational behavior—were required at twenty-three of the twenty-five schools; two additional courses—macroeconomics and management information systems—were required at fifteen or more schools. Moreover, required courses typically accounted for about half of each program, with a range of between 40 and 55 percent. This is hardly differentiation on a massive scale.

A more recent study of the fifty top U.S. business schools reported similar results.[9] It too sought to cluster schools into thematic categories and identified six different groupings. But again, despite a smattering of distinctive offerings such as multidisciplinary exercises, experiential field projects, and team competitions, the amount of differentiation was limited. Clusters were usually distinguished by small shifts in the set of required offerings, slightly different mixes that reflected the inclusion or exclusion of a course in communications, ethics, globalization, information technology, or leadership. Again, there were striking levels of commonality, and thirty of the fifty schools fell into a single cluster. The same seven courses—marketing, corporate finance, financial accounting, operations and supply chain management, corporate strategy, managerial economics, and quantitative analysis (including statistics)—were required at least 85 percent of the time, and five additional courses—managerial/cost accounting, management information systems, management communications, organizational behavior, and macroeconomics—were required at least 50 percent of the time. Here too the picture was mixed, but was largely one of standardization.

These studies, although suggestive, are limited in that they do not provide comprehensive, multidimensional portraits of MBA programs. In particular, they use an extremely narrow definition of the curriculum, focusing almost entirely on course mix while saying little or nothing about pedagogy, architecture, or purpose. A number of critical questions remain unanswered. How is the core curriculum structured and sequenced? Are students grouped into cohorts or teams, and, if so, for how long do they stay together? What options do students have? For example, can first-year students waive requirements by taking qualifying exams, enroll in different levels of required courses (basic, intermediate, or advanced), or pursue electives amidst their required courses? Prior studies have been silent on these questions. They have been equally silent on issues of course content and pedagogy. Schools may require similar sets of courses, but how similar or different are they? Do courses focus on the same topics and devote comparable amounts of time to each one, or do they differ in coverage and emphasis? Do different programs favor different teaching approaches? To what extent do they rely on textbooks, articles, cases, and exercises?

These distinctions are important because they provide a baseline for assessing current critiques of business education and for calibrating the concerns of deans and executives that we review in the next chapter. They also help us understand the degree to which differentiation has already occurred, and the degree to which schools are operating from a common base. Without this information, we simply cannot say, at a granular, refined level, how MBA programs compare and the degree to which they are truly similar or different.

Putting MBA Programs Under the Microscope

To address these questions, we conducted a detailed analysis of the 2006 and 2007 curricula of eleven leading MBA programs: Carnegie Mellon (Tepper), Chicago Booth, Dartmouth (Tuck), Harvard, INSEAD, MIT (Sloan), NYU (Stern), Northwestern (Kellogg), Stanford, Wharton, and Yale. The sample consists entirely of highly ranked schools, including all five programs that are profiled in the case studies of part II. We collected detailed data on program purpose, architectures, course offerings, course content, and pedagogy by first accessing each school's Web site and online syllabi and then supplementing that information based on interviews with faculty and deans and with additional background materials they sent to us.[10] In addition to examining programs as a whole, we looked closely at three core courses—financial accounting, strategy, and organizational behavior/leadership—with very different disciplinary roots, analytical methods, and maturities as academic fields, and compared their content, length, materials, and pedagogies. To the extent possible, we standardized our data, creating common categories for better comparability; we also occasionally excluded schools from the analysis when their data were incomplete or inconsistent. Inevitably, these decisions involved judgment calls.

Our goal was to answer three questions: (1) How uniform are the curricula of leading business schools today? (2) To the extent that differences exist, where are they most pronounced? (3) Are there any emerging trends that suggest the likely shape or direction of future MBA offerings? Among our major findings were the following:

- At the level of content—particularly the core curriculum and the subjects covered—we found programs to be much alike. Schools offer the same basic mix of requirements, with coverage of many of the same topics. At times, they even use the same textbooks and assign the same articles and cases. Most core courses focus on "the basics" and feature the same well-accepted concepts, frameworks, tools, and techniques. However, schools differ considerably in the precise amount of time and attention that they devote to particular topics and also vary in the breadth of coverage of subjects they include in the core.

- At the level of pedagogy—particularly the use of cases, exercises, and problem sets—schools are diverse. Some schools vest heavily in a single teaching technique such as lectures or the case method, whereas at the other extreme are schools that rely on a wide mix of alternative pedagogies. These differences vary somewhat depending on the course and the maturity of the field.

- At the level of architecture—particularly regarding issues of structure, sequence, and requirements—we found a large number of highly differentiated approaches. Those approaches are distinguished along relatively few dimensions of choice: the proportion of all coursework that is required, the sequencing of courses, the degree to which the sequence of required courses is rigid or flexible, the existence of required courses pitched to different levels of student experience and expertise, the extent of integration, the presence and extent of electives in the first year, the allowance for formal specialization in the second year, and the existence of a capstone course or experience. These dimensions are combined in many different ways, leading to considerable differences among programs. Some of these differences lead to substantially different types and degrees of student learning. In other cases, it is unclear whether, and to what extent, the differences are meaningful educationally.

- At the level of purpose—the animating ideas or educational goals of the program—we found both commonality and differences. All programs seek to educate students simultaneously for their first jobs and for their careers. All seek to create both generalists and specialists by combining breadth and depth of exposure to essential business topics. All expect their students to master both "hard" (analytical) and "soft" (organizational and managerial) skills, although seldom in equal measure. However, programs often differ sharply in their primary orientations and centers of gravity. Many schools differentiate themselves on the basis of one or two themes, citing, for example, their commitment to globalization, general management, or integrated thinking. We explore these differences in much more detail in the case studies in part II of the book.

- In terms of trends—broad directions common to multiple programs—we found a number of efforts to offer greater flexibility, with increased, and earlier, student choice. As recruiters place more and more weight on summer jobs as the route to full-time employment, schools have responded by adding electives and opportunities for increased specialization in the first year of their programs. They have also increased the number of courses stratified by different levels of student preparation and experience. Small-group work is similarly on the upswing. Most programs include team-based exercises, as well as opportunities for action learning, although these still occupy only a small proportion of the curriculum. Programs are also innovating in the areas of globalization, leadership development, integrative thinking, and course sequencing. In other areas we see inaction: partial or limited response to calls for more applied offerings. In areas such as communications, creativity, and implementation skills, schools are still wrestling with the extent of their commitments, and only a limited number of programs have developed required courses. The same is true of more traditional fields such as managerial accounting and corporate finance, where schools remain split on the degree to which these courses should be required. The economic crisis has led many business schools to contemplate giving greater attention to risk management, the systemic effects of decisions, the role of institutions and public regulation, and developing responsible leaders. As yet, it is too early to tell whether these efforts will result in deep or significant changes to the structure or content of MBA curricula. Most changes to date have involved the addition of a small number of crisis-related sessions to one or more existing courses.

Program Design

Ten of the eleven business schools we examined offer two-year degree programs, with the first year devoted primarily to core courses and the second year devoted largely to electives. INSEAD is the lone exception, with a ten-month program. Ten of the eleven schools divide their incoming classes into cohorts (also known as sections, clusters, and blocks), groups of students that remain together and, for some stretch of time, take classes as a unit. Cohorts range in size from fifty-five students at Chicago Booth to ninety students at Harvard, with seven schools falling in the range of sixty to seventy students. Some cohorts stay together for a full year (Harvard, Wharton, and Yale), others stay together for a semester or quarter (MIT, NYU, and Stanford), and still others stay together for only one or two classes (Chicago Booth and Northwestern). INSEAD keeps students in cohorts for six of its ten months, whereas Dartmouth assigns students to one section in the fall and a different section in the spring. Nine of the eleven schools further assign incoming students to small teams, ranging in size from four to fifteen people, and use these teams, to varying degrees, for graded projects, experiential exercises, and class preparation.

Programs also operate on very different schedules and divide up their calendars in very different ways. Six schools divide the year into semesters, four schools divide the year into quarters, and one, INSEAD, divides its program into periods of eight weeks each.[11] Some schools, such as Northwestern and Wharton, have a required pre-term session that begins in the summer before the first year; others, such as Harvard, offer optional pre-term classes. These variations lead to differences in the number of required courses, the amount of time devoted to each required course, and the total time spent in core classes.

The key comparisons appear in table 3-1. The number of required courses ranges from eight to twenty, with the vast majority scheduled during the first year. The most telling comparison, however, is in the number of "required course weeks," which we calculated to adjust for differences in class and term length. This figure represents the entire period of time that students spend in required classes. Programs cluster into three groups. At the high end are Stanford, Wharton, INSEAD, and Harvard, which require students to spend about half of their total time in required classes.[12] At the low end are MIT, NYU, and Yale, which require students to spend a third or less of total time in required classes. The remaining schools fall in between.[13] Nor is this the only basis on which core curricula differ. Programs differ in the degree to which they dictate the sequence of required courses. The order in which topics are introduced varies as well. For example, in its recent MBA program redesign, Stanford chose a sequence markedly different from most other schools. Whereas the first-year curriculum usually starts with disciplines, moves to functions, and ends with broad, integrated topics, the Stanford curriculum opens with courses that provide a larger integrated context and perspective, such as Global Management and Strategic Leadership, before moving to disciplinary and functional courses.

In terms of flexibility and choice, programs cluster into three groups. Seven schools insist on a rigid sequence of courses: they tell students exactly when, and in what order, core courses must be taken. Three schools allow for variations; we call these programs "semi-flexible" because they dictate the sequence of some courses but allow choice in other areas. The remaining school, Chicago Booth, anchors the flexible end of the spectrum. Requirements are minimal, and students may take core courses in any order, in any combination, and at any time in the program. We discuss Chicago Booth's approach in more detail in chapter 7.

In the same spirit, schools differ in the degree to which students can tailor their first-year classes. Students at Carnegie Mellon, Dartmouth, INSEAD, NYU, Northwestern, and Wharton can place out of required courses and take electives or more advanced courses instead. Four schools offer students the option of different levels of core courses, although most do so only for those courses that are technical or analytical. Stanford, however, does so for a large number of core functional courses; we explore its tailored, customized approach in detail in chapter 12. Nine of the eleven schools also offer electives in the first year, allowing students to take additional courses in fields such as finance or marketing that might give them an edge in their summer job searches. Several deans reported that this shift to a more flexible first year, with greater tailoring and offering of electives, was a relatively recent move, undertaken in response to recruiting pressures and students' desires to be better prepared for their summer jobs.[14]

Opportunities to concentrate or specialize in the second year of the program are offered formally by several schools and informally by all, because most schools have minimal requirements after the core is completed.[15] At many schools, the number of second-year elective courses is as high as 90 or 100. As table 3-2 indicates, schools also offer a dizzying array of joint, dual, and specialized degree options, with

TABLE 3-1

Program structures and architectures

School	Required Courses/Areas	Required Course Weeks[a]	Order of Core Courses	Multiple Levels of Core Courses	Choice of Core Course Subject Areas	First-Year Elective Courses	Second-Year Required Courses	Concentrations, Majors, or Specializations
Carnegie Mellon Tepper	15	120	Rigid	No	Choose 1 of 2	4–6	1: Management Game[b]	Tracks and 1 concentration
Chicago Booth	10	110	Flexible	Yes	Choose 4 of 6	Many Choices	None	Up to 3 from 14 concentrations
Dartmouth Tuck	15	119	Rigid	No	No	1	None	No
Harvard Business School	11	160	Rigid	No	No	None	None	No
INSEAD	13	104 of 200 weeks	Rigid	No	No	Minimum of 10.5[c]	N/A	No
MIT Sloan	8	90	Rigid	No	Choose 1 of 2	Second semester	None	1
New York University Stern	9	104	Semiflexible (4 rigid, 4 flexible)	No	Choose 5 from 7	1–3	Professional Responsibility[b]	Up to 3 from 22 specializations
Northwestern University Kellogg	10	120	Semiflexible (5 rigid, 5 flexible)	2 choices for quantitative courses	No	3–4	Values and Crisis Decision Making[b]	Up to 3 majors

School						Synthesis seminar[b]	Certificate program option
Stanford Graduate School of Business	20	Up to 169	Rigid	12 core classes at 3 levels	No	0–1	None	1 from 17 majors
Wharton School of the University of Pennsylvania	18	Up to 165	Semiflexible (14 rigid, 4 flexible)	Only for Financial Accounting and Corporate Finance	No	None	None	No
Yale School of Management	17	109	Rigid	No	No	1–3	None	No

Note: N/A = not applicable.

a. Of 320 total course weeks, except where noted.

b. Denotes capstone.

c. This number is not strictly comparable with first-year electives offered by the other ten schools in this study because INSEAD has a ten-month MBA program. Courses in the INSEAD core curriculum extend over three periods. No elective courses are offered in the first two periods. Four elective courses are offered in the third and fourth periods, and three electives are offered in the fifth period.

TABLE 3-2

Joint, dual, and specialized degree options

Schools	Percentage of Students Enrolled	JD/MBA	MD/MBA	MPP, MPA, MA/MBA/MSPPM	MPH or Healthcare/MBA	Other
Carnegie Mellon Tepper	2–3	w/ University of Pittsburgh School of Law	—	MSPPM w/ H. John Heinz III School of Public Policy & Management	MBA/Healthcare policy & management	MS in computational finance MSE in software engineering MSCEE in civil & environmental engineering MS in quantitative economics
Chicago Booth	4	w/ University of Chicago Law School	w/ Pritzker School of Medicine	MPP w/ Harris School of Public Policy		MBA and master's in area studies or international relations MA w/ School of Social Service Administration
Dartmouth Tuck	5	MELP with Vermont Law School's environmental law program	w/ Dartmouth Medical School	MPA with the Harvard Kennedy School MA with the Paul H. Nitze School of Advanced International Studies at Johns Hopkins University	w/ Dartmouth's Institute for Health Policy & Clinical Practice	MEM w/ Dartmouth's Thayer School of Engineering MALD with the Fletcher School at Tufts University
Harvard Business School	3–4	w/ Harvard Law School	w/ Harvard Medical School	MPP or MPA-ID w/ the Harvard Kennedy School	—	—
INSEAD	0	—	—	—	—	—

School					
MIT Sloan	18	—	MPA or MPP w/ the Harvard Kennedy School	MBA/Masters in health science in the Biomedical Enterprise Program	SM in the Leaders for Manufacturing Program MIT Sloan Fellows Program in Innovation and Global Leadership (SM) SM in system design and management
New York University Stern	4–5	w/ NYU Law School	MBA/MA in politics MPA w/ Wagner School of Public Service	—	MA in French studies MFA in fine arts MS in biology HEC, France/NYU Stern MBA
Northwestern University Kellogg	12–14	w/ Northwestern University's School of Law w/ Feinberg Medical School	—	—	Master of management and manufacturing (MMM) earns MBA and MEM (master of engineering management), w/ Northwestern University's McCormick Engineering School
Stanford Graduate School of Business	10	w/ Stanford Law School w/ Stanford Medical School	MPP w/ School of Humanities and Science	—	MS in environment and resources/MBA MA in education "Students have the option to apply for an MBA with a dual degree in another field from Stanford or another university."

(continued)

TABLE 3-2 (*continued*)

Schools	Percentage of Students Enrolled	JD/MBA	MD/MBA	MPP, MPA, MA/MBA/MSPPM	MPH or Healthcare/MBA	Other
Wharton School of the University of Pennsylvania	8–9	w/ Penn Law School	MBA/MD with Penn Medical School	Wharton School of Advanced International Studies (SAIS)	—	MB/MBA in biotechnology with the School of Engineering and Applied Science and School of Arts and Sciences
			MBA/DMD with Penn Dental School			MBA/MSE in engineering with the School of Engineering and Applied Science
			Medicine, and MBA/VMD and MBA/MS with Penn Veterinary Medicine School			MBA/MArch, MBA/MLA, MBA/MCP, MBA/MHP with the School of Design
			MBA/MSN, MBA/PhD with the School of Nursing			MBA/MSW in social work with the School of Social Policy and Practice
Yale School of Management	7	w/ Yale Law School	w/ Yale School of Medicine	MBA/MA with Yale Graduate School of Arts and Sciences	w/ Yale School of Public Health	MBA/MEM or MF with Yale School of Forestry and Environmental Studies
						MBA/MARCH with Yale School of Architecture
						MBA/MFA with Yale School of Drama
						MBA/MDIV or MAR with Yale Divinity School
						MBA/MA in Russian and East European studies with Yale Graduate School of Arts and Sciences
						MBA/PhD with Yale Graduate School of Arts and Sciences

students able to combine their MBA with programs in law, medicine, public policy, design, and other fields. The proportion of students electing these options varies, ranging from a very small number (less than 5 percent) at Carnegie Mellon, Chicago, and Harvard to a considerably larger proportion (as much as 18 percent) at MIT and Northwestern, where joint or specialized programs frequently involve an engineering component.

What is one to conclude from these comparisons? At a broad level, they suggest an extraordinary amount of diversity in MBA programs. Beyond the existence of a set of required courses to be taken early in the program, a set of electives to be taken later, the wide use of cohorts and teams, and the division of programs into modular, interrelated pieces, it is difficult to find much that programs have in common. There is no dominant, universally accepted design, and the approaches are hardly "cookie-cutter." If anything, these comparisons suggest that no two programs are alike. Focusing on course offerings and course content, however, leads to a slightly different assessment: it shows that MBA programs are alike in some important ways but sharply different in others.

Course Offerings

Table 3-3 presents the basic data on required courses. At most schools, students are required to take the same eight courses: financial accounting, finance with a capital markets emphasis, microeconomics, strategy, organizational behavior or leadership, operations, marketing, and decision sciences or statistics. There are a few exceptions—Harvard does not require microeconomics or decision sciences, and MIT does not require strategy or operations—but by and large schools have the same foundational requirements. These courses, which are largely analytical and functional, might be called the "primary core." At the next level are a set of courses required by roughly half of the schools: managerial accounting, corporate finance, macroeconomics, ethics, and communications. These courses might be called the "secondary core"; they are sometimes required and sometimes not, depending on the program. Finally, there are a mixed bag of courses, including capstones, presentation skills, team projects, and negotiations, that are required

TABLE 3-3

Required courses

School	Accounting		Finance		Economics		Strategy	Org Behavior/ Leadership	Global Business		Operations	Marketing	Decision Science/ Statistics	Ethics	Communication	Presentations	Team Project	Negotiation	Other
	Fin	Man	Corp	Cap Mrkt	Micro	Macro			Micro	Macro									
Carnegie Mellon Tepper	1	1	½	½	1	1	1	1	—	—	2	1	2	1	1	1	1	—	—
Chicago Booth	1	1	—	1	1	1	1	2 1	—	—	1	1	1	—	—	—	—	—	—
Dartmouth Tuck	1	—	1	1	1	—	1½	2	—	1	1½	1	2	—	1	—	1	—	—
Harvard Business School	½	½	1	1	—	—	1	2	—	1	1	1	—	1	—	—	—	1	—
INSEAD	1	1	2	—	1	1	1	2	—	1	1	1	1	1	—	—	—	—	—
MIT Sloan	1	—	—	1	1	—	—	1½	—	—	—	1	1	—	1	½	1	—	—

New York University Stern	1	—	—	1	1	1	—	1	1	1	1	1	—	—	—
Northwestern University Kellogg	1	—	—	1	1	1	—	1[a]	1	1	2	1	—	—	—
Stanford Graduate School of Business	1	1	—	1	2	3	½	½	2	1	2	1	—	—	—
Wharton School of the University of Pennsylvania	1	1	1	1	2	2	1	1	2	2	2	1	1	—	—
Yale School of Management[b]	1	—	1	1	2	5	—	—	1	1	1	1	—	1	1

Note: ▨ = student is required to take 1 of 2 courses; ▧ = student is required to take 4 of 6 courses; ▥ = student is required to take 5 of 7 courses; ½ = half the class covers this discipline, and the other half of the class covers another discipline.

[a] As of June 2008, a global course was required at Kellogg.

[b] For the Yale School of Management, which introduced a new core curriculum in the fall of 2006 (see chapter 11 for details), we have coded The Investor as finance; The Competitor and The Innovator as strategy; Integrated Leadership Perspective, Employee, Interpersonal Dynamics, Managing Groups and Teams, and Careers as organizational behavior/leadership; The Operations Engine as operations; and The Customer as marketing.

by a minority of schools. They often involve hands-on managerial skills. These courses might be called the "peripheral core" because they remain outside the mainstream of most programs.[16]

Yale's redesigned curriculum is different. Rather than emphasizing traditional functions such as marketing, finance, and strategy, it is built around stakeholders, both external (e.g., competitors and customers) and internal (e.g., employees and innovators). The goal is to provide students with an integrated perspective on each of these different constituencies. For example, the customer course, which is taught by faculty from multiple disciplines, integrates learning from fields such as marketing, operations, and accounting. Like Yale, a number of schools are also introducing courses such as Problem Framing, The Innovator, and Critical Analytical Thinking into their required curriculum in order to develop a new set of cognitive skills that have not previously been part of the traditional MBA curriculum.

We looked closely at the content and formats of three foundational courses: financial accounting, strategy, and leadership/organizational behavior. The basic data appear in tables 3-4 through 3-6.[17] All schools require students to take thirteen to twenty-five sessions of financial accounting (on average, nineteen sessions), usually during the first semester or quarter (table 3-4). These courses cover much of the same material. All eleven courses cover statement of cash flows; ten of eleven cover accounting principles and the accounting cycle, financial statement analysis, long-term and short-term assets, and long-term and short-term liabilities; and eight of eleven cover acquisition and intercorporate ownership. Four schools assign the same popular textbook, and three schools assign another.[18] Schools differ, however, in the amount of time they devote to individual topics and the perspective they take. Some schools teach accounting from the standpoint of the preparer, others from the standpoint of the analyst, and still others from the standpoint of the manager. Schools also differ in their pedagogies, especially their reliance on case studies and the importance they attach to class discussion. Here, Harvard anchors one end of the spectrum, teaching all financial accounting classes by the case method and making 40 percent of a student's grade dependent on class participation, and Northwestern anchors the other end of the spectrum, with no assigned cases and 90 percent of a student's grade dependent on

TABLE 3-4

Core courses in financial accounting: Topics, number of sessions, and teaching method

Schools	Accounting Principles and Accounting Cycle	Revenue Recognition	Income Statement	Financial Statement Analysis	Statement of Cash Flows	Long-Term Assets	Short-Term Assets	Long-Term Liabilities	Current Liabilities	Stockholder Equity	Acquisition and Intercorporate Ownership	Other (intro., exams, review, less common topics)	Total Sessions	Teaching Method[a]
	S	S	S	S	S	S	S	S	S	S	S	S		
Carnegie Mellon Tepper	2	0	1	1	2	0	1	2	0	2	2	2	15	R/P: 9 C: 4
Chicago Booth	2	0	1	1	2	3	4	5	0	1	0	3	22	R/P: 10 C: 9
Dartmouth Tuck	1	1	2	4	2	1	1	3	1	2	0	1	19	R/P: 3 C: 15
Harvard Business School	2.5	2	0.5	5.5	1	1	0.5	3	0	2	2	3	23	R/P: 0 C: 20

(continued)

TABLE 3-4 (continued)

Schools	Accounting Principles and Accounting Cycle	Revenue Recognition	Income Statement	Financial Statement Analysis	Statement of Cash Flows	Long-Term Assets	Short-Term Assets	Long-Term Liabilities	Current Liabilities	Stockholder Equity	Acquisition and Intercorporate Ownership	Other (intro., exams, review, less common topics)	Total Sessions	Teaching Method[a]
	S	S	S	S	S	S	S	S	S	S	S	S		
INSEAD	3	1	1	2	1	1	1	1	1	1	1	3	17	R/P: 6 C: 8
MIT Sloan	2	2	0	2	1	3	1	4	1	1	1	6	24	R/P: 13 C: 6
New York University Stern	4	0	1	1	3	1	1	1	0	0	0	3	15	R/P: 8 C: 3

School													Total Sessions	R/P & C
Northwestern University Kellogg	4	0	3	2	2	2	4	2	1	0	0	2	22	R/P: 20 C: 0
Stanford Graduate School of Business	5	1	0	6	1	3	2	2	0	1	0	4	25	R/P: 6 C: 14
Wharton School of the University of Pennsylvania[b]	1	1	2	0	1	2	2	3.5	0	0.5	0	2	15	R/P: 8 C: 4
Yale School of Management	3	0	3	3	3	0	0	0	0	0	0	1	13	R/P: 11 C: 2

Note: S= Number of sessions, R/P = Readings/Problem sets, C = Cases.

a. For most schools, the number of sessions listed under Teaching Method is less than the number of Total Sessions. The remaining sessions are miscellaneous sessions (such as, lectures, videos, visitors, reviews, and exams) that have no required reading as preparation.

b. Used 2007 Acct 621 syllabus.

exams. Other schools fall midway between these two, relying on a combination of readings, cases, exercises, and problem sets for conveying ideas and computing grades.

The picture for strategy, a somewhat less mature field, shows a bit more diversity (table 3-5). Nine of the eleven schools expect students to take a strategy course—seven as a core requirement and two as a core elective. The course's position in the program varies, with some offerings in the fall, some in the winter, and some in the spring, indicating different views on whether the course is formative or summative. The number of sessions varies as well, ranging from eleven to thirty, with an average of sixteen. Cases are used far more widely than in financial accounting and are the dominant form of material at most schools, although they vary from being the focus of the class to serving as illustrative examples. Not surprisingly, class participation is weighted more heavily in grading strategy courses than in grading financial accounting courses; the same is true of individual case write-ups and team projects. Only one textbook is used by more than a single school.[19] Even so, courses cover much of the same material. All nine courses cover competitive dynamics; all nine cover scope, diversification, and multibusiness strategy; eight of nine cover industry analysis; eight of nine cover the positioning perspective; and seven of nine cover competitive advantage. As with financial accounting, the time and attention devoted to topics varies, and schools differ in whether they emphasize single-business or multibusiness topics. All courses, however, have a strong analytical bent, based primarily on industrial organization theory and microeconomics.[20]

Leadership and organizational behavior courses show the most diversity (table 3-6). All eleven schools require students to take courses in these areas; in many programs, multiple courses are involved. Titles include Managing Organizations, Organizational Processes, Leading People and Groups, and Management of People at Work. The number of sessions range from fourteen to fifty-nine, with an average of roughly thirty-one.[21] All schools rely on case studies to some degree, but vary in their use of surveys, exercises, simulations, and other experiential and action learning methods. Chicago Booth and Stanford rely most heavily on experiential methods, whereas Harvard and MIT use them much less frequently. Schools also differ strongly in the perspective

TABLE 3-5

Core courses in strategy: Topics, number of sessions, and teaching method

Schools	Industry Analysis (S)	Competitive Advantage (S)	Positioning Perspective (S)	Resource-Based View (S)	Capability-Based View (S)	Competitive Dynamics (S)	Multibusiness/Scope/Diversification (S)	Corporate Scope (S)	Global Scope (S)	Other (Intro., exams, review, speakers, less common topics) (S)	Total Sessions	Teaching Method[a]
Carnegie Mellon Tepper	—	—	—	—	—	—	—	—	—	—	—	—
Chicago Booth	1	0	1	0	0	6	0	2	0	1	11	R: 1 C: 9
Dartmouth Tuck	2	0	4	0	0	4	1	0	0	5	16	R: 0 C: 12
Harvard Business School	3	3.5	4.5	0	0	7.5	2.5	1.5	2.5	5	30	R: 0 C: 28

(continued)

TABLE 3-5 (*continued*)

Schools	Industry Analysis	Competitive Advantage	Positioning Perspective	Resource-Based View	Capability-Based View	Competitive Dynamics	Multibusiness/Scope/Diversification	Corporate Scope	Global Scope	Other (Intro., exams, review, speakers, less common topics)	Total Sessions	Teaching Method[a]
	s	s	s	s	s	s	s	s	s	s		
INSEAD	1	3	2	2	0	1	2	0	1	1	13	R: 4 C: 8
MIT Sloan	—	—	—	—	—	—	—	—	—	—	—	—
New York University Stern	1	1	1	0	0	2	4	1	1	3	14	R: 0 C: 12
Northwestern University Kellogg	2	2	2	0	0	6	0	2	0	5	19	R: 8 C: 9 (all cases: 11 sessions split in half, and there is always a case in the second half)

School												
Stanford Graduate School of Business	1	1	1	0	0	2	3	0	0	10	18	C: 17
Wharton School of the University of Pennsylvania	2	3	0	1	0	1	2	1	0	3	13	R: 1 C: 11
Yale School of Management	0	4.5	1	0	0	2.5	0	1	0	3	12	R/E: 8 C: 4

Note: S = Number of sessions, R = Readings, E = Exercises, C = Cases.

a. For most schools, the number of sessions listed under Teaching Method is less than the number of Total Sessions. The remaining sessions are miscellaneous sessions (such as, lectures, videos, visitors, reviews, and exams) that have no required reading as preparation.

TABLE 3-6

Core courses in leadership/organizational behavior: Topics, number of sessions, and teaching method

Schools	Course Titles	Organizational Behavior S	Human Resource Management S	Teams S	Leadership S	Communication S	Interpersonal Relationships S	Decision Making S	Other (intro., exams, review, less common topics) S	Total Sessions	Teaching Method[a]
Carnegie Mellon Tepper	Managing Organizations	4	1	1	1	0	1.5	0	5.5	14	R: 8 C: 11 Si: 1 Pr: 1
Chicago Booth[b]	Managing in Organizations; LEAD (+1 more course students can take for core area requirement, not coded)	3	0	7	5	3	3	1	5	27	R: 10 C: 8 V: 2 LOE: 3
Dartmouth Tuck	Leading Organizations; Analysis for General Management	9	0	2	5	0	3	2	5	26	R: 11 Su: 2 C: 8 Pr: 1 N: 1 E: 1

School	Course										Codes
Harvard Business School	LEAD (parts of Entrepreneurial Mgr and Leadership & Corporate Accountability, not coded)	12	0	6	8	0	6	0	6	38	C: 24 E: 2 V: 2
INSEAD	Leading People & Groups; Leading Organizations	8	1	4	6	2	3	0	6	30	R: 11 C: 9 P: 1 V: 2 Si: 1 Su: 2 E: 2
MIT Sloan	Organizational Processes (works closely with two required courses: Leadership & Personal Effectiveness; Coaching and Team Project Class; last two not coded)	7	1	2	2	14	3	1	2	32	R: 14 C: 11 D: 1 E: 1
New York University Stern	Managing Organizations	8	0	2	0	0	4	2	7	23	R: 9 C: 8 E: 1 V: 1
Northwestern University Kellogg	Leadership in Organizations	6	0	2	2	0	6	2	3	21	R: 7 C: 5 V: 2 E: 3 Si: 1
Stanford Graduate School of Business	Leadership Labs; Organizational Behavior; Managing Groups and Teams; Human Resources (last three not coded)	0	2	2	4	0	2	0	2	12	C: 5 E: 3 Si: 2

(continued)

TABLE 3-6 (continued)

Schools	Course Titles	Organizational Behavior	Human Resource Management	Teams	Leadership	Communication	Interpersonal Relationships	Decision Making	Other (intro., exams, review, less common topics)	Total Sessions	Teaching Method[a]
		S	S	S	S	S	S	S	S		
Wharton School of the University of Pennsylvania	Management of People at Work; Foundations of Leadership and Teamwork (also courses on management communication and on ethics and responsibility, not coded)	6	4	4	3		3	1	7	28	R: 21 C: 14 E: 6 P: 2
Yale School of Management	Integrated Leadership Perspective; Employee; Interpersonal Dynamics; Managing Groups and Teams; Careers	7	6	8	10	6	0	0	22	59	R: 36 C: 19 E: 8 V: 4

Note: S = Number of sessions, R = Reading, C = Cases, Si = Simulations, Pr = Presentations, Su = Survey/Questionnaire, N = Negotiation session, E = Experience/Exercise, V = Video, P = Paper, D = MIT Sloan's Team Day, where students "spend a day working on the role of teams in organizations," LOE = Leadership Outdoor Experience.

a. For most schools, the number of sessions listed under Teaching Method is less than the number of Total Sessions. The remaining sessions are miscellaneous sessions (such as, lectures, videos, visitors, reviews, and exams) that have no required reading as preparation.

b. Chicago's mandatory LEAD class is very exercise oriented and does not map easily onto the categories we use for topics. Also, students can take two to three other leadership/organizational behavior courses to fulfill their area requirement. We chose to code the syllabus for the popular class Managing in Organizations as a representative example.

and orientation of their classes. Some programs focus primarily on organizational theory and behavior; some focus primarily on leadership theory, skills, and development; and some focus primarily on teams and teamwork. Some courses spend considerable time on the topics of human resource management and interpersonal relationships; others do not.

Overall, the picture that emerges from this analysis of schools' course offerings is one of considerable commonality in key topics, especially in the more established disciplines, but considerable diversity in course coverage, emphasis, perspective, and pedagogy. Despite strong overlaps in their basic subject matter, required courses in financial accounting, strategy, and leadership/organizational behavior vary on multiple dimensions: length, point of view, coverage, number of sessions devoted to essential topics, and their relative emphasis on lectures, case-based discussions, problem sets, and exercises.

Surveys of core finance courses at top MBA programs by Professor Kent Womack of Dartmouth support these findings and present an equally mixed picture of commonality amidst diversity, and stability coupled with change.[22] Between 2001 and 2005, required finance courses changed little in their topics and relative emphasis. Portfolio theory, the capital asset pricing model, and capital budgeting continued to top the list of topics that received the most time and attention. Courses continued to devote significant amounts of time to present value and other basic background topics in order to level the playing field for students before more difficult subjects are introduced. The time devoted to options and capital structure and dividend policy has increased slightly, and the time devoted to equity valuation has fallen. Bond valuation continued to receive only limited attention. On average, roughly one-quarter of class time was devoted to case studies, with the bulk of time spent in lectures. The same two textbooks continued to dominate the market. However, on each of these dimensions there was also considerable variation across schools. There was equally wide variation in the total class time devoted to core finance courses, ranging, in 2005, from twenty-four to eighty hours, with an average of forty-four hours. The general trend has been toward an increase in the time spent on finance. In fact, between 2001 and 2005, the proportion of top MBA programs requiring two finance courses rose from 20 to 50 percent.

Taken together, these portraits paint a picture of both standardization and differentiation. Much of the content is common, but it is subject to myriad variations and permutations. At leading MBA programs, students are exposed to many of the same subjects and take many of the same courses, but each comes in its own flavor. The structures of the programs are different, as are the underlying pedagogies. As the case studies in part II vividly demonstrate, programs differ in purpose; they are animated by different principles and organizing themes. At Chicago Booth the theme is flexibility and deep roots in the disciplines, at Harvard it is the general management perspective, at INSEAD it is globalization, at Stanford it is customization and the tailoring of courses to students' experiences and skills, and at Yale it is integration. Each orientation leads to differences in substance, shading, and tone, even when the same courses and topics are being taught.

These differences in content and purpose drive different program architectures as well as the associated pedagogies. For example, the case method complements Harvard's general management perspective, leading to a very different student learning model relative to programs that use other teaching techniques. Moreover, Harvard's program architecture reinforces its orientation and emphasis. Keeping students in ninety-person cohorts for a full year results in groups that, because of their great familiarity with one another, are more comfortable and practiced in dealing with complex, ambiguous, and contentious issues. Programs that rely less heavily on the case method or other discussion-based approaches frequently favor smaller cohorts and keep them together for shorter periods to extract most of the benefits of an intact learning group while avoiding the staleness and occasional dysfunctions of groups that stay together for too long.

The choice of a rigid versus flexible core similarly leads to different student experiences. A flexible core caters to heterogeneous student backgrounds and preparation. It is frequently presented as enhancing student engagement by challenging students to reach their full potential. The disadvantage is that it does not always bring together students with the varying experiences and points of view that are so critical to having multiple perspectives represented in class. A rigid core, by contrast, allows for more integration because of common educational experiences.

Without question, these architectural, pedagogical, and design choices result in different educational experiences for students. Each alternative has an associated set of advantages and disadvantages. Each also has strong supporters—frequently alumni who enjoyed their MBA training and now attribute their success to its distinctive features, or long-serving faculty whose teaching and classes have always conformed to a particular architecture or design. Our own view is that no single approach is superior on all dimensions. When designing programs, one has to think about trade-offs. At the same time, we strongly believe that schools should avoid spending too much time fine-tuning and reengineering their program structures and architectures without changing the substance of their school's offerings. Changing an element such as size of cohort, course length, and number of required courses without thinking through the overall purpose is unlikely to add educational value.

Despite these variations, there is one element of commonality at leading business programs that has persisted over time and, in recent years, has attracted increasing criticism and concern: the analytical and technical orientation of MBA training. We turn to that topic in the next chapter.

A Rising Chorus of Concerns

T O BETTER UNDERSTAND current concerns about the MBA, one must begin with some history. From its start in the late nineteenth century, graduate business education has been the subject of nearly continuous debate. As one dean put it over twenty years ago, "No professional field of study has been more consistently inspirational both to its friends and critics."[1] Surprisingly, the substance of these debates has changed little over time. There have been alternating waves of suspicion and support, each motivated by the same basic tension: how to balance the demands of scholarship and practice.

The "Two Cultures" Problem

The development of university-based business schools is, in many ways, a story of aspiration and acculturation—a quest for legitimacy within the wider world of the university.[2] The earliest university-based business schools, such as Wharton (1881), the University of Chicago (1898), Berkeley (1898), Tuck (1900), Northwestern (1908), and Harvard Business School (1908), were founded largely to meet the demand for more rigorous and systematic business and management training. Education at these schools was to be in marked contrast to the vocational orientation of apprenticeships and private commercial colleges. Faculty members would be accountable to the university and its values, committed to the pursuit of teaching, research, and scholarship without bias or a prescribed ideological or commercial agenda. By participating in these programs, business leaders would, it was hoped, attain the status and social standing of a profession.

And so the debate was joined. Some academic leaders welcomed business into the university community, whereas others disdained it. Business schools quickly found themselves pulled in two directions simultaneously. They struggled to meet the intellectual demands of their academic audiences while attending to the practical demands of their professional audiences. Two cultures, each with its own agenda, norms, and frames of reference, struggled for control: "the soldiers of organizational performance and the priests of research purity."[3] What topics should be the focus of teaching and research? Should the curriculum feature analytical tools or managerial problems? Should the emphasis be on rigor or relevance?

Eventually, rigor won. In 1959, the now famous Ford Foundation and Carnegie Corporation reports were published.[4] Both roundly criticized business schools for falling far short of their scholarly aspirations. As one expert observed, "the desire for breadth[,] . . . combined with the lack of developed subject matter in business fields per se, left many programs lacking in coherence or underlying logic."[5] Business school curricula were, for the most part, still narrow and vocational. The advice they offered to managers was largely anecdotal. The associated research and theories were often unsophisticated and incomplete. The solution, the reports argued, was for programs to model themselves ever more closely on traditional arts and sciences departments. Students would be provided with "a high level of analytical ability" as well as "a sophisticated command of analytical and research tools derived from the fundamental disciplines."[6]

These reports, coupled with the subsequent funding of research programs and curriculum reforms at several leading business schools, led to dramatic changes: a sharp rise in analytical courses, an increase in the research orientation of business school faculty, a tighter alignment with traditional academic disciplines such as applied mathematics, economics, statistics, and social psychology, and a greater commitment to rigorous, theory-based scholarship.[7] These were necessary steps in legitimizing business schools' presence within the modern research university, but they came with problems of their own. Business school faculty began to look increasingly like faculty in other academic disciplines. They were recruited from traditional PhD programs, were well versed in the latest research methods, and were expected to publish their work in the best academic journals. But they were frequently lacking in business knowledge—or even an interest in business.[8] The result, according to critics, was that business schools soon "lost their way . . . the focus of graduate business education . . . [became] . . . increasingly circumscribed—and less and less relevant to practitioners."[9]

This argument has several threads.[10] Because business schools are increasingly modeled on academic disciplines, business school research is seen as having only limited impact on managers and the problems they face. Whether it is best-selling business books or influential management ideas, the authors are increasingly consultants or managers, not business school faculty. A recent look at the world's fifty most important management innovations (an admittedly subjective grouping that included such concepts as brand management, strategic business units, and T-groups) concluded that none of the fifty had its origins in academic research or scholarship.[11] Why? Because young professors have simply responded rationally to the incentives they face. To get promoted they need academic publications, not books or articles aimed at a popular audience. The former count when it comes to career advancement, whereas the latter do not. And because the most prestigious academic journals prefer theory and methodological rigor to applied problem solving and managerial topics, those are the types of papers that young scholars produce.[12]

The result, according to critics, is a growing "gap between theory and practice," and the coexistence of two largely separate, independent communities.[13] Some of the criticisms from within the academy have been sharp:

> Business schools appeal to one another as scholarly communities through a plethora of academic journals that are utterly divorced from the challenges of everyday management.[14]

> [O]ur elite scholarly journals have, on the whole, become a means of communicating with those within our discipline,

leaving our research at risk of failing any reasonable test of applicability or relevance.[15]

A number of executives we interviewed shared these views, noting their lack of interest in business school research. One executive put it bluntly: "As for using business school research, I don't do that, and my colleagues don't talk about it."

Most deans disagreed with these critiques, arguing that business school research was indeed practical and relevant.[16] They gave a number of examples. Modern finance theory, several deans noted, has, for better and worse, had a profound impact on practice. Recent work in strategy, accounting, and organizational behavior has also affected practice through incorporation in textbooks and practitioner-oriented journals such as *Harvard Business Review*, *Sloan Management Review*, and *California Management Review*.[17]

Our own view lies somewhere in the middle. Although examples of relevant research can be readily identified, we believe that more needs to be done to build useful and usable models that bridge the gap between academic business school research and the knowledge needs of practicing managers. There is, unfortunately, little work that synthesizes and translates discipline-based research to make it relevant and accessible to practitioners. Too little attention is given to field-based research that explores real-world management practices and offers insights into how managers actually respond to the contingencies and complexities they face. Too often, research lacks an interdisciplinary or problem-focused lens, and so misses the multifaceted challenges that managers must address. A recent AACSB report makes many of the same points.[18]

For related reasons, critics view MBA training as having limited value in preparing students for their careers. Most courses emphasize analytical frameworks and quantitative techniques, not softer, hard-to-measure organizational skills. This approach has the advantage of teaching students how to dissect and solve complex problems, such as valuing a potential acquisition, balancing an assembly line, or positioning a new product, as well as providing essential functional knowledge in fields such as accounting, finance, marketing, operations, and strategy.

Students learn the language and frameworks of business. Particularly at those schools that rely heavily on the case method, they also learn a way of thinking: how to identify underlying assumptions, assess alternatives, take a position and defend it, critique plans and proposals, and place business problems in a larger, multifunctional context. Even though these attributes were highly regarded by executives and deans—several cited them as *the* primary value of MBA training—they were generally viewed as incomplete.

Why? Because students learn analysis, but not action. They develop skill in attacking problems, but learn little about implementing solutions. They become knowledgeable about business, but remain untutored in the art and craft of management.[19] "MBA education," one dean argued, "is creating technocrats, people with a great toolbox who are not able to accomplish the things that organizations need them to accomplish." Another dean added, "We are training people to do what we faculty know how to do. We are analysts. We are weak in equipping people to run something—motivating, building teams, or building consensus. Most of our faculty have never tried to do something through a team outside academia."

Despite the research orientation of faculty and their need to be at the cutting edge of their fields, analytical courses continue to feature many of the same fundamental concepts and frameworks that emerged years ago: decision trees, the five forces of strategy, statement of cash flows, and the capital asset pricing model. To be sure, new ideas such as real options, behavioral finance, supply chain management, and sustaining competitive advantage have been steadily added to the curriculum. Nevertheless, a few deans believed that too much of the curriculum has remained unchanged. As one of them put it, "If I look back at the 1960s and 1970s, new students were really ahead of practice. During that time, the curriculum changed a lot. That isn't happening now."[20]

Moreover, many companies have sought to keep their executives current by beefing up in-house training programs and sending managers to attend short, specialized programs on campus. The result, according to critics, is that newly minted MBAs no longer enjoy privileged access to the latest business frameworks, concepts, or techniques. One dean noted, "Twenty years ago, MBAs were seen as value-added for what they brought. Today, there is a structural change in the value of the MBA. Now we need to go deeper. We need to show progress and develop new concepts. We can't impress just based on the jargon." Executives agreed, citing the rapid spread of knowledge among firms in their industries:

> Today we get much less cutting-edge knowledge from MBAs. There is much more commoditization of investing banking knowledge. In most cases, the information is already out there.

> We are not hiring MBAs for their ability to bring cutting-edge research to the firm. There's been a commoditization of knowledge among consulting firms.

In light of the recent economic crisis, the last two quotations are even more disturbing. They suggest that although knowledge of key business frameworks, concepts, and techniques may have been widespread in investment banking and consulting, their knowledge base remained partial and incomplete. Post-crisis, executives and deans identified a number of gaps in MBA teaching, largely in applied areas such as risk management, internal governance, the behavior of complex systems, regulation and business/government relations, and socially responsible leadership. Critics also raised questions about the mind-set and perspective that MBA graduates absorbed from a steady diet of technical, analytical courses. Few students were made aware of the limitations of the theories they were learning, the complexity of the trade-offs they would face, and the skeptical, critical lenses they would need to accurately evaluate data and draw correct conclusions.

Together, these criticisms raise serious questions about MBA education. As business schools have modeled themselves increasingly on the academic disciplines in order to secure their foothold in the university, their research and teaching have become less and less relevant to executives and students. Both groups have responded rationally and predictably: the former by viewing MBA graduates as often in need of additional hands-on training and development, and the latter by disengaging from their academic studies.

A Decline in Student Engagement

At many business schools, faculty and deans complain of a steady erosion of student interest in, and commitment to, academics. Classes are no longer the centerpiece of the MBA experience, having been replaced by other activities. "When was the last time," one dean asked, "that you heard an MBA student say, 'I came here because of the curriculum?'" One result has been a lessening of effort and a widely shared concern among faculty that students no longer devote themselves as diligently to coursework as they did in the past. Several deans reported that measures of the academic work week—the total amount of time students spend in, or preparing for, classes—have declined significantly over time. At one institution, the figure fell from forty-five to fifty hours per week in 1975 to thirty hours per week in 2003–2004. Another institution found that its students were starting to prepare for the next day's classes later and later each day (and presumably were spending less time on preparation as a result). A third institution, with a class of a few hundred, discovered that it was home to over sixty-five student clubs, meaning that virtually every member of the class had the opportunity to serve as a club officer. Rather than devoting themselves to academics, students were spending increasing amounts of time networking, attending recruiting events, planning club activities, and pursuing the best possible job. As one dean noted, "The focus has shifted from learning to earning."

This shift has several roots. In part, it reflects the increased prominence and influence of business school rankings.[21] In 1988, *BusinessWeek* published the first business school rankings; other publications, such as the *Wall Street Journal*, *Financial Times*, and *U.S. News and World Report*, soon followed suit. Many ranking systems give great weight to salary, career advancement, and recruiters' evaluations when calculating scores. This creates a vicious cycle. High rankings mean better job placement and faster progression through the ranks; students, like most people, are responsive to those factors and weigh them heavily when selecting a program. Business schools, not surprisingly, frequently cite these same advantages in their marketing and promotional materials (especially if they have recently jumped in the rankings), further promoting a careerist orientation. Over time, success at recruiting and job placement has become increasingly important.

The emphasis on careers has been exacerbated as employers have shifted their recruiting practices. Companies that continue to hire MBAs from two-year, full-time programs are doing so earlier and earlier, before classes have proceeded very far. This suggests an increase in emphasis in the recruitment process on prior experience and the personal qualities of applicants. A number of recruiters made essentially the same observation:

> Ten years ago the summer internship program yielded 50% of our full-time MBA recruits. Now the summer program yields 85% to 90% of full-time recruits. Today, we view the summer work experience as a full-time job, expecting that they will accept an offer.

> We are hiring for summer jobs early in the second semester of the first year. So, their previous experience is important, and the business school doesn't have much time with students before we evaluate them.

> The summer program is much more important now than it used to be, and it takes up much more of our recruiting time. Now, we spend 75% of our recruiting time on the summer job and 25% on the second year. Twenty years ago, it was the reverse. Now we only fill holes with the recruiting in the second year.

Such early hiring suggests that MBA programs are being valued increasingly for their screening and selection role. The top business schools attract intelligent, hard-working, accomplished students, who have already displayed an interest in business or an aptitude for leadership—exactly the qualities that companies are looking for. Students, not surprisingly, often respond with reduced interest in their coursework, especially those classes that come later in their programs.

At the same time, the decline in student engagement also reflects a change in demographics: the increased diversity of students, many of them from less traditional backgrounds, and the difficulty of shepherding them all through the same set of basic, required courses. As chapter 3 showed, the first-year curricula at most business schools cover many of the same topics, techniques, and theories. Most schools require both experts and novices to wade through these same materials. This means that students who already have deep exposure to the field ("rocket scientists") often sit side by side with students who are largely unfamiliar with the basics ("poets"). The gaps between these two groups are frequently large; for this reason, especially in quantitative or analytical courses such as finance, accounting, and strategy, it becomes difficult to pitch the material in a way that does not disengage a significant proportion of students. Oversimplifying the course means boring the experts; moving too quickly to more advanced material means losing the novices. The implications, one dean observed, are especially troubling for the most advanced students because "bringing in highly successful people and trapping them in a rigid, required core curriculum raises the question, 'What is the value-added of putting these students through the core?'"

This problem, it should be noted, is not shared by all professional schools. In fields such as medicine, dentistry, and law, the vast majority of entering students are on relatively equal footing because they come to graduate school with limited prior knowledge of the subject. Neither undergraduate courses nor prior work experience provides more than a cursory introduction to essential medical, dental, or legal knowledge. The same cannot be said of business schools, where differences in undergraduate majors and post-college jobs often create sharp disparities in preparation and prior knowledge among members of the entering class.

Opportunities and Unmet Needs

Despite these concerns about the value added by MBA education, the future is filled with possibility. There is a growing consensus about the changes needed to make programs more relevant. Deans and executives consistently identified the same set of opportunities and unmet needs, topics that they viewed as poorly or incompletely addressed by business schools today but that, if they were to be well researched and properly taught, would make the degree have far more impact. All reflect the changing nature of business today and an expanded notion of the essential skills required of business leaders. As later chapters will show, experiments are already under way in many of these areas, encompassing both individual courses and entire MBA programs.

A Global Perspective

First on the list is the desire for a more global perspective. It is by now virtually a truism that information, capital, and trade flows are increasingly global; that countries such as Brazil, Russia, India, and China are the marketplaces, service centers, and production sites of the future; and that businesses must learn to adapt to a wide variety of local, national, and regional rules, regulations, institutions, business practices, and social norms. Even so, one dean noted, "globalization is not something that any school has fully grasped."[22] Executives agreed, zeroing in on the need for students to develop greater "cultural sensitivity" and "cultural awareness." Students, they argued, had to learn to work comfortably and effectively with people who had sharply different values and behaviors. A new set of skills and sensitivities was required, a kind of "cultural intelligence"—the ability to interpret and respond appropriately to the unfamiliar and often ambiguous words, gestures, and behaviors of people from countries and cultures other than one's own.[23]

The goal, both deans and executives emphasized, was not simply for students to acquire abstract, theoretical knowledge about the world's many different economic and political systems. Rather, they needed to understand, at a granular, how-to-get-it-done level, the challenges and requirements of living and working in differing societal, organizational, and commercial contexts. At times business strategies and management styles will generalize, allowing for a single, global approach; at other times they will have to be tailored to local or regional requirements. At times markets will be so deeply interconnected that they can be treated as seamless or "flat"; at other times they will remain segregated and distinct because of political, economic, or technological barriers.[24] If students are to operate successfully on a global stage, they must develop the ability to distinguish these situations and act accordingly. Several executives expanded on this theme:

> The first truly global generation is now coming through business school. But we're not yet at the point of "one world," in the sense that cultural norms are collapsing to a single model. Students need to understand how to do business in different countries and cultures. They need training in asking the right questions.

> _____

> Outside the U.S., there is much greater government and NGO involvement in business. You're also dealing with people with a different worldview. Students need to develop a sense of the differences that they may not be aware of.

> _____

> There are simple, practical aspects to globalization—time differences, the stress of travel, the need to establish relationships before videoconferencing. Then there are the harder, more complex issues that involve cultural differences. If you know the culture, you'll see it reflected in the business. For instance, our Japanese organization doesn't tick the way our other units do. Then the questions become: What do you accept, and what not? What do you tolerate because that's just the way things are? What do you understand, but reject?

> _____

> It's the ability of executives to be global citizens, to have a real understanding of global issues. They don't have singular, simplistic responses keyed to one culture. When they discuss an issue, I listen for how quickly they begin to build in a contingency based on their context.

These views suggest that business schools still have much work to do before they can claim to be fully equipping their students with a global mind-set. There are challenges of both knowledge and action. Not only must students gain an understanding of the world's many differing business and economic environments, but also they must develop a set of conceptual, behavioral, and interpersonal skills that will allow them to navigate their way successfully through these environments, enabling them to work effectively with unfamiliar, culturally diverse customers, colleagues, partners, and suppliers.

Leadership Development

A second area of broadly recognized need is leadership development. Virtually all of the top business schools aspire to "develop leaders," yet their efforts in this area are widely viewed as falling short. In part, the problem is the state of knowledge in the field—the fact, as one dean put it, that "the research underpinnings are weaker than they should be." Many schools have been reluctant to move forward aggressively without a stronger theoretical base. Even so, executives cited a number of concrete steps that MBA programs could take to further their students' development as leaders.

Perhaps most important was the need to foster heightened, and more accurate, self-awareness. This was viewed as the starting point of leadership because, as one executive observed, "you can't understand others without understanding yourself." To get that understanding, students have to be offered more frequent, detailed feedback about their behavior—especially their interactions with others—as well as the opportunity to reflect, draw lessons, and make subsequent changes.[25] Several executives spoke in nearly identical terms:

> You need to be aware of how you act and how people respond to you. You need an awareness of how you appear to others, especially peers, and the impressions that you make. Give students enough so that they know how to go about pursuing this understanding through self-assessment.

_____

> Self-awareness is very important. To be a business leader, you have to understand yourself. I love the idea of increased emphasis on coaching, personal development, leadership skills, and small group experiences.

_____

MBA programs are heavy on IQ but poor on EQ [emotional intelligence]. Those who have EQ have a much clearer path to long-term success. High intellect and command of the toolkit are not enough to make it. The problem often comes down to a lack of self-reflection and self-examination.

All leaders benefit from having a mirror held up to themselves and receiving rich, regular, and rapid feedback on how they interact with other human beings.

One executive summarized these views by noting, "Any opportunity that allows the business leaders of the future to be more introspective is a plus."

Coupled with the desire for greater self-awareness was an interest in improving MBAs' interpersonal skills. Their ability to work well with others, especially in team or small-group settings, was viewed as weak. This is a critical deficiency, because most studies agree that "interpersonal influence" and the "mobilization of others" lie at the heart of effective leadership.[26] Here too executives shared a common view of the problem:

How do you lead? How do you get people to do what must be done? That requires knowledge about what moves others. Students need to understand situations from a psychological and interpersonal perspective, not just a cognitive point of view.

MBAs need to learn to work as members of a team. Immediately after business school, they're rock stars—they outproduce and outperform everybody else. But those same skills get in the way after the first few years on the job. Then they need to be able to do different things: build a well-functioning team, motivate a team, and delegate. It's important for them to be good at both leading and following, and helping others.

It's important for MBAs to think about how to move from an individual to a team mind-set. Preparing students for that shift is important because the more senior you get in an organization, the more it is about people. Leaders get things done through others.

————————————

Students need small-group experiences. To get the most out of them, they also need training, guidance, and structured opportunities for reflection to help them unearth those things that will be difficult for them in the work environment.

In addition to developing self-awareness and interpersonal skills, a number of deans and executives urged business schools to pay more attention to the ethical development of MBA students. This need has become even more acute in the wake of the economic crisis. As one dean observed, "People don't simply lack trust in business schools; they actively distrust them . . . In order to reduce people's distrust, business schools need . . . to teach that principles, ethics, and attention to detail are essential components of leadership, and they need to place a greater emphasis on leadership's responsibilities—not just its rewards."[27]

Executives raised similar concerns, encouraging schools to train students to prepare for, and to think through, ethical dilemmas they might face in their careers, ranging from insider trading to bribes and side payments to how best to deal with employees in the face of cutbacks and restructuring. As one executive put it, "Ethics is very high on my list. Students need to learn frameworks . . . a clear sense of right and wrong, and how to think through difficult situations." Another executive argued that such training was essential because some MBA students "take full advantage of the firm . . . they bend the truth to get what they want and engage in fast and loose behavior. We need to train and reinforce commitment, loyalty, and truthfulness."

Action-learning projects were cited by both deans and executives as the best vehicle for developing self-awareness, interpersonal skills, and ethical sensitivity. In their view, critical leadership capabilities such as exercising influence, creating engagement, driving toward completion, and behaving ethically in stressful, competitive situations are best learned by doing. That, in turn, requires immersion in challenging, real-world projects.

This approach has strong support from scholars: "It is now taken-for-granted that managers learn leadership skills by practice and observation, and therefore, learn most from direct work experiences . . . [O]ne of the most significant advances in executive development has been the increasing reliance on methods that take place *in situ*, notably action learning and coaching."[28] Within MBA programs, this would require teams of students to work together for extended periods in the field, under the oversight of faculty members and executive sponsors, collectively framing problems, assembling and analyzing data, assigning and completing tasks, brainstorming solutions, and preparing, presenting, and (to the extent possible) implementing their recommendations. As one executive pointed out, this approach would help overcome a common weakness in the training of MBAs: "the absence of fieldwork to challenge their thinking. MBAs try to argue and debate instead of just doing." Moreover, the coupling of collective responsibility with concrete deliverables, pressing timelines, and demanding clients would elicit many of the same behaviors—and dysfunctions—that one encounters in the workplace, providing students with rich opportunities for learning real-world leadership skills.

Integration

Business schools have long organized their faculties and course offerings by function and discipline. As chapter 3 has shown, functional courses such as finance, marketing, and operations and discipline-based courses such as micro- and macroeconomics remain the building blocks of most MBA programs today. Each course addresses problems from its own relatively narrow, specialized point of view, and topics are seldom integrated or coordinated across courses or fields. A silo mentality pervades business schools, just as it does many corporations. One former university president terms this the "Home Depot approach to education," in which knowledge is atomized "by dividing it into disciplines, sub-disciplines, and sub-subdisciplines," the curriculum "is little more than a collection of courses," and programs are in danger of "becoming academic superstores . . . [with] . . . courses . . . stacked up like sinks and lumber for do-it-yourselfers to try to assemble into their own meaningful whole."[29]

Business problems, unfortunately, seldom respect functional or disciplinary boundaries. Especially when problems are complex, effective solutions usually require an integrated, holistic perspective: the ability to apply multiple lenses and link differing points of view.[30] As one executive put it:

> What's missing from business schools is boundary spanning. Most business education today rests in silos. It is disciplinary-based. There's very little opportunity to deal with real problems that cross boundaries, yet that is the nature of problems that people confront in work settings. Think of an M&A deal where you have to weigh the value, complementarity, and conflict in brands, consider tax and manufacturing issues, and recommend how to finance and value the deal. If you walk into a meeting with the CEO of a merger candidate with a Blue Book [the written analysis of the deal] that doesn't address these issues in detail, you're cooked.

Both executives and deans noted that a multifunctional, multidisciplinary perspective was especially important when addressing the most pressing business challenges today, such as sustainability, innovation, and the global economic crisis. Such a perspective was regarded, almost by definition, as essential for those managers who sit atop their organizations and must balance and trade off the frequently competing demands of diverse functional groups.

Our interviewees differed on precisely what they meant by integration. Some defined it as a form of thinking, very much akin to synthesis: "the ability to knit together information from disparate sources into a coherent whole."[31] In business settings, "a highly-skilled integrator can see how the parts of a firm fit together and how they might fit together differently. The parts in play may be functional silos, separate product lines, individual divisions, or different geographic regions."[32] A second group argued that integration was a multistep reasoning process in which you "hold two opposing mental models in your head at the same time and come up with one that is better than both."

A third group defined integration as skill at applying multiple perspectives or viewpoints, but in a serial, linear fashion—as one executive put it, "the ability to go through the same problem using different functional lenses and look at it in a multitude of ways."[33] A fourth group defined integration as a problem- or solution-centric point of view, often from the vantage point of a CEO, business unit head, or general manager who is steward of a complex organization, oversees multiple functions, and is evaluated on an integrated P&L. According to this perspective, "An organization is like a tangle of rubber bands: tugging on one affects all the others. In dealing with a specific issue, the manager must recognize that it will always influence and be influenced by the general situation. How he or she deals with a problem in the sales department, for example, may affect overall company operations. The effective manager must think about the organization holistically and behave accordingly."[34]

Although there was general agreement that business schools needed to do a better job of teaching integration in one (or more) of these forms, deans and executives issued several caveats. The primary one, which we heard repeatedly, was that increased attention to integration must not come at the cost of downplaying or minimizing basic, foundational material. As one dean put it, "Integration should not be at the expense of deep knowledge. Every MBA must understand the key functional areas. You really need the basics before you start integrating, just as a cook needs the ingredients, an engineer must learn calculus, and a bridge designer must understand physics."

A second caveat was to avoid approaches to integration that relied too heavily on team teaching. Having faculty from different disciplines take responsibility for different portions of the same class, with few additional efforts to link concepts, frameworks, or readings, was described variously as "a recipe for disaster," an idea "that looks good on paper, but not so good in practice," and an approach that is "difficult to execute" and "tends to fail each time it has been tried because of high coordination costs." Although deans were almost uniformly negative about team teaching, we believe the jury is still out. A number of innovative team-teaching experiments are now under way, and there are clear educational benefits to bringing multiple perspectives into the classroom. Nevertheless, we agree that having faculty from different departments co-teach presents a difficult implementation challenge.

A final caveat from deans was to get the balance right: to include some sessions or pedagogies that were explicitly integrative in nature—here, the case method and capstone exercises or courses were cited repeatedly—but also to recognize that, as one dean observed, "you don't have to force it too much. Students are doing some of the integration themselves."

Organizational Realities: Power, Politics, and the Challenges of Implementation

Despite their years of work experience, MBAs, according to experienced executives, are often surprisingly naïve about organizations. They take a highly rational view of implementation and action, while failing to recognize that "organizations . . . are fundamentally political entities."[35] Newly minted MBAs frequently underestimate the power of hidden agendas, unwritten rules, long-term loyalties, behind-the-scene coalitions, and other potent political forces. They lack execution skills to get things done because they fail to fully understand basic organizational processes: how priorities are set, decisions are made, and tasks are accomplished.[36] As one executive put it, "They're not too good at the chess game." Two other executives expanded on these concerns:

> MBAs do not have a good sense of how business works. They don't have a good understanding of how a decision is made. More should be done to help students understand that the right answer on paper is not necessarily the right answer in practice. There should be more attention paid to process, and more emphasis on politics and power. In other words, there should be more focus on organizational realities.

> There is a level of naïveté, especially when it comes to resolving problems. Students need to understand why rational plans don't get implemented, why logical arguments don't get accepted,

why people say "yes" and then don't follow through. They need to understand how people think about initiatives that relate to their budgets and their organizations, and how to determine who is their boss and who is not. The MBA curriculum is thin in these respects.

These observations not only suggest that MBA students would become far more valuable to employers if they had a deeper understanding of the realities of power, politics, and implementation, but also reinforce the importance of action-learning projects focused on real-world problems. Projects give students firsthand knowledge of the difficulty of introducing initiatives, solving persistent problems, and getting groups of people to move in new directions. They are certain to teach students a great deal about the nuts and bolts of management, the levers of organizational action, and common barriers to change. One executive put the challenge bluntly: "In terms of managerial competence, MBA students are at a 'B' level. That needs to be higher."

In part, this problem reflects a larger shift in the world of organizations, from a world dominated by high-authority, low-conflict environments to a world in which low authority and high conflict are the norm.[37] This shift is both internal and external. For decades, large corporations have been tightly structured and hierarchical, with distinct, segregated functions and divisions, clear lines of authority, and well-defined roles and responsibilities. Conflict has often been viewed with concern and was compartmentalized to the extent possible.[38] Today, however, many global organizations have shifted to matrix and network forms. Two-boss structures, cross-functional teams, multidivisional councils, and committees with overlapping responsibilities are common, even at the highest levels. One senior executive acknowledged this reality by noting, only partly in jest, "It's not as lonely at the top as I'd hoped."

In such settings, conflicting agendas, diverse positions, and competing points of view are frequent occurrences. They can seldom be resolved by fiat. In fact, these tensions have often been consciously and deliberately built into the organizational fabric to force individuals and groups to surface and resolve difficult trade-offs. Matrix organizations, for example, have proliferated for precisely this reason: to ensure that attention is paid to conflicting, but equally legitimate, objectives and that the resulting choices are made consciously and carefully. When should the needs of country managers take priority over the needs of business unit leaders? When should functional agendas be emphasized—the pursuit of scale economies in manufacturing, rationalized supply chains, and uniformity in human resource practices— and when should business units be allowed to tailor functional policies to their idiosyncratic needs? Faced with conflicts like these, skilled executives rely far more on negotiation and discussion than direction or command.[39]

Several of our interviewees made a point of emphasizing the need for MBA students to learn how to implement more effectively when influence skills were essential for resolving divergent points of view. One executive noted, "I don't think people come out of MBA programs with a sense of trade-offs. In my organization, it's rare that you're picking the right decision. Usually, you're picking a good one and making it right." A senior executive at a consulting firm called for more "how-to-get-it-done insight," noting that "people who are really, really powerful in organizations are those who can get things done." An executive at a large consumer products company added: "We seek people who can influence others, who can articulate how they got things done. We want to know you can lead in a matrix environment." The same sentiment was voiced by an executive from Silicon Valley:

> When my peers and I get together, the discussion is all about how to influence others. You need to be able to persuade and negotiate, to communicate your ideas in a powerful way. In a large company, you have to be able to influence across the organization, not elevate up the chain of command. Even as a venture capitalist, you can't tell the CEO of a company to do anything. You have to be able to sell.

One dean summarized these views as follows: "What executives want from students is knowledge about how to execute. A good decision well executed will always beat a perfect decision poorly executed. Students analyze too much and don't pull the trigger when they should. Unfortunately, nobody teaches this well."

Much the same challenge exists externally. With the rise of activist shareholders and nongovernmental organizations (NGOs), large global corporations are now increasingly exposed to the threat of consumer boycotts, potentially damaging publicity, and other challenges to their brand or reputation.[40] Confrontation is a common tactic because many activists view public conflict as the primary means for realizing their goals. Corporations have limited authority over these organizations, yet they must frequently respond to their claims and demands. The global financial crisis has similarly heightened executives' public exposure and led to increased demands for legislative and regulatory oversight. Here too students need to understand and be able to respond to new business realities. According to the leader of a large multinational, "For me, the biggest challenge is, how do I deal with my opponents? Is it better to hold them at a distance or have a dialogue? Which ones do I trust? These are people who oppose me, and my organization, because of dogma and differing perspectives. To succeed, one must understand their agendas and be good at communication."

Creative, Innovative Thinking

Even though MBAs are well trained analytically, many executives and deans believe that they still lack essential innovative thinking skills. Faced with a clearly defined, targeted problem, MBAs are in their element, ready and able to apply spreadsheets, decision trees, financial models, and high-powered statistical methods. But faced with unstructured problems, ambiguous data, rapidly changing environments, and information overload—challenges that are common today, especially in emerging industries, nascent markets, and newly regulated or deregulated sectors of the economy—MBAs, critics contend, are less likely to be effective. Their current repertoire of tools and techniques is inadequate.[41] Instead, they must master a new set of skills: the ability to find and frame problems; collect, synthesize, and distill large volumes of data; exercise creativity and imagination; and develop, test, and revise ideas.

Lectures and case studies provide only limited training in these skills. Lectures are a passive form of learning and do little to teach unstructured problem solving. Case studies are more active, but they too are bounded and prepackaged; the instructor has already narrowed the problem down to manageable proportions and supplied the data required for essential calculations. The problem is usually stated as one of the assignment questions. But many business settings are much less obvious or clear-cut. They are, to use the technical term, "ambiguous," meaning that they are subject to multiple possible interpretations and remain plagued by many unknowns.[42] Case studies can get at these issues, but they would need to be written and used very differently, with broader descriptions of the business situation, lots of open-ended exploration, and no targeted questions. Other pedagogies such as field or project work lend themselves more naturally to problem finding and innovative thinking. Several executives cited the ability to work in unstructured environments as crucial to the future of business and the education of MBAs:

> We are all suffering from an increase in the signal-to-noise problem. When students develop business plans, they are flooded with information and have trouble teasing out the critical nuggets in their projects and proposals.

———————

> Students need to learn how to handle emergent situations. They need to learn when is the right time to act—when it is too soon, and when it is too late.

———————

> The most important thing that business schools do is prepare students for a world that is unpredictable. They need to learn how to cope with problems that are totally different from those that they have been exposed to. There is too much belief in models and data-based thinking. Students are not able to think originally; they aren't good at working from a blank sheet of paper.

———————

> In the future, MBAs need to learn how to assess the importance of things while they are still emergent. They need to be able to identify trends like Green-tech or Clean-tech and get ahead of

the curve. They don't have to know it all, but they have to know where to look for information and how to synthesize it.

There are several interrelated challenges. First is the need, as one dean put it, to be able to identify and define critical issues through "opportunity sensing and project scoping." Management challenges and business opportunities seldom come prelabeled; they must usually be culled from the environment, articulated, framed, and rated in importance. These skills are essential but have often taken a back seat to analysis. According to a leading scholar:

> As a result of research over the past twenty years, a number of extremely effective analytical techniques are currently available for the solution of management problems . . . But the manager's job is not simply to solve well-defined problems. He must also identify the problems to be solved . . . To many managers and students of management, the availability of formal problem solving procedures serves only to highlight those parts of the manager's job with which these procedures do *not* deal: problem identification, the assignment of problem priority, and the allocation of scarce resources to problems . . . These tasks may be among the most critical of the manager's decision making responsibilities.[43]

Executives noted that success at these tasks required a range of skills: "anticipation," "knowing where to look for data," and "the ability to synthesize." In emerging industries, especially those based on novel, cutting-edge technologies, there is the further challenge of coping with scattered, hard-to-validate information. As one experienced executive put it, "It's difficult to find marketplace insights for a market that doesn't exist."[44] In such settings, another executive observed, "Problem finding is need finding. Often, the future is already here but unrecognized. MBAs are not good at seeing around corners or detecting discontinuities. They need to learn how to collect information—how to cultivate and develop great sources, to find the expert wheel-maker and learn from him."

Once problems or opportunities have been identified, students must learn to tackle them creatively. Here too executives highlighted the need for projects that provide practice in "generative," "innovative," and "lateral" thinking and offer the opportunity to develop "game-changing ideas." They noted that, in their experience, creativity required "the ability and willingness to question authority and rules that seem true or immovable." Most important, they urged students to "overcome the skepticism that comes with an MBA, the tendency to say 'I've seen this tried before and it didn't work.'" Instead, they wanted to see "more of an adventurous attitude," a willingness "to come in and say, 'Let's give it a try,' to take risks and fail, to learn from experiments and iterate." Resilience—the ability to bounce back from failures, setbacks, and dead-ends—was viewed as absolutely essential to success. All of these capabilities and skills, executives argued, were best learned through practice: by wrestling repeatedly with unfamiliar, open-ended problems. As one of them put it, "The future will be based on innovation and creativity. So how do you prepare students for a world that is unpredictable? By throwing them into situations they know nothing about."

Oral and Written Communication

Managing is a social process, and managers' "working life is a never-ending series of contacts with other people. They must talk and listen, telephone, call meetings, plead, argue, negotiate."[45] Success requires skill at crafting and communicating proposals, presentations, and positions in ways that are logical, coherent, and persuasive. They should have a compelling point of view, marshal supporting evidence in a convincing fashion, distinguish fact from opinion, and flow logically and consistently from beginning to end. Clear thinking and effective communication are closely linked.

Unfortunately, MBAs are frequently weak in these areas.[46] Executives and deans agree strongly on this point. One executive observed that "even the students we hire from the best schools can't communicate," and another noted that "communication skills are poor, and without them you cannot lead." A dean added: "The ability to communicate is lacking. Students don't know how to present in front of groups, nor how to express their concerns in a frank but non-aggressive way." Although deficiencies were identified in both written and oral communication, the focus was on the latter. This is not surprising, because "virtually every empirical study of managerial time allocation draws attention to the great proportion of time spent in verbal communication."[47] Several executives singled out presentation skills as an area of special weakness:

> Students fail to deliver the important message up front. I'm often asked to review their five-minute pitch for a business plan, but after the first minute they still haven't given me a reason to listen for the next four. I'm looking for clarity with accuracy, precision, and conciseness.

> MBAs' basic presentation skills are weak. They lack confidence and don't make eye contact. They need to be able to get to the bottom line more quickly and to present the correct level of information for their audience.

> Students need to master the art of storytelling. They must learn to sell their ideas in a powerful, succinct way.

Case method classes overcome many of these weaknesses, but are not curative. Especially in first-year required courses, which are normally taught in sections of sixty to ninety students, comments are frequently brief, and few students get the opportunity to speak more than once per class. Only the opening speaker presents at length, with a fully developed position or point of view, and even he or she is usually interrupted or redirected frequently by the professor. Case method classes certainly develop rhetorical skills and the ability to contribute to an ongoing discussion, but are less effective at teaching students how to make extended presentations or to craft complex, nuanced arguments.

The six areas of opportunity presented to this point were highlighted by both deans and executives in our first round of interviews, which were conducted before the economic crisis. Post-crisis, we reinterviewed several deans and spoke further with a large number of executives. They reaffirmed these six areas of opportunity, but also introduced two new ones that we describe next.

The Role, Responsibilities, and Purpose of Business

Business executives have long been subject to public scrutiny, and never more so than in the recent past. As the global economic crisis has deepened, the public, already greatly concerned about high levels of executive compensation, a lack of transparency, and accounting irregularities, singled out business leaders as largely responsible for the economic downturn and the ensuing rise in unemployment. Their motives were questioned, as were their decision making and choices. Were business leaders guided by private interests alone, or did they also weigh the social consequences of their actions? Public distrust only increased as companies such as AIG and Merrill Lynch paid multimillion-dollar bonuses to the very same executives whose flawed decision making led to the government bailouts. Opinion polls repeatedly confirm the depressingly low regard in which business and business leaders are now held. The results have been predictable: greater government intervention, increased regulatory oversight, and tighter control of the private sector.

These shifts have prompted considerable soul searching at business schools. Many now recognize the need to reexamine the role and purpose of business and have students wrestle with complex questions of companies' responsibilities to stakeholders, such as customers, employees, and society at large, in addition to shareholders. The current generation of students seems to be inspired by this challenge. They are much more motivated to think of business success in terms of making money while being sensitive to work-life needs of employees and recognizing their responsibilities to the environment and society. In the words of several deans:

> Business and society is a huge issue today. This generation of students will force our hand on the topic. There is pressure to do more around social responsibility.

> There will be increasing pressure to get environmental, ethical, and corporate responsibility issues into the curriculum.

We're not raising the awareness of students or pushing them hard enough to think about their responsibility to the community or the wider society.

These issues revive an age-old debate about the purpose of the corporation and its role in society. On one side are scholars who argue for the primacy of shareholder value, and on the other side are scholars who favor a multiple-stakeholder approach.[48] At the heart of the debate is a deceptively simple question: What does it mean to be a good corporate citizen?[49] Although there is clearly a need for more research on this question, there is no doubt that the current crisis has accelerated the demands from society for more responsible leadership and for deeper discussion of these issues by MBA students.

Risk, Regulation, and Restraint: Understanding the Limits of Markets and Models

Not surprisingly, in the post-crisis interviews we conducted in 2009, both executives and deans cited the topics of risk and risk management as important gaps in MBA programs today. Among their comments:

There should be more focus on risk and governance. We have created students who are smart, but not necessarily as street smart and skeptical as they should be.

_____

So much of what we teach in strategy and entrepreneurship is about the upside and the right-hand tail of the distribution. We need to do a better job on the left-hand tail. We need to teach a lot more about the downside and potential failures.

_____

We need to understand risk. When you break it down into functions, you lose the bigger perspective and don't integrate the individual piece into the macro environment.

In particular, several executives raised concerns about the modeling of risk, especially by managers at many financial institutions, who often based their decisions prior to the economic crisis on probability distributions of future housing prices drawn from the most recent housing price data. These managers failed to consider longer-term trends; they relied too heavily on mathematical risk models and not enough on good judgment. Other executives pointed to links between incentives and risk taking and the related pursuit of short-run gains. Again, the issue was one of prudence and proper restraint, and how best to train students to design incentive systems so that they were aligned with long-run value maximization. What assumptions should one make about managerial behavior when designing compensation systems and the governance institutions that guide them? How powerful should incentives be, and what unintended consequences might they produce?

Several deans and executives emphasized the need for a deeper appreciation of macroeconomic issues. In particular, they noted the importance of exposing students to "lost decades," such as the 1930s in the United States and the 1990s in Japan and Latin America, in order to develop a better understanding of how and when speculative bubbles occur. The recent economic crisis also suggests a related gap in students' understanding of the public-private nature of capitalist economies, and the role of regulation and institutions in shaping the markets in which businesses operate. In the voices of executives and deans:

> We need to talk more about regulation and focus more on the political economy perspective.

———————

> It is important to understand business/government relationships, with regulation as a special case. The future will see more intrusive government policy and intervention. Students need to understand more on the public policy front.

A final set of concerns revolves around the sense of surety and certainty of belief that an MBA education often engenders. Critics questioned whether business schools do a good job of alerting students to the imperfections and incompleteness of the models and frameworks they teach. This is hardly a new issue. Friedrich von Hayek, in his 1974 Nobel Memorial Lecture "The Pretense of Knowledge," described the dangers posed by scientific pretensions in the social sciences.[50] Hayek's main point was that social phenomena are more complex, contingent, and context dependent than scientific phenomena, so that the application of scientific methods that has yielded such brilliant progress in the physical sciences may not provide the same definitive conclusions in the social sciences.

Our point here is not to debate how much of management is science, driven by markets and the laws of economics, and how much is art or craft, influenced by human behavior, judgment, and intentions. The scientific approach has led to significant progress in our understanding of management practice and clearly needs to continue. At the same time, we agree with deans and executives about the need to train students to think more critically about models as simplifications of complex phenomena, as providing insights rather than answers, and as vehicles for raising questions that then require the exercise of careful judgment.

A Shift in Emphasis

Taken together, these criticisms and concerns suggest the need for a careful rethinking of MBA education. Business as usual will not close the gap between the two cultures, nor will it produce the skilled, self-aware leaders who are so desperately needed to tackle global problems, deal creatively with uncertain, ambiguous environments, get things done in complex, multilayered organizations, and act prudently in the face of risk. The enrollment data presented in chapter 2 suggest increased challenges for the full-time, two-year MBA degree and, more recently, for part-time and executive MBA programs, particularly at midranked schools. To respond to these challenges, schools need to consider substantial changes in their course offerings and pedagogical approaches.

Equally important is an underlying shift in perspective. That shift is best understood by drawing on a leadership framework developed by the U.S. Army and enacted in a series of curriculum reforms at West Point.[51] According to the framework, leadership always involves three interrelated components: "knowing," "doing," and "being."[52]

Professional education must focus on those same three components, whether it is aimed at military officers, doctors, lawyers, or businesspeople. The first component is knowledge: the facts, frameworks, and theories that make up the core understandings of a profession or practice. There are, for example, things that every business leader should *know*—the difference between assets and liabilities, the forces determining industry structure, the meaning and measurement of return on capital, and the four P's of marketing. The second component is skills: the capabilities and techniques that enable one to practice one's chosen field. There are things that every business leader should be able to *do*—execute tasks as a member of a team, manage and implement a project, conduct a performance review, and deliver an effective presentation. The third component is values, attitudes, and beliefs: the commitments and purposes that constitute one's character, worldview, and professional identity. There are things that every business leader should *be* (or, more precisely, should reflect on and be aware of)—the line between right and wrong, the preferred treatment of others, the purpose and goals of organizations, and the behaviors that exemplify integrity, honesty, and fairness.

Ever since the Ford and Carnegie reports, most MBA curricula have emphasized knowing at the expense of doing and being. In part, this was by necessity. To overcome legitimate concerns about their lack of scholarly rigor and the associated questions about their place within the university, business schools had to work hard at creating and disseminating knowledge, providing proof that they were capable of developing and teaching well-grounded concepts, theories, and techniques. In this they succeeded, although there are clearly many areas of knowledge where understanding remains limited. For example, despite the importance of the sales function, business schools still impart meager knowledge about how to sell effectively. A further problem, critics contend, is that the knowledge that is currently taught is increasingly technical and analytical and provides limited guidance to practicing managers. As our discussion of risk, regulation, and restraint suggests, financial and economic models are normally parsimonious and focus on a few key tensions, whereas the real world is complex. Opportunities to translate knowledge into practice, to understand the limitations of theories, to acquire essential judgment and skills, and to develop deep self-knowledge are less and less central to the curriculum. The result is a persistent "knowing-doing gap."[53]

A natural question at this point is whether certain pedagogies are better than others at balancing knowing, doing, and being. We are admittedly biased, but we believe that cases are superior to lectures in this respect. As one of us has written elsewhere, "Cases provide practical, relevant examples that can be linked to executives' prior experiences; anchor concepts and theoretical frameworks in accessible, analogous settings; provide drama and colorful stories that improve attention and retention; stimulate involvement and class participation; and couple knowledge acquisition to decision making and action"[54] At the same time, cases are well suited to addressing many of the unmet needs identified in this chapter. They can be used, for example, to integrate thinking around the general manager's perspective, introduce students to organizational realities, and improve oral communication skills. But to teach the full complement of knowing, doing, and being, more needs to be done. Business schools will have to continue to experiment with new pedagogies, such as reflective exercises, supported by individual coaches, to develop leadership skills; small-group work to teach innovative, integrative, or critical thinking; and experiential learning to gain a global perspective and learn about the challenges of implementation. We describe a number of ongoing efforts in chapters 5 and 6.

In summary, the concerns presented in this chapter are a ringing endorsement of the need for a more nuanced understanding of knowledge and its limitations, coupled with more doing and more being, in MBA education. They call for a pronounced rebalancing of the curriculum. Students need to understand the *hows* and *whys* of business management as well as they understand the *whats*. Learning to work well with colleagues from other countries, expanding one's capacity for creative problem solving, developing the resilience to overcome inevitable setbacks, and cultivating insight into problems that arise from one's own dysfunctional behaviors—all of these require guided practice and reflective understanding.[55]

Certainly, functional and disciplinary knowledge will continue to be the foundation of business school education. Every dean we interviewed insisted that rigorous, scholarly research was essential to the mission and continued vitality of their programs. Many feared a return to the "trade school mentality" of the past. We agree on both points. But we also believe that the gaps in knowledge, how knowledge is used, and the unmet needs discussed in this chapter, as well as the experiments and reforms that we describe later in this book, show that a reorientation of MBA programs is absolutely essential—and, to a considerable degree, already under way. The standardization of the past, with its near exclusive focus on analytical knowledge, is slowly but surely being replaced by innovation and differentiation, with greater attention to action, implementation, exercising judgment when applying knowledge to practice, skill building, and personal development—all aimed at developing leaders and entrepreneurs who are able to create, build, and sustain organizations.

5

Meeting the Challenges of Globalization, Leadership, and Integration

I N CHAPTER 4, we identified a set of opportunities and unmet needs that deans and executives viewed as poorly or incompletely addressed by business schools today. In this chapter, we examine some of the progress to date, describing several initiatives already under way at business schools in the areas of globalization, leadership development, and integration. All examples are drawn from our case studies and interviews. Chapter 6 completes the story, presenting curricula innovations in the areas of understanding organizational realities; fostering creativity and innovative thinking; strengthening oral and written communication; contemplating the roles, responsibilities, and purpose of business; and understanding the limits of markets and models.

Globalization: A Continuum of Options for Knowing, Doing, and Being

Chapter 4 described several goals that deans and executives identified for teaching globalization. They ranged from developing broader, more inclusive conceptual frameworks to building greater cultural sensitivity, awareness, and intelligence. These goals can be further categorized using the "knowing-doing-being" framework. The "knowing" component involves helping students identify, analyze, and explain which business strategies, selling tactics, and management styles generalize across the globe and which need to be tailored to local or regional requirements, what the essential political and institutional differences are across nations, and which markets are interconnected and which remain largely segregated and distinct. For example, Ghemawat proposes a CAGE framework to distinguish the *c*ultural, *a*dministrative, *g*eographic, and *e*conomic dimensions of differences across countries and their implications.[1] The "doing" component of globalization involves helping students learn the skills needed to manage diverse teams of individuals with differing assumptions and expectations. As one executive described the task, "Can I take a newly hired MBA and put her in charge of a team of software developers working in India— either virtually from the United States or on the ground in Bangalore?" The "being" component involves helping students to reach a deeper psychological understanding of themselves and how different cultures shape their own, as well as others', values, behavior, and interactions.[2] For example, MBAs need to develop the ability to listen and act in cultures and contexts that are different from their own by gathering tacit knowledge through attention to signals such as body language and implicit cultural rules.

There is broad consensus among business schools about the need to globalize MBA programs, but more variation in the strategies employed. Responses fall into eight major categories. Ranging from the least to the most demanding, they are as follows:

- Increasing the percentage of international students and faculty at the school

- Increasing the global content of functional courses

- Creating integrative global management courses

- Developing international exchange programs

- Organizing treks and immersions that take students abroad for several weeks or months

- Offering global field studies and projects

- Establishing global research centers

- Building an overseas campus

For each alternative, we discuss both its strengths and weaknesses and provide a number of representative examples.

Increasing the Percentage of International Students and Faculty

The international presence in the MBA student body has steadily risen over the years. In 2008, international students constituted 34 percent of the students at the top fifty-five MBA programs in the United States and 85 percent of the top MBA programs in Europe (table 5-1).[3] International students bring greater diversity of views to class discussions, contribute the experience of other cultures to study groups and team projects, and increase other students' opportunities for personal interactions with individuals from very different backgrounds. A discussion of a U.S. insider trading case is significantly richer when

TABLE 5-1

The internationalization of students and faculty of all U.S. and European business schools listed in the 2009 *Financial Times* Global MBA ranking

	PERCENT INTERNATIONAL STUDENTS		PERCENT INTERNATIONAL FACULTY	
	United States	Europe	United States	Europe
Highest	56	99	63	100
Lowest	10	40	2	16
Average	34	85	26	46

Source: *Financial Times* Global MBA ranking 2009.

students from other countries contrast how insider trading regulations and enforcement practices work in their countries, just as a discussion of performance reviews benefits from comparisons of differing cultural norms around delivering critical feedback. With their very high percentage of international students, European business schools such as INSEAD offer a classroom experience with no dominant culture. However, finding qualified applicants from diverse backgrounds and countries of origin in sufficient numbers is no easy task. As the pace of globalization continues, business schools will need to cast their admissions nets even further, without diluting the quality of students admitted.

The percentage of international faculty at business schools has also been on the rise, reaching 26 percent at the top fifty-five U.S. schools and 46 percent at the top European schools by 2008 (see table 5-1).[4] These faculty members, with their international backgrounds and knowledge of business practices and cultures in different regions of the world, bring more global experiences and perspectives into the classroom. Nevertheless, a major challenge for globalizing MBA programs is aligning the global focus with faculty interests. Conflicts can arise in many forms: a desire on the part of faculty to contribute to basic disciplinary or functional knowledge rather than global research, often motivated by the editorial policies of leading scholarly journals; lack of training in how to design and conduct global research projects; and the inherent difficulties and costs of empirical research on a global scale. Fortunately, there has been considerable progress in recent years in alleviating each of these challenges. Many journals today encourage research on globalization. The quality and consistency of data have also markedly improved, and globalization research has begun to attract some of the best scholars in a range of fields, resulting in higher quality research and better-trained students. Still, there is a long way to go, and the faculty issue remains a challenge.

Faculty members face additional pedagogical challenges as business schools increase the percentage of international students in their MBA program, problems that they would not likely encounter with a more homogeneous group of students. One example is the problem of cultural relativism. Some INSEAD faculty report that "for every example you use, you need to have a culturally based response" to deal with the criticism that a proposed action would not be effective in a different culture. For example, a diversification strategy may be seen as less desirable in developed market economies but more valuable in developing economies, where imperfections in product, capital, and labor markets cause more value to reside in the brands and reputations of business groups.

Increasing the Global Content in Functional Courses

Over the years, business schools have increased the global content of such core courses as strategy, marketing, and operations. For example, by 2007 about 34 percent of strategy cases at American business schools involved international (non-U.S.) markets or companies. At the same time, according to a leading critic, "few courses . . . teach global strategy tools and concepts . . . such as locational advantages, scope decisions, adaptation and arbitrage."[5] Much more global content needs to be infused into functional courses before business schools can truly claim that they teach business functions from a global perspective. The trade-off, of course, is that allocating more sessions to global issues can reduce the time available to teach functional content.

Creating Integrative Global Management Courses

More recently, MBA programs have begun developing courses about what it means to be a general manager in the era of globalized product, labor, and capital markets. An example is Stanford's Global Context of Management course, which is taught in the first quarter of the first year. According to the syllabus, "[t]he course center[s] on the political, economic, financial, and cultural drivers of the global marketplace. It develop[s] students' understanding of both the global and individual markets that comprise the world economy. By focusing on markets, the course provide[s] students with general and specialized knowledge to help them ask necessary questions and take appropriate actions when entering a new market." A second example is the "Globalization of Business Enterprise" (GLOBE) course that will be introduced into the first year of the MBA curriculum at IESE during the 2009–2010 academic year. GLOBE is based on an "interlock" model that provides a "cross-functional launching pad for discussions throughout the rest of the first and second year of the program." Focusing on cross-country differences and their implications for business, and informed by the CAGE framework, the GLOBE course "takes students from macro to managerial perspectives and from data analysis to judgment."[6] Both the integrative approach and the previous one of infusing more global content into functional courses focus on the knowledge component of the knowing-doing-being framework.

Leaders of MBA programs have often debated which of these two approaches is the better option: should MBA programs focus on adding more global content in functional courses or on teaching a separate course on globalization? Like Ghemawat, we see these approaches as complements, not substitutes.[7] A separate course on globalization, particularly if it is scheduled early in the first year, provides useful context, structure, and perspective for the functional courses that follow. It also gives voice to the views and experiences of international students, who may otherwise be more reticent to share their ideas about why a particular theory, framework, or approach may not work in their countries. A separate course on globalization also sensitizes all students to thinking about how they need to adapt what they are learning in functional courses to different global environments. For example, what are the implications of weak capital, labor, and product markets for corporate strategy? What effects do cultural differences and limited distribution channels have for marketing? It is much easier to infuse functional courses with global content if students already have a framework and mind-set for considering the global context.

Developing International Exchange Programs

A fourth approach is one that Hawawini refers to as the "export model"—focusing the school's attention outward by sending students and faculty abroad, setting up international facilities and campuses, and organizing international programs.[8] Many schools have established exchange programs that give students the opportunity to spend a quarter or semester taking courses at a business school in a different country. These programs, modeled along the lines of undergraduate "study abroad" programs, have the advantage of helping students build global knowledge through coursework in a foreign country, global skills through team projects with diverse students and interactions with managers and organizations in a foreign country, and global attitudes and cultural understanding through time spent with peers from other countries. Exchange programs place more emphasis on doing and being than the approaches discussed earlier. The biggest challenge for students is the opportunity cost of missing out on the courses offered only at their home institutions. For example, if students take a full set of required courses in the first year of their MBA program, spending a semester abroad in an exchange program would cause them to miss out on fully one-half of their elective courses. Many students see this as an excessively high cost.

Exchange programs are a more attractive option at schools like Chicago Booth that have highly flexible course requirements in their MBA program. Other than one required course on leadership, every course in Chicago's program is an elective, subject to distribution requirements across ten areas such as economics, quantitative methods, strategy, and organizations. Moreover, as noted in chapter 3, students can take courses and satisfy their distribution requirements in any order. This flexibility reduces significantly the opportunity cost of an exchange program. Consequently, Chicago reports that 10 percent of its students study abroad at one of its thirty-three partner schools.

To facilitate exchange programs, some schools have aided the establishment and continued operation of associated business schools. For example, Instituto de Estudios Superiores de la Empresa (IESE), the business school of the University of Navarra, has helped to found and support business schools in a total of fifteen different countries, including Argentina, Brazil, China, Guatemala, Kenya, Mexico, Nigeria, Peru, and the Philippines. IESE shares cases and educational materials with these schools and arranges student and faculty exchange programs.

Organizing Treks and Immersions

Intensive travel programs are a relatively recent addition to the portfolio of approaches to globalization. Like exchange programs, they immerse students in a foreign culture, but they do so for shorter periods and on a more ad hoc basis. Treks and immersions take various forms. Some involve visits to companies and organizations in foreign countries with little preparatory work, advance reading, or project requirements. Others require students to meet in class sessions, prepare background readings, and do other advance work in preparation for the trek. Still others require students to conceptualize and complete a study project related to the trek or immersion. At the Yale School of Management, during a weekly class in the fall, faculty lead discussions about the country that students will visit during their winter break. Students also hear perspectives about the country and learn from outside experts about how business operates in that country, and then carry out small-group projects and presentations on the political, situation, general economic issues, and specific industries in the countries where they will travel. During the break, groups of twenty-five students travel with a faculty member to different countries and companies. When they return, students write a paper on a specific topic related to their trip and discuss the lessons learned.

Deans and executives had varying reactions to these treks and immersions. All felt that they were better than no such program, but the general consensus was that the most effective ones were those that, through classroom and project work, engendered a deeper engagement in a foreign country so that they focused on knowing, doing, and being. For example, one school's trek to China involved a day of market research, in which U.S. students were paired with English-speaking Chinese business school students. Together, they spent the day interviewing Chinese consumers. During the evening debriefing, one U.S. student complained about the project, disparaging her "translator," whereas a second student praised the project and the experience with her "partner." The faculty member leading the trek used these contrasting experiences to produce a vivid lesson about the power of preconceptions and relationships in effective partnerships and alliances.

Offering Global Projects

Several business schools offer global project and laboratory courses. Whereas the goal of immersions and treks is to provide students with a general overview and understanding of a particular country and its business environment, the goal of project and laboratory courses is to allow students the opportunity to do a deep dive into a specific project in order to better understand the realities of doing business in a foreign country. Chicago Booth, for example, offers an International Entrepreneurship Lab in which students develop a business plan for opening a new international business venture. This program combines classes with a ten-day trip to an international location, such as China, focused on field-based work for developing the business plan. In a similar vein, the international Multidisciplinary Action Projects (MAP) at the Ross School of Business at the University of Michigan has teams of students, in the spring of their first year, spending seven weeks working on in-depth international projects. Examples include developing a market analysis and growth strategy in China for Ryder Systems, a transportation company; designing a market entry strategy in the Czech Republic for Arbel Medical Ltd., a medical devices company; and assessing the feasibility of renewable energy solutions in Mozambique for BHP Billiton, a natural resources company. Students spend a significant portion of the seven weeks devoted to the project on site at the international location.

Global projects of this sort have several advantages. They allow students to experience first hand the effects of different cultures and institutions on business practices, reinforcing the knowledge they have gained in global courses. Developing a more refined understanding of how workers and managers in different countries think and act is particularly valuable. The most effective learning in the psychological realm often involves taking students out of their comfort zone by placing them in situations where their expectations, values, and assumptions are not necessarily shared by their local sponsors or coworkers. The biggest challenges for implementing global projects include releasing faculty time, training faculty in how to support students in these activities, and securing the resources necessary to offer them at scale.

Establishing Global Research Centers

Our interviews with deans and executives underscored the importance of encouraging faculty to be more global in their research and case writing—major engines for innovation in the MBA program. Some schools organize faculty field trips to foreign countries, whereas others establish programs that encourage faculty exchanges and collaborations with foreign business schools. Still others set up and staff international research centers in foreign locations. INSEAD, for example, has centers in Israel, the United Arab Emirates, and South Asia. Harvard Business School has research centers in Europe, Latin America, Asia Pacific, and South Asia. A typical Harvard Business School research center has a research director and one or two research associates who work with faculty collecting data for research or support faculty in their case writing and course development. A recent collaboration between a faculty member and the school's Japan Research Center is representative. Together, they developed a case on the Nippon Steel Corporation to explore the relationship between Japanese corporations and diverse stakeholders—customers, employees, and society at large, but not shareholders. The Tokyo-based research team first identified a salient issue to analyze, then located a company willing to take part in the case, scheduled interviews, and secured and translated documents central to the case.

The goal of research centers is to facilitate learning about the latest business developments and best practices in particular nations or regions and increase faculty members' ability to conduct research and write cases on emerging national or regional problems. They also enable business schools to build relationships with local academic institutions, alumni, and practitioners. A major advantage of research centers is their capacity to engage a broad cross section of faculty. Harvard Business School's research centers have helped faculty do research on such diverse topics as the tensions between country and company cultures in multinational organizations, the different philosophies of capitalism practiced around the world, and how best to manage in fast-growing developing economies. The challenge is that research centers require a major commitment of financial resources and human capital.

Building an Overseas Campus

The most intense commitment to globalization for a business school is to build and staff a second campus located overseas. By developing strong connections with business communities in another country, having a strong and permanent local faculty presence, and allowing students to live in a different location for a considerable length of time, a second campus combines all the benefits of exchange programs, project courses, and global faculty research described earlier. It gives students a deep appreciation of different market contexts, institutions, and cultures, and of the combined effect of these factors on how business is done. INSEAD, which we discuss in detail in chapter 8, became our primary case study on globalization because it is the only business school that has an overseas campus for full-time MBA students. (Other business schools, such as Wharton, with its facility in Singapore, and Chicago Booth, with its facilities in London and Singapore, have overseas campuses, but only for their executive MBA programs.)

In 2000, INSEAD opened an Asian campus in Singapore to complement its European base in Fontainebleau and deliver on its mission to "bring together people, cultures and ideas from around the world" as a global business school. The Singapore campus has a full-time residential faculty, and students are given the option of starting their MBA programs there or at Fontainebleau. Most students spend significant amounts of time on both campuses. About 20 to 25 percent of students complete the entire program at one of the two campuses (these students are known as "stickers"). Thirty-five to forty percent of students are "switchers," who start at one campus and complete the program at another, and roughly the same proportion are "swingers," who start and end at the same campus but sandwich a period at the second campus in between.

The Singapore campus provides faculty and students with direct, frequent, and consistent access to businesses and projects throughout Asia. Several INSEAD faculty members argued strongly that their research benefited from the existence of the Singapore campus. One professor observed, "I did research and wrote cases on topics that I probably would not have written if I had not been in Singapore." INSEAD students were equally enthusiastic about the extent to which their cultural awareness and sensitivity were enhanced by exposure to different cultures during their time in Singapore. One student noted, "Everything on the Asian campus, including cases, simulations and events, is influenced by Asian economic, strategic, and political developments." Other students recognized the recruiting advantages offered by the Singapore campus: "The campus allows people to go to industry meetings and gatherings and meet entrepreneurs and guest speakers."

Despite its many advantages, INSEAD is still the only major business school that has a second campus for its full-time MBA program. The reason is clear: the enormous commitment of money, time, and faculty resources required to establish and operate such a facility. INSEAD invested $27 million just to build the Singapore campus. Most schools believe that, based on their current financial constraints, a second campus does not meet the cost-benefit test.

As a school moves along the spectrum of approaches from globalizing material taught in the MBA curriculum to exchange programs, immersions, and projects to international research centers and second campuses, it is increasingly shifting the balance from knowing to doing and being, from simply understanding how business works in a different country to developing skills for working in diverse teams and building cultural sensitivity and intelligence. But these increasing benefits come with escalating costs in terms of faculty time and financial resources. Different schools will therefore choose different points on the globalization continuum as they consider their own distinctive cost-benefit calculus, purpose and commitments, and strategic priorities.

Leadership Development: Conventional and Experiential Courses

Chapter 4 presented several objectives that deans and executives argued were important elements of teaching leadership. They ranged from increasing self-awareness to developing interpersonal and influence skills to learning how to resolve divergent points of view. These too can be further specified using the knowing-doing-being framework. The "knowing" component of leadership involves helping students understand theories of leadership, the responsibilities of leaders, alternative approaches to influencing and guiding others, and ethical challenges that leaders must resolve. The "doing" component of leadership involves helping students learn how to work more effectively as members of a team, conduct a performance review, frame and articulate a point of view, and give difficult feedback. The "being" component involves helping students understand their strengths and weaknesses, their values and attitudes, and the impact of their actions and behaviors on others.

Leadership is a topic of increasing importance to business schools, and is now highlighted in many of their mission statements. There is a remarkable degree of overlap in schools' stated missions. Examples include Yale ("educate leaders for business and society"), Harvard ("educate leaders who make a difference in the world"), Stanford ("develop innovative, principled, and insightful leaders who change the world"), Wharton ("prepare business leaders who fuel the growth of industries and economies"), and Darden ("improve society by developing leaders in the world of practical affairs").[9] A further indication of the increasing importance of leadership is the prevalence of the terms *leader* or *leadership* in articles in the *Harvard Business Review*. Until the early 1990s, the two terms rarely appeared in the title or subtitle of *Harvard Business Review* articles. In contrast, from the mid-1990s to mid-2000s, the two terms appeared in the title or subtitle of such articles more often than the terms *manager* and *management* (figure 5-1).[10]

Approaches to teaching leadership fall into three broad categories. Ranging from the least to the most demanding, they are as follows:

- Adding leadership courses to the curriculum

- Developing leadership laboratories and small-group work

- Creating experiential learning programs

Adding Leadership Courses

For many years, business schools taught leadership as a part of their course offerings in organizational behavior. More recently, corporate scandals at companies such as Enron and WorldCom have caused schools to broaden their approaches to teaching leadership to include issues of ethics, governance, and corporate accountability. Some schools believe that these topics are best taught in the context of existing, typically functional courses, such as marketing, accounting, and finance; others favor freestanding offerings. Just as in the case of globalization, the trade-off for increasing ethical content in established

FIGURE 5-1

Analysis of *Harvard Business Review* article titles

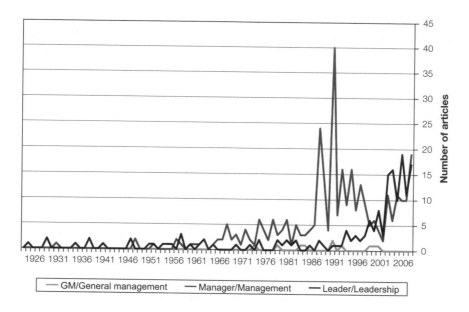

Source: Benjamin C. Esty, "The Harvard Business School MBA Degree: Educating Leaders, General Managers, or Tradespeople?" working paper, 2007.

courses is the reduced time available to teach functional content. Faculty members teaching functional courses are also often less comfortable dealing with ethical issues because they have not been part of their doctoral training. As a result, tough ethical questions are at times given limited attention. In response, a number of schools have begun offering courses whose principal focus is to build student knowledge in leadership issues involving ethics, values, and corporate accountability.

One example is the Harvard Business School course Leadership and Corporate Accountability (LCA), which we discuss at length in chapter 6. LCA, a required course in the second semester of the first year, focuses on the responsibilities of business leaders to diverse constituencies, such as investors, customers, employees, suppliers, and the public at large, and the need to simultaneously weigh the economic, legal, and ethical implications of decisions. Students are faced with a range of difficult dilemmas, such as how to behave when personal values collide with the values of the company and how to balance profitability against social and ethical concerns, and are required to take a position and defend it. The course also includes a number of reflective exercises designed to help students think through their personal leadership philosophies.

An alternative approach, used at Yale, is to teach a small module on leadership and ethics early in the program to provide context, structure, and perspective for the discussion of ethical issues in courses that follow. Yale's Leadership Development Program (LDP) aims to help students align their actions with their personal values and beliefs. During the 2007–2008 academic year the LDP program began with an assignment that asked students to develop a concept for a viable enterprise at a selected location in New Haven. Each concept was required to reflect both the economic situation of the local environment and the school's mission of educating leaders for business and society. The assignment emphasized group work to give students an early opportunity to collaborate with peers, develop leadership skills by influencing the group's decisions, and help shape the final presentation. A faculty member or a second-year student provided feedback on the group's interactions. Much of the learning about leadership development occurred during the debriefing stage of the assignment, in which groups of twenty students reflected on the exercise together with faculty and second-year students. After the orientation sessions, LDP classes met six times. The three classes in the fall focused on developing self-awareness through, for example, values clarification exercises. The three classes in the spring were oriented toward actions and behaviors. In one session, for example, students examined the leadership that emerged within their group during their January international experience trip.

In our interviews with executives, we probed the wisdom of offering courses such as LCA and LDP when academics lament that the field of leadership lacks "a widely accepted theoretical framework or a cumulative empirical understanding leading to a usable body of knowledge."[11] The absence of such a framework was of little concern to executives, who argued that well-designed courses help students learn how to ask the right questions and provide a valuable lens through which to consider "gray area" issues. Their bigger concern was with teaching leadership in large classes, where the focus was on imparting knowledge in much the same way as accounting or finance. Building leadership skills, they argued, requires practice and deep reflection on a student's own values and attitudes, not just mastery of concepts and frameworks.

Developing Leadership Laboratories

Business schools have only recently begun offering laboratories and small-group work to help students develop their leadership skills. But other organizations have provided leadership development for executives, both individually and in small groups, for years. One of the best known is the Center for Creative Leadership (CCL), based in Greensboro, North Carolina, which was founded in 1970 and since then has provided leadership training for over 400,000 executives. As discussed at length in chapter 9, CCL has developed a specific model for leadership development called assessment, challenge, and support (ACS). ACS is a combination model—one that encourages both practice and reflection on the part of the participant. It provides a template for how to conduct leadership training and development.

Assessment tools, designed to collect information on a participant's style, personality, and approaches to problem solving, are sent to participants and their workplace colleagues several weeks before programs begin. This information is then processed and analyzed by CCL and compared with the benchmark data in its massive database. The results are fed back to, and reviewed with, participants. The second aspect of ACS is challenge. Exercises or simulations of demanding work environments push participants out of their comfort zones, prompting reexamination of their abilities, approaches, and effectiveness. Breaking with habitual ways of thinking requires participants to develop new capacities and adapt their ways of understanding. The last element is support, which comes through an empathetic climate that provides security in the face of new challenges. During the programs, support comes from facilitators, coaches, and peers. Afterward, participants are encouraged to build supportive networks to continue their leadership development. Participants often need reassurance and continued reinforcement as they change ingrained habits and pursue a new, more constructive relationship with superiors, subordinates, and peers.

Leadership laboratories at many MBA programs have similar goals and objectives and use many of the same techniques and approaches as CCL. At several schools, students fill out a number of personal assessment tools over time. They complete a 360-degree tool before coming to campus and again at the end of their summer internship experience, as well as several years after graduation. They also complete the Myers-Briggs Type Indicator (MBTI) tool and the Thomas-Killman Conflict Mode Instrument to identify their preferred individual conflict resolution style. Early in their first year, students are challenged with multiple simulations, which culminate in post-mortem discussions and feedback. Besides the lab sessions, students meet with their fellows (second-year MBA student coaches) for further reflection and discussion of what they learned in the course. Leadership labs shift the scales of leadership development from knowing to doing (e.g. how to do a performance review or give difficult feedback) and being (e.g. understanding strengths and weaknesses, values and attitudes, and the impact of actions and behaviors on others).

The aim of these courses is to encourage students to view their leadership laboratories as safe places to try new or unfamiliar behaviors, to fail if necessary, to receive feedback from coaches, and to implement that feedback. Through several cycles, students become more self-aware, begin to rethink their attitudes and behaviors, and develop their leadership styles as well as their abilities to listen, inspire, and influence. As one dean put it, such courses "hold a mirror up to students to help them see how others see them."

In chapter 4, we described a shift in the world of organizations from high-authority, low-conflict environments to ones such as matrix organizations and network forms, where low authority and high conflict are the norm. To cope and thrive in such a world requires leadership skills centered on empathy and a deep understanding of others' points of view. Such skills inform the art of persuasion and the ability to identify common interests despite apparently conflicting agendas. These "doing" and "being" capabilities are much more likely to emerge in leadership laboratories than in traditional classrooms.

Nevertheless, some deans question whether these laboratories help in the teaching of leadership. In particular, several wondered whether leadership could actually be taught to typical MBA students—young people in their mid- to late twenties who have limited work experience. As one dean put it, "At mid-career they 'get' leadership. Most MBAs don't yet understand it." The executives we interviewed generally disagreed, arguing that such training was invaluable. Many recalled their own experiences and those of others in their companies who benefited from early leadership coaching, frequently by organizations such as CCL. One executive remarked, "It is never too early, and you can never do enough." Another commented, "Building self-awareness before you go into the workplace helps you avoid some major pitfalls."

Leadership laboratories do come with certain downsides and difficulties. For one thing, they are costly to implement; they are built around individual coaching and mentoring, which are hard to operate economically at large scale; and they use different teaching formats and approaches. This is uncharted territory for most faculty members, requiring significant faculty development or, alternatively, the hiring of new faculty (and coaches) trained and experienced in these methods of teaching. Small-group formats also imply a higher ratio of faculty (plus coaches) to students and require different physical facilities, a large number of small breakout rooms rather than a few large classrooms.

Creating Experiential Learning Programs

Experience has long been regarded as important in the honing of leadership skills. It is leadership in action: in the process of doing, leaders learn what it means to make difficult decisions, what it takes to gain trust, and what is required to bring people together to achieve a common purpose. Experience makes leadership real, personal, and consequential. Not surprisingly, both deans and executives believed strongly in the virtues of experiential learning for leadership development. Some schools design outdoor experiences involving a variety of group activities that teach team-building concepts; others develop group exercises around real-world projects for business clients. Immersion in demanding real-world projects, many argue, helps students learn how to work on a team, develop interpersonal skills, engage and motivate each other to complete a task, and resolve conflicts—all essential skills of leadership.

To realize these benefits, projects need to be scheduled under tight timelines and with clients who demand excellence. The Multidisciplinary Action Projects at Michigan, discussed at length in chapter 6, use this approach to target the development and testing of leadership capabilities. Teams "confront real business challenges with real stakes in real time." They learn to "overcome unexpected obstacles" and to "successfully navigate organizations, perspectives, and cultures."[12] In one project, students discovered that executives in a particular unit were not committed to the project, contrary to what they had expected. Yet the team had to find a way to complete the project amid the conflicts and differences that inevitably surface under these circumstances.

The "being" element of experiential learning holds particular promise for helping students develop a neglected, but critically important, facet of managing and leading: empathy. Designing experiential learning projects around interactions with frontline and midlevel employees such as assembly-line workers, clerical staff, and salespersons can help students learn about the aspirations, motivations, and desires of individuals different from themselves. It can provide them with the kind of insight they might otherwise never gain. As one faculty member put it, "We should work on developing empathy as an intellectual (not emotional) skill. One of the underemphasized skills is to see things from a different perspective. A traditional course is not going to get there."

Experiential learning requires significant commitments of faculty time. Moreover, the discipline-based training of many faculty members is seldom well suited to developing and running multidisciplinary projects. For this reason, schools sometimes assign adjunct faculty members with executive experience to work alongside or in place of tenure-track faculty to staff experiential learning courses. In addition, the organization, planning, coordination, and execution of experiential learning courses require substantial financial resources.

As we highlighted in chapter 4, a significant number of executives and deans we interviewed believe that business schools need to do more leadership development using leadership laboratories, small-group simulations, individual coaching, and experiential learning.[13] These pedagogies allow students to experiment with different personal styles and receive feedback on how others judge and perceive them. They represent a shift in emphasis from knowing to doing and being, from reading about the actions of others to learning for oneself how to perform, motivate, and be more self-aware. These larger benefits come with higher claims on faculty time and on organizational and coaching infrastructure, as well as higher costs. Many schools, though, see some form of leadership development as essential and long overdue.

Integration: From Student Responsibility to Institutional Requirement

When it comes to integration, curricula-wide changes in MBA programs have followed two divergent paths. Many programs, as we noted in chapter 3, have reduced core requirements in favor of greater choice and flexibility. Even schools like Stanford, with a large required core, now allow students to choose from three different levels of functional courses—basic, intermediate or fast-paced, and advanced applications. At Chicago Booth, the program is so flexible that students can fulfill each of their distribution requirements by selecting from one of five to seven courses in any order at any time during the program. Schools such as Stanford and Chicago argue that MBA programs need to adapt to the growing complexity of the business environment by allowing students to take a richer, more diverse, set of courses.

Other schools see a different imperative in the changing demands of the workplace: the need for improved integration. They argue that the traditional function-based MBA curriculum became the dominant approach when executives' careers tended to follow a linear path, rising stepwise through the same function and industry during most of their working lives. In such settings, unless they had unusual cross-functional responsibilities or became one of the few who reached the highest levels in their organizations, most executives were not required to have more than a basic knowledge of functions or disciplines beyond their areas of specialization.

Over the last twenty years, business careers have broadened substantially as globalization, information technology, and intense competition have reshaped the environment. Today's executives increasingly encounter issues and challenges that cut across multiple functions. As we noted in chapter 4, a number of deans and executives argue that the traditional function-based MBA curriculum is no longer the most effective model for the management challenges of the future. Instead, they call for a more tightly integrated program. For example, the Report of the Core Curriculum Subcommittee at the Yale School of Management, whose program we examine in detail in chapter 11, stated, "Management education is compartmentalized by function even though management challenges no longer are. The result is a disconnect between what is taught and what is needed."

To remedy this disconnect, business schools such as Yale and Toronto have reformed their MBA programs to integrate content from multiple functions. They argue that an integrated curriculum reflects the way the business world operates. Decisions and challenges do not typically present themselves as discrete, compartmentalized marketing or finance problems, but rather as incompletely defined issues that require cross-disciplinary solutions, often involving areas different from those where the problem first arose. The solution to what appears to be a pricing problem (marketing) may in fact reside in a better product or process design (operations), whereas an acquisition decision (finance) might require large-scale cultural and behavioral change (organizational behavior) to have any hope of succeeding.

At its most basic level, an integrated curriculum knits together functional knowledge in a way that is useful for problem solving. It also helps students develop the ability to frame problems comprehensively. Too often, students in a particular functional course frame problems only in the context of that course: the same problem will be viewed as a marketing or communications problem in a marketing course, but as a competitive positioning problem in a strategy course. An integrated curriculum forces students to think about issues from diverse, shifting angles and to then frame the problem holistically.

A final objective of an integrated curriculum is honing students' ability to make decisions based on multiple, often conflicting, perspectives. Beyond teaching specific content or frameworks, an integrated approach forces students to build judgment and intuition in messy, unstructured situations. For example, the decision to acquire a business in another country may be strategically valuable but difficult to manage given marketing and human resource constraints. Students learn to evaluate those conflicting trade-offs based on how they can best be managed.

There are five main approaches to teaching integration. They vary in the degree to which faculty rather than students take responsibility for making the connections across functions. Ranging over an array of options, they are as follows:

- Giving students responsibility for integrating across a portfolio of functional courses

- Embedding integrative thinking in required functional courses

- Creating capstone courses with a general management point of view

- Developing an integrated curriculum

- Organizing the curriculum around integrative thinking skills

Giving Students Responsibility for Integrating Across a Portfolio of Functional Courses

This approach makes little attempt to teach the principles of integration; instead, it assumes that well-rounded managers/leaders are trained largely through exposure to multiple functions and specialties. This is a "sum of the parts" approach. The expectation is that students themselves will provide the necessary integration by finding the connections among courses and creating their own holistic views. Some schools augment this approach with brief capstone experiences that cross course boundaries and demand integrated thinking. For example, the joint teaching of new product development by faculty from marketing and operations management forces students to grapple with balancing opposing tensions: meeting the needs of diverse customers by proliferating features versus accepting the practicalities of designing and manufacturing products at an affordable cost. The problem with this approach is that integration skills are difficult to master on one's own. They are best developed actively and explicitly, through debate, discussion, and repeated practice, rather than through private, personal reflection.

Embedding Integrative Thinking in Required Functional Courses

In this approach, there are no separate, freestanding integrated courses, nor do cases typically include detailed descriptions of multiple functions. Instead, each functional course—either throughout the course or at selected intervals—takes an integrated, general management view of the topic, in part because cases and readings feature business unit heads as frequent protagonists. Functional issues are considered from an enterprise or whole-unit perspective, secondary effects and other cross-functional impacts are discussed in detail when evaluating options and making decisions, and tools and frameworks are taught from the perspective of what a general manager or business unit leader needs to know to make informed choices, not from a specialist's or function head's point of view. The Ivey School of Business at the University of Western Ontario infuses its courses with this "issues-centered," general management perspective, as does Harvard Business School, which we discuss at length in chapter 10.

Creating General Management Capstone Courses

A third approach teaches integration through one or more capstone courses designed with a general management point of view. The capstone courses supplement the separate functional courses, usually at the end of the first year, encouraging students to focus on integration. At many schools, business policy courses have long played this role. The associated cases nearly always featured CEOs or other general managers as protagonists, included descriptions or profiles of multiple functions, and focused on cross-cutting strategic, organizational, or operational decisions. Courses in entrepreneurship sometimes play this role today, as do some leadership and ethics courses. The Entrepreneurial Manager and Leadership and Corporate Accountability courses at Harvard Business School, described in chapter 10, are representative examples.

Some schools offer a capstone experience rather than a conventional course. Carnegie Mellon, for example, pioneered an extended business simulation that required first-year students to engage in simultaneous operating, marketing, staffing, and other functional decisions, which played out across multiple periods as student teams competed to be the most successful firm. Such exercises can foster integrative thinking and a multidimensional point of view, although their effectiveness rests, to a great extent, on the quality of the reflections and debriefings that conclude the activity.

Developing a Fully Integrated Curriculum

This approach organizes either the entire curriculum or a large subset of courses by categories of problems, issues, or business challenges rather than by functions. Separate courses in finance, marketing, or strategy are not offered or else play a less central role in the program; they are replaced by multifunctional, multidisciplinary courses. Yale has gone the furthest in this direction, as described in chapter 11. It has revamped its first-year curriculum so that, after an introduction to the basic language, concepts, tools, and methodologies of business, all courses are presented from the viewpoint of key internal or external roles, stakeholders, or constituents, such as investors, customers, competitors, innovators, and employees. Although each of these courses addresses a core discipline or field (the Investor course is rooted in finance, the Customer course in marketing, the Competitor course in strategy, and so on), each course also draws on multiple disciplines to examine cross-cutting managerial questions. The Customer course, for example, draws on multiple instructors and insights from accounting, finance, operations, organizational behavior, and political science in addition to marketing. As just one instance of integrated course content, the accounting professor introduces concepts of life cycle customer profitability analysis as an important input to the discussion about which customers to target and pursue.

Organizing the Curriculum Around Integrative Thinking Skills

Beyond finding ways to integrate functional knowledge, Toronto's Rotman School of Management takes the view that integrative thinking in itself is a fundamental management function requiring specialized skills. In other words, it is a meta-skill, a capability needed to successfully mesh two or more skills developed by specialized training, such as training in finance or strategy. Rotman defines integrative thinking as "the ability to constructively face the tensions of opposing models, and instead of choosing one at the expense of the other, generat[e] a creative resolution of the tension in the form of a new model that contains elements of the individual models, but is superior to each."[14] Integrative thinking serves as an organizing conceptual framework for the entire Rotman MBA program, providing students with the tools to analyze problems holistically and to synthesize competing perspectives.

Rotman's approach offers students an interactive pedagogical model for practicing integrative thinking. First, it trains students to become *model builders* rather than *model takers*: they are encouraged and taught to build their own representations of complex business problems and situations, using the specialized language systems of the social sciences as building blocks.[15] Students also learn and practice *assertive inquiry*, the craft of rapidly but precisely understanding other people's mental models and representations in typical business interactions, as well as analyzing their own and others' defensive moves and maneuvers that raise barriers and blockages to achieving authentic mutual understanding. Finally, students are taught to use these tools as elements of *generative reasoning* in problem situations—reasoning that creates novel explanations, worlds, and courses of action as opposed to justifying or refuting available options, and that stresses thinking abductively (by assessing how well a theory of a situation fits the observed evidence or facts) rather than merely inductively (looking for a general law that follows from finite data) or deductively (inferring the particular or general statements that follow from a set of accepted premises).[16]

An example from the world of open source operating systems serves to illustrate the Rotman approach. The advent of Linux, the open source operating system, created a new business model. However, it did not do so by itself. Rather, it took a special kind of integrative thinking on the part of a few entrepreneurs to realize its inherent potential. In the existing, proprietary software model, companies such as Microsoft and Oracle sold the operating software, but not the source code, at a high price. If problems arose, customers called the software maker's customer service department, which provided debugging services, sometimes for an additional fee. The only enhancements and modifications available were the upgrades that the companies offered from time to time. Linux promised to change all that. By making the source code available to the end user, the Linux environment promised to break the monopoly of established software vendors by making it possible for thousands of programmers and developers to offer upgrades, improvements, and services on a platform that would be owned by the end user. However, this abundance of supply created problems for developers and end users; competition among developers whittled profits down, and the incompatibility of different versions and modules of Linux made it risky for a large business to place a big bet on products based on the platform. Two models emerged, each unattractive for a different reason.

Enter Bob Young, the founder and CEO of Red Hat Software, Inc. Young's approach combined elements from each of the two models to take advantage of the open source movement while also adding value for the customer.[17] Rather than *choosing* between the two dominant models, Young decided to build his own model of the situation and, subsequently, to build a new business model for the industry. Such a model would have to account for three key facts. First, although Linux was capable of handling large corporate applications as early as the 1990s, executives were confused by the many competing versions of the freely available software and unwilling to make big bets given this much ambiguity. Second, corporations only wanted to buy from a vendor who would be around to support Linux for several years. Third, systems administrators could not manage and deploy multiple, daily updates of the nearly one thousand different packages that made up Linux. So, any "good" business model that would lead to profit in the open source ecosystem would have to jointly minimize ambiguity about which version to buy, uncertainty about the future of the supplier, and the complexity of coordination among different developers.

A *model* comprises a set of variables and a set of causal or logical links among them: what depends on what, and how much? Young began identifying the basic variables of the model and building his own causal chain to connect them. He reasoned that increased acceptance of a particular "certified" brand of Linux among corporate users would lead to the establishment of both greater credibility with customers and lower coordination costs among developers, who could all target the same platform and be guaranteed to interoperate with one another. Access to more applications would in turn increase the attractiveness of the platform as a whole to corporate buyers, which would decrease prospective buyers' uncertainty about the future of the software provider. The resulting lock-in of Red Hat Linux as the "official version of the Linux kernel" would also decrease ambiguity among customers about which version of the code would turn out, years hence, to have been "the right one." Young's next course of action was as simple as it was unthinkable in the world of shrink-wrapped software, in which many small manufacturers competed for infinitesimal revenues by selling CDs: giving Red Hat Linux away by allowing it to be downloaded free from the Internet. This allowed it to catch on, and then allowed the forces of positive feedback and lock-in to work their magic. As sales grew, Young began imposing order and control over the process of developing and capturing Linux enhancements, helping systems administrators to manage and deploy Linux updates.

In designing and executing this business model, Young displayed exemplary integrative skill: rather than accepting existing models, he built a new model that combined the low cost and easy adaptability of the open source model and the organized management of updates from the proprietary model, a service that customers were happy to pay for. He required the model to fit the facts and constraints of the situation at hand, in typically abductive fashion, rather than reasoning from established principles (deductive) or extrapolating from the past experiences of other vendors (inductive). He tested this model assiduously, through repeated dialogue and interactions with end users, Linux developers, and his own programmers—who, by his own admission, were appalled, at first, by the idea of giving away what they had worked so hard to build. In the process, Young found profit in a world of free software code once thought impossible. By 2000, Red Hat held over 50 percent of the global market for Linux systems.

Other examples of integrative thinking abound. Richard Currie at Loblaws introduced President's Choice high-end private label products as an integrative solution to the problem of charging low prices to consumers while maintaining high margins. Jack Welch at General Electric delinked strategic planning and budgeting to resolve the tension between ambitious stretch goals and efficiency-focused budgets. Rejecting causal reasoning that higher internal R&D spending increased innovation output, Procter & Gamble's CEO, A. G. Lafley, developed a new model, "Connect & Develop," to obtain 50 percent of P&G's innovations from innovators outside the company while focusing P&G on developing, testing, and commercializing breakthrough ideas. Each of these leaders used integrative thinking in making his decisions.[18]

Rotman teaches integrative thinking using a range of pedagogies: lectures and discussions, exercises and reflections, role-plays, and projects with local businesses. In one exercise, students contrast the arguments in Milton Friedman's essay "The Social Responsibility of Business Is to Increase Its Profits" (which argues that "there is one and only one social responsibility of business—to use its resources and engage in activities designed to increase its profits so long as it stays within the rules of the game") with Sumantra Ghoshal's article "Bad Management Theories Are Destroying Good Management Practice" (which takes issue with Friedman's arguments for their negative assumptions about people and institutions and its exhortation to focus on economic responsibility to the exclusion of social responsibility).[19] The two articles reach different conclusions about the role of managers as agents of shareholders to maximize shareholder value. Students practice generating and building new models by asking questions such as the following: Under what assumptions, conditions, and mechanisms are the propositions in each of the articles true or valid? Can Friedman's case be made with Ghoshal's argument, and vice versa? What should be true if Friedman's claim was false while Ghoshal's was right, and vice versa? Are there more general laws or mechanisms that would make both models right, albeit in different particular conditions? Students practice assertive inquiry by attempting to understand each others' models and interpretations of the debate, and explicitly learn to think interactively, which entails thinking about what their classmates think and about what their classmates think they think.

Two integrative thinking courses serve as bookends to Rotman's required MBA curriculum: Foundations of Integrative Thinking and The Integrative Thinking Practicum. The Foundations course, scheduled early in the program, infuses the curriculum with a mode of thinking—model based and data driven—that students practice in the courses that follow and get to use in real-time, real-world business settings in the Practicum. Several second-year elective courses—The Opposable Mind, Business Problem Solving: An Integrative Approach, Learning to Learn, and Managing with an Integrative Thinker's Stance—build on the basic integrative thinking skills seeded in the first year.

Integrated curricula and integrative thinking help to rebalance the MBA program from knowing to doing and being. To be sure, integration across courses and ideas teaches new concepts ("knowing"), but its emphasis is on building capabilities and techniques, such as connecting with organizational realities, recognizing trade-offs, and using different modes of thinking and different logics, that enable managers to practice their craft ("doing") and on engaging with complex and ambiguous problems to construct better solutions ("being").

Despite its many advantages, an integrated curriculum poses several challenges. On numerous occasions, schools have tried to introduce greater amounts of integration into their curricula. Many of these attempts have foundered in the face of the challenges and trade-offs. Perhaps the greatest challenge is faculty time and resources. At a minimum, faculty must coordinate content across different classes and identify opportunities for integrative learning. A key question is whether integration can be delivered without excessively taxing faculty resources and good will. The training and reward system for faculty members, after all, encourages the development of deep expertise in a particular field, whereas integrated courses require faculty to develop broad knowledge across multiple areas and hone the skills to teach subjects outside their primary expertise. Senior faculty members are often in the best position to do this and have the most relevant experience, but requiring too much of senior faculty time may come at the cost of research productivity and junior faculty mentoring. An integrated curriculum poses special challenges for junior faculty, who often lack the breadth to handle general management topics and at times find the subjects disconnected from their narrower, discipline-based research. Most academic journals have a discipline and functional focus. Consequently, there is a paucity of integrated, multidisciplinary research for faculty to draw on when designing or teaching integrated, multidisciplinary courses.

Wholly integrated programs also raise concerns that basic functional knowledge and skills may not be taught in sufficient depth. Time spent by students on integrated coursework is seen as time diverted from disciplinary knowledge. Several deans spoke of the risk that students in an integrated curriculum might not learn enough financial, marketing, and other core discipline-based tools to meet the demands of employers and successful careers. Moreover, students with limited business experience might find ideas concerning integration difficult to grasp. At a minimum, these deans argued, students need sufficient grounding in the functions to appreciate the tensions and trade-offs that must be faced when integrating across functions.

Teaching integrative thinking skills requires faculty to teach students how to think. Some of these skills—such as probing models, building causal maps, designing experiments, and testing hypotheses—are familiar to faculty from their PhD programs. But faculty also need to develop other skills, such as how to deal with ambiguity and complexity to resolve tensions across opposing models, that are novel and likely to be new to many of them.

Even so, the need for more integration in business school curricula remains a perennial challenge. As schools move to more differentiated and flexible core curricula, students need some vehicle for pulling the pieces together. We believe that it is unlikely that fully integrated MBA programs will become the norm, except perhaps for a few schools with relatively small enrollments. A viable alternative is careful, tailored integration in one of the other forms we have described.

Innovations in Pedagogy
and Course Design

I N THE PRECEDING CHAPTER, we discussed a range of diverse initiatives under way in the areas of globalization, leadership, and integration. All are curriculum-wide and involve a broad spectrum of courses and MBA programs. In this chapter we focus on innovations in the "small," that is, innovations in the form of individual courses and new pedagogies designed to respond to other opportunities and challenges identified in chapter 4. We begin with critical thinking and oral and written communication, then move to creativity and innovative thinking, experiential learning, the role, responsibility, and purpose of business, and conclude with understanding the limits of markets and models.

Oral and Written Communication:
The Critical Analytical Thinking Course

Executives and faculty have long recognized that critical thinking and its expression as oral and written communication are important skills required of business graduates throughout their careers. What has often been debated is whether incoming MBAs already have these skills and, if they do not, whether they can be effectively taught at this stage of their development. Increasingly, business schools are staking out this territory, introducing "thinking and communication courses" as important components of major overhauls to the MBA program. In the last three years, for example, Stanford's Critical Analytical Thinking course, Yale's Problem Framing course, and Washington University's Critical Thinking for Leaders course have all taken aim at the need to develop and refine these skills, deeming them essential to effective decision making and action.

Executives and recruiters agree. Many seek to hire MBAs who can think about problems and articulate solutions in unique and logical ways, especially when faced with imperfect, ambiguous, or excessive information. As two of our interviewees observed:

> We want people who can take an unstructured problem, or a structured problem they can deconstruct, and look at it in a completely different way. We want people who can x-ray through to a different problem while using the same material everyone else has seen.

> _____

> We need people who can look at a problem and see it differently from others. [That way] you break the log jam.

But what exactly is critical thinking? And how can it be taught? The best way to answer both questions is by looking closely at an innovative example, Stanford's Critical Analytical Thinking (CAT) course.

To think critically is to reason clearly. It is a form of disciplined analysis, but one that is useful whatever the discipline or subject matter. Arons, for example, defines critical thinking as an approach that focuses on "the thinking and reasoning *processes* that underlie analysis and inquiry," and Paul and Elder identify eight essential elements: purpose, questions, points of view, information, assumptions, concepts, conclusions, and consequences.[1] The CAT course is cut from the same cloth. Its vision is "to improve students' reasoning and argument building skills, while also helping them to read and listen critically." The course develops these skills by "help[ing] students to think about causal inference, ask the right questions, be more critical, work out the logic behind an argument, and uncover assumptions."

CAT employs a small-group, seminar-style format.[2] A tenure-line faculty member or an adjunct faculty member with significant practitioner experience leads a group of fourteen to sixteen students. The course comprises seven weekly cycles. Each week, students write a three-page paper—typically, one thousand words—that they turn in late Wednesday evening. Professors grade the papers and return them with comments by Friday.

Writing coaches assigned to each section also review the papers, offering detailed advice on everything from structure to punctuation. Review by the writing coaches is mandatory for the first several weeks, but is optional later in the course, giving the coaches more time to work with students who need the most assistance. Meanwhile, the seminar group meets on Thursday evening or Friday to discuss the topic on which students have written.

The recommended reading list offers insight into the range of skills CAT seeks to develop. It includes three types of materials:

- Writing resources, such as the *Chicago Manual of Style*, Roget's Thesauri Online, and *A Plain English Handbook: How to Create Clear SEC Disclosure Documents*

- Readings on reasoning, such as *Reflections on Reasoning* by Raymond Nickerson and *The Art of Deception* by Nicholas Capaldi, as well as short notes prepared by faculty members on topics such as arguments, (mis)using evidence, and reasoning by analogy

- Books that provide context, as well as business and nonbusiness examples, such as *Reinventing the Bazaar: A Natural History of Markets* by John McMillan, *Blink: The Power of Thinking Without Thinking* by Malcolm Gladwell, and *The End of Poverty: Economic Possibilities for Our Time* by Jeffrey Sachs

Each week, CAT builds different reasoning skills in the context of a single substantive topic. For example, week 1 of the 2008 course focused on Google's presence in China and centered on issues of corporate social responsibility and ethics. Students were asked, Should Google launch versions of its search and news Web sites in China that censor material deemed objectionable to authorities? Was offering Chinese users limited access to content better than offering them none? Reasoning skills focused on the basics of constructing, communicating, and analyzing deductive arguments. Deductive reasoning, also called deductive logic, is a valuable reasoning skill that involves the construction of arguments that move from given statements (premises) to conclusions, which must then be true if the premises are true. It makes explicit implicit premises and the logic underlying the conclusion. In other sessions, students learn inductive reasoning, which reasons from a large number of similar situations or examples to arrive at a general rule.

Faculty and writing coaches evaluated students' answers across several dimensions. Were the assumptions clearly stated, or were there implicit, unarticulated assumptions behind a line of reasoning? Were inferences correctly drawn from the assumptions and evidence? Were the relevant principles and constraints properly considered? Did the student recognize when inferences could not be drawn? Was the document structured and sequenced logically to support the conclusions? Was there a compelling conclusion that synthesized the thinking? Were the style and language (sentence structure, word choice) and grammar and mechanics (subject-verb combinations, pronoun references, punctuation) correct? In the seminar discussion, students further explored the different conclusions they had reached and the logic and judgments they had employed.

Later sessions of CAT focused on different substantive topics as well as different modes of reasoning. For instance, the topic one week was the California Air Resources Board (CARB) Zero-Emission Mandate, circa 1990, which led to the production of electric vehicles. CARB subsequently weakened and then canceled the Zero-Emission Mandate, leading automobile manufacturers to withdraw their electric vehicles. CAT instructors posed the question, Why did this happen? This time, the goal was to help students learn to reason better abductively, that is, to assess how well their theory of the situation fit the observed evidence or facts. In abductive reasoning, critical questions include the following: What do we know? How do we know x? Why do we accept or believe x? What is the evidence for x? Are we clearly and explicitly aware of gaps in available information? Are we taking something on faith? Are we discriminating fact from conjecture? Is there sufficient evidence to fit our theory?[3]

A third CAT topic was the relative power of intrinsic and extrinsic motivators on employees. Students were given survey data on how employees in a large multinational corporation responded to questions about how powerful, on a scale of 1 to 7, each of several categories of motivators were for them and for their peers. The list of motivators included such categories as pay, praise, doing worthwhile things, and the opportunity to learn and practice new skills. Four of the eight motivators were extrinsic (e.g., pay, praise), and four were intrinsic (e.g., doing worthwhile things). The data presented had two characteristics, reflecting an almost universal result of such surveys: individuals saw themselves as substantially intrinsically motivated, and they saw their peers as much more extrinsically motivated. Students were asked to respond to the following question: Given these data, what conclusions do you draw for the human resources policies of the firm? The aim was to talk about the uses (and misuses) of data, especially survey data, with particular emphasis on the question of whether data are really actionable.

Many CAT sessions engaged students in a range of difficult, divisive questions and debates. At times the questions were focused on business topics: What responsibilities do corporations have to society? How do corporate culture and national culture interact? When do markets perform well and when do they perform poorly? On other occasions, they examined broader social questions: Should K–12 education be publicly provided and publicly financed? Can extreme poverty around the world be alleviated? A CAT instructor observed, "We expose students to conflicting perspectives about how to address complex issues such as poverty. The challenge lies in trying to construct good inductive arguments from imperfect data, and that struggle produces tremendous insight and learning for students and faculty alike."

Throughout the course, students analyze, write about, and debate fundamental questions and phenomena that arise in many business and nonbusiness settings. These issues transcend any single discipline or function of management. In the process, students hone their analytical and persuasive capabilities by developing a portfolio of thinking skills: the abilities to identify critical questions when exploring unfamiliar issues; parse issues into smaller, more manageable chunks; understand cause and effect; recognize when it is appropriate to use simple theoretical constructs in complex contexts; develop reasoned, defensible positions; make compelling arguments using a variety of reasoning skills; and recognize the limitations of different types of reasoning.

Beyond improving these reasoning skills, CAT also improves students' written and oral presentation abilities. Success comes through repetition and practice, as students engage in active debates week after week. Moreover, by positioning CAT at the beginning of the program, Stanford ensures that students have the opportunity to further deploy their newly acquired critical thinking and communication skills in the courses that follow.

Courses in critical thinking, logical reasoning, problem framing, and communication are not without challenges. They require high faculty-to-student ratios and a cadre of writing coaches, which can be costly. They do not fit neatly within the traditional MBA curriculum, which is dominated by the teaching of functions. Moreover, the research foundations of these fields—at least within business studies—are not well developed, even though the academic training of business school faculty, with its emphasis on rigorous analytical thinking, offers promise for developing courses in these areas. But such courses require faculty "to move beyond the hard skills of analytic thinking and incorporate . . . softer skills of purpose (for example, how does one begin to frame the problem), point-of-view (for example, theory on decision biases) and consequences (for example, a discussion of what happens next after the recommendations are implemented)."[4]

In summary, courses such as CAT help students practice the skills of oral and written communication that executives noted were sadly lacking in many MBA graduates: the ability to reason and argue effectively; read, write, and listen carefully; test conclusions for internal consistency; develop confidence in one's thinking and reasoning processes; and, in the words of a faculty member, cut through "a world of jargon and bombast, in which the medium is mistaken for the message."

Creativity and Innovative Thinking: The Creating Infectious Action Course

No one doubts the role of innovation in fostering the economic growth of countries and the competitive advantage of companies. Much has been written about innovative methods and how innovation has powered the success of companies such as Apple, Google, Johnson & Johnson, and Toyota.[5] Yet, as we described in chapter 4, many executives and recruiters express concern that MBA programs have failed to develop innovative and creative thinking skills in their graduates. These concerns focused on the following criticisms:

- Analytical skills are readily available. People who are creative and innovative are far rarer.

- MBAs lack creativity. They don't think outside the box. Business schools have to find a way to encourage creativity.

- Few graduates are capable of formulating "game-changing ideas." In many sectors of the economy, it is innovation and creativity that add the highest value, yet business schools have, at best, a modest record of developing these skills.

Why this modest record? According to many deans and faculty members, it is because innovative thinking skills are difficult to teach. In this section, we describe an effective approach to teaching innovation: Creating Infectious Action (CIA), a novel course offered by the Hasso Plattner Institute of Design at Stanford University.

CIA takes the view that teaching innovative and creative thinking requires a fundamentally different approach from the lecture- and case-based pedagogies that dominate most business school courses. The CIA approach emphasizes learning in multidisciplinary, diverse teams with the support of faculty and coaches rather than in large lecture hall formats. The pedagogy centers on student exercises and projects and emergent problem solving, in contrast to lectures and analytical assignments. The core activities are based on doing and on debriefing and learning from experiments and failures, rather than purely thinking and debating. The focus is on rigorous testing and on building process expertise for innovating, in contrast to rigorous analysis and subject expertise about innovations.[6]

The CIA course is founded on design thinking, "a discipline that uses the designer's sensibility and methods to match people's needs with what is technologically feasible and what a viable business strategy can convert into customer value and market opportunity."[7] At the core of design thinking is the ability to develop a deep understanding, through direct observation, of what a target group of customers wants in a product—for example, a cellular phone. What aspects and features do they like? Why? How do they use the product? A design team uses these insights to brainstorm many potential design solutions, taking into account multiple perspectives, such as look and feel, features, technology, and ease of use. Many alternative designs are explored by building prototypes, experimenting, and learning directly from the marketplace. The final design combines and integrates the best features from these experiments. In the CIA course, the goal of design thinking is to create infectious action: to design market offerings that delight customers and spread in a viral fashion through society.

The underlying philosophy of the CIA course is learning by doing: a strong belief that design thinking is best learned through practice. Consequently, CIA is a project-based course with a bias toward action. The teaching team for the course consists of one tenured professor and three adjunct faculty members with practical experience in design thinking. Twenty-four students are grouped into teams of four. Each multidisciplinary team is comprised of a mix of students from the Product Design Program, engineering school, business school, law school, and the school of arts and sciences. An industry coach supports each team.

Students undertake three projects during the eight-week course. The first project introduces students to the principles of design thinking by exploring one of several topic areas, such as, Why are some people so passionate about buying organic foods? Why do people use Wikipedia and why do they contribute to it? Why are people so excited about iPhones? The goal is to get students to talk to real people and collect data and evidence to gain deep insight into, and to develop hypotheses about, observed behaviors. Week 2 starts with a second project: how to increase the adoption of Firefox, Mozilla's Web browser. This project, which we describe in detail later in this section, takes three weeks. The final project focuses on how to build the user base for an entity such as Global Giving, a social venture organization that runs an online marketplace to connect individual donors to social entrepreneurs.

Instructors assign no pre-reading before the projects. However, students are given course handouts on design thinking; links to various Web sites about business, marketing, entrepreneurship, and change; and a variety of reference books to access during the projects, including *What Sticks: Why Some Ideas Work in the World and Others Don't* by Chip

Heath, *Pattern Recognition* by William Gibson, *Permission Marketing: Turning Strangers into Friends and Friends into Customers* by Seth Godin, *Diffusion of Innovations* by Everett Rogers, and *Influence: The Psychology of Persuasion* by Robert Cialdini. Instructors and coaches guide students to relevant reference material during the projects. The goal is not to require students to do specific readings in advance but rather to help students learn experientially about how to set their own frame by "discovering their way to a solution."[8]

An effective way to understand how CIA teaches creativity, innovation, and design thinking is to review in some detail one of the projects. We describe the Firefox project from the spring quarter of 2007. The project required student teams to find and implement ways to encourage downloads of Firefox in a user population beyond Internet-sophisticated and early-adopter populations, by creating a market offering (such as a Web site) tailored to particular user groups. Besides downloads, instructors asked the teams to consider "adherence"—the number of users who would continue using Firefox a few weeks later. Design thinkers call the problem or opportunity that prompts the search for a solution the "inspiration" for the project.[9]

In the first phase—*understand and observe*—students chose the user groups to focus on, informed by real-world evidence. The choice of user group was open ended, with very little guidance from instructors. Some student teams focused on religious groups, others on groups with similar interests, such as dog lovers, and still others on users with common behaviors, such as eBay users. Over three days, students contacted several groups through the Internet and in person to understand why they were not using the Firefox browser, paying close attention to less technologically adept users. This user- and consumer-centric, almost anthropological, understanding helped the team to address questions such as the following: Who should be the target users? What do they need? How do you know? The key deliverable was an actionable point of view, defined as answering all three questions.

As an example, if the target group were eBay users, it would not be enough to say "eBay users need to surf quickly." This point of view lacks deep insight because it answers the first two questions but not the third—it does not reveal a guiding principle for how users can be enticed to move to Firefox. A good point of view would be "eBay users need to surf quickly *and*, based on our observations, would move to Firefox from another browser if they could access eBay faster from Firefox." This insight could help a team identify first users (for example, key bloggers who could spread the word) and to find ways to spread the method of recruiting to other users (for example, by designing an attractive Web site).

The second phase entailed *brainstorming* potential solutions. Initially, the team focused on issues, not solutions, allowing for idea expansion by asking such questions as the following: What types of Firefox browser plug-ins should we consider? What should we optimize: ease of use? Speed? Look and feel of the Web site? The goal was to stay focused but to encourage ambitious ideas, build and expand on others' ideas, apply integrative thinking, and defer judgment to avoid interrupting the flow of ideas. For two days, all ideas were posted on classroom walls, and the entire team, rather than a single team leader, chose the best ideas to pursue.

The third phase involved *rapid, iterative prototyping*—building, testing, learning, and refining the team's Web site and plug-ins. Students built and tested two or three generations of prototypes during the next three days. "The goal of prototyping . . . [was] to learn about the strengths and weaknesses of the idea and to identify new directions that further prototypes might take."[10] In building various generations of prototypes, students designed prototypes to optimize each desired feature, such as speed or ease of use, and then integrated the best aspects of each prototype. In making these choices, team members revisited the insights and latent user needs generated during the understand-and-observe phase. In addition to users, students also considered the likely impact on other parties, such as Mozilla and competitors. The second and third phases together are sometimes referred to as *ideation*—"the process of generating, developing, and testing ideas that may lead to solutions."[11] According to one of the instructors:

> The CIA class takes the form of a traditional Beaux Arts class. Users, faculty, industry coaches, and students from other teams offer critiques of each prototype. Taking the critiques into account, each team evaluates and refines the prototype, in an iterative process that is characteristic of design thinking.

Students learn how enlightened trial and error, building lots of prototypes, and running quick experiments leads to more rapid success by generating knowledge faster and eliminating unfavorable options early and at low cost. They also learn the value of diverse perspectives, idea sharing, respecting contributions regardless of status and background, and teamwork.

The final phase is *implementation*—launching the Web site once the testing phase is complete. Over several weeks, Mozilla Corporation monitored Firefox downloads for the different teams, and each week the number of downloads were reported by each team to the rest of the class. The results varied significantly. The most successful prototype targeted eBay users by designing a plug-in that would allow them to surf eBay directly from the Firefox toolbar, and the least successful team targeted dog owners. Teams had the opportunity to learn from each other and from their instructors during meetings in which the results were discussed.

In line with the "think to build" philosophy and the emphasis on creating prototypes, CIA instructors do not present any theory in the class. Instead, they help students understand the various steps that support design thinking. Students then derive the underlying design principles that distinguish success from failure "by getting their hands dirty" and reflecting on their experience.[12] As the Mozilla example suggests, the pedagogical approaches used in the CIA course are a valuable way for students to learn about applications of information technology (IT). One of the major changes occurring in business today relates to how IT is reshaping business processes and operations. For example, the advent of the Internet has fundamentally changed how businesses reach customers, gather information, and coordinate their activities. Advances in IT have also allowed businesses to experiment cheaply, obtain rapid feedback, and quickly assess the impact of their actions. Much of the learning about these technologies is best achieved by doing and debriefing rather than through lectures and debate.

Teaching innovative thinking and creativity raises several challenges. The pedagogy of courses like CIA differs from the lecture- and case-based approaches that dominate at most business schools, but it is a pedagogy that faculty can learn with the help of coaches experienced in design thinking. Nevertheless, it requires faculty to move beyond an analytical mind-set centered on thinking and debating to one that concentrates on emergent problem solving based on doing and debriefing. Working with small teams of students also places more demands on faculty time and imposes greater financial costs.

Teaching innovative thinking and creativity also represents a shift in emphasis from knowing to doing. In CIA, students undertake ethnographic research to gain firsthand market knowledge that informs decisions. They experiment, build prototypes, obtain feedback, iterate, and learn from experience. The focus is not on theory but on understanding design processes and principles by actually trying them out. Innovative thinking and creativity, much like swimming and biking, is a skill best learned through practice, reflection, and repeated application. Listening to lectures or discussing cases about innovation does not develop this skill. Only by honing and testing these skills in real-life situations while still in business school will students become comfortable and well prepared for applying them in the workplace.

Understanding Organizational Realities: Multidisciplinary Action Projects

Experiential learning has been a recurrent theme in those sections of chapters 5 and 6 that focused on globalization and cultural sensitivity, leadership development and self-awareness, integration and integrative thinking, and innovative thinking and customer-centric design. As we noted in chapter 4, executives and recruiters are critical of MBA graduates for their limited understanding of organizational realities and underdeveloped execution and implementation skills. In this section, we focus on the benefits of experiential learning as a pedagogy that holds much promise for closing the knowing-doing gap.

The enthusiasm for experiential learning in MBA programs comes from deans, faculty, and executives increasingly recognizing that critical aspects of managing and leading are learned most effectively through practice rather than through traditional classroom-based pedagogies. In recent years, a growing number of business schools, including Michigan, MIT, Cornell, Case Western, and Harvard, have increased the experiential learning content of their MBA programs. According to

Michigan's Ross School of Business, "action-based learning enriches business education by connecting theory with practice. It deepens understanding of analytical concepts and tools, builds confidence in their use, and hones skills essential for their successful application."[13]

During our interviews, many deans strongly endorsed this approach to learning:

> Experiential learning is the new hallmark in MBA programs across the country.

> We are thinking about changing the curriculum so that the required curriculum and electives are finished in four quarters, and the last two quarters will be devoted to experiential learning in the form of a practicum. This could be a way to make business education more relevant.

Several executives echoed the deans' views. One of them observed, "Much of future success will not yield to a focus on rigorous analysis. A new approach is needed. The old, deliberate way was to talk to experts, think and plan, analyze in the classroom, work in headquarters, and present at meetings. Emergent discovery is different. It comes from doing—being out in the field. It is experiential and involves rigorous testing and experimentation."

As an approach to education, experiential learning has a long heritage. The foundations for much of the recent work in the field can be traced to such scholars as John Dewey, Kurt Lewin, and Jean Piaget—all of whom saw experience as central to understanding learning and development.[14] David Kolb then built on the work of these pioneering scholars to develop a more comprehensive experiential learning theory, which is becoming increasingly influential in management education.[15]

Kolb defines experiential learning as "the process whereby knowledge is created through . . . grasping experience and transforming experience."[16] Keeton and Tate expand on Kolb's definition by emphasizing that learning achieved through internships, work study programs, and field projects is experiential in that "the learner is directly in touch with the realities being studied . . . It involves direct encounter with the phenomenon being studied rather than merely thinking about the encounter or only considering the possibility of doing something with it."[17] The "direct encounters" with organizations enable students to learn about organizational realities, as Raelin explains: "Learning by experience is important to new practitioners because once they enter the world of practice, no matter how hard they try to apply theoretical criteria, use advanced analytical techniques, or recall a case study, they confront a host of unexpected contingencies associated with organizational life."[18]

Courses that provide students with real-world experience in dealing with "unexpected contingencies" help them to recognize, appreciate, and adapt to organizational realities by tempering their theoretical knowledge with practical constraints. They force students to identify and define problems, understand and navigate formal and informal structures, identify implementable actions, and exercise judgment when making decisions. Experiential learning takes aim at remedying many of the concerns presented in chapter 4 that characterized MBAs as highly analytical yet naïve about organizational realities, and knowledgeable about concepts and theories yet unable to apply them effectively in real-world settings. It seeks to make knowledge more practical and useful.

Kolb's model of experiential learning contends that effective learning is achieved through a cycle, in which each step is connected: "Immediate, concrete experience is the basis for observation and reflection. These observations are assimilated into a 'theory' from which new implications for action [are] deduced. These implications or hypotheses then serve as guides in acting to create new experiences."[19] This cycle helps students to understand how and when to apply the concepts and theories learned in the classroom to real-world settings.

We illustrate Kolb's experiential learning model using an example from a market entry project.

1. *Concrete experience:* "Learners . . . must be able to involve themselves fully, openly, and without bias in new experiences."[20] In a market entry project, concrete experience involves identifying target users and deeply understanding their needs, often through direct contact and personal engagement.

2. *Reflective observation:* "Learners . . . must be able to reflect on and observe their experiences from many perspectives."[21]

Reflective observation in a market entry project involves developing insights to meet customer needs by recognizing patterns, commonalities, and trends.

3. *Abstract conceptualization:* "Learners . . . must be able to create concepts that integrate their observations into logically sound theories."[22] Abstract conceptualization occurs during the brainstorming that teams engage in when considering alternative customer groups and differentiation strategies for establishing a position in the marketplace.

4. *Active experimentation:* "Learners . . . must be able to use these theories to make decisions and solve problems."[23] In a market entry project, active experimentation occurs during the testing of various strategies with customers, making improvements, and experimenting repeatedly to constantly learn from doing.

The challenge for experiential learning is to develop all of the capabilities Kolb describes in both individuals and teams. To understand these challenges in more detail, we review experiential learning projects from the MBA curriculum of the University of Michigan's Ross School of Business, which has engaged in a sustained and intensive action-learning effort since 1992.

The Ross School's Multidisciplinary Action Projects (MAP) course consists of intensive projects executed on site by MBA students in collaboration with a wide range of organizations, with the support of faculty advisors and coaches. The Ross School seeks complex projects in ambiguous contexts that require students to identify problems, navigate organizational politics, and formulate multidisciplinary solutions. Although most schools offer students the opportunity to do real-world projects, MAP is different in both scope and scale.

A required component of the Michigan MBA program's first year, the MAP course is scheduled for a seven-week period in March and April. During that time, students take no other courses. In recent years, 430 students each year have completed approximately eighty projects. The process begins in February, when students are assigned to a project as part of a team of four to six students based on their preferences. All students rank their top ten projects in order of preference and are assigned to teams based on an optimization algorithm, which typically results in 75 percent of students receiving a placement in one of their top three choices. About half of the projects are based in the United States. The others take place in a wide range of countries. Recent examples of international MAP projects include the following:

- *Aravind Eye Care System (nonprofit/health care), India:* Develop financial statements

- *Arbel Medical Ltd (medical devices), Czech Republic:* Design a market entry strategy

- *BHP Billiton (natural resources), Mozambique:* Assess the feasibility of renewable energy solutions

- *Rainforest Expeditions (hotel management), Peru:* Create a framework for mission and capabilities

- *Ryder System, Inc. (transportation), China:* Perform a market analysis and develop a growth strategy

- *Uniplen Industria de Polimeros (rubber/plastics), Brazil:* Propose a cost accounting method for products

- *Whirlpool Europe (consumer goods), Russia and Italy:* Develop strategic and marketing plans to grow revenue

MAP's learning objectives span three broad categories. In the first category, core business knowledge, students address the knowing-doing gap by applying concepts, theories, tools, and frameworks from their functional courses, such as strategy, marketing, finance, statistics, and accounting, to the problems of the sponsoring organization. Students integrate material from multiple disciplines and approaches, but more important, they begin to recognize the limitations of their theories and frameworks and the need to adapt these ideas to particular problems. For example, in thinking about strategy in countries such as Russia and China, students learn to explicitly consider the more active role that government policy plays in strategy formulation.

A second category of objectives, critical thinking skills, requires students to identify and characterize opportunities and hurdles, locate relevant data to conduct analysis feasible within the project length, engage in innovative problem solving, and exercise judgment. As one faculty member describes it, "Critical thinking is what MAP is all about because it is needed to both define the problem and then execute an appropriate analysis." The project on waste management, outlined later in this section, provides an example of the combination of analytical techniques and judgment that characterizes many MAP projects. One student found MAP to be "a test of my skills in visualizing the logical outcomes of different strategies and choosing the best alternative."

In the final category, leadership capabilities, students develop team-building and communication skills while learning how to navigate organizational politics. Students identified several areas, such as dealing with ambiguity and managing expectations, in which leadership qualities were enhanced:

> As a leader, now I feel more confident of handling situations and tasks with a lack of clarity, inadequate information, and no precedents.

> To turn an ineffective team into a highly effective team, understanding and analyzing what's going wrong is far from enough. A true leader must be able to push him- or herself to take initiative and make a change.

> As a leader, I learned the importance of determining expectations and goals at the start of each meeting (both within our MAP team and with sponsors) . . . As an individual, I have come to learn that it is vital to have a Plan B for all major steps.

> You can be effective leading teams without being excessively vocal. Quiet diplomacy may actually be more effective.

> I learned that I can lead a team, manage conflicts of personalities and personal styles, and manage my personal expectations.

To deliver on these objectives, the Ross School selects projects that are useful for both the students and the sponsoring organization. This means that projects cannot be so narrow that they do not challenge students (for example, a simple process improvement problem, such as how to collect cash on a flight), or so broad that they cannot be completed in seven weeks (for example, creating a market entry strategy for all of Asia). Faculty advisors play an important role in MAP. Each team has two faculty advisors, one of whom visits the sponsoring site during the project. Both advisors provide research support and grade the final paper. In addition, faculty coaches help teams to improve communication skills, create surveys, and conduct diagnostic interviews, and second-year MBA coaches help students with team dynamics. A librarian is also assigned to each team to assist with background research.

MAP projects are implemented through four phases that align closely with Kolb's model of experiential learning, providing opportunities for concrete experience, reflective observation, abstract conceptualization, and active experimentation. In the first phase, project entry, each team focuses on project scoping and planning and works together to define its goals. This is often a major challenge for the team because the issues or problems to be addressed are not immediately clear. During this phase, students immerse themselves in an often ambiguous situation. They ask: What are the key issues? What are the opportunities, challenges, and constraints? What is the anticipated output? Although teams do not receive specific training in how to scope the project, they have access to databases of scoping documents from previous years. The project entry phase concludes with a "Letter of Engagement" that confirms the understanding between the team, faculty, and sponsor regarding "project goals, boundaries, expected deliverables, and a summary work plan for completing the project successfully."[24]

Once the scoping and planning stage is complete, teams enter the second phase, diagnosis. In this phase, students refine the problem, collect available data, identify additional data that are needed, and formulate potential solutions. In developing these solutions, students consider several issues: Have various organizational realities been considered? How will different individuals in the organization react to this proposal? Can the proposal be implemented? Should an alternative proposal be recommended because it is easier to implement? A key learning for students is recognizing how the challenges of execution temper the direct application of theories and concepts. In this phase, the preliminary findings and diagnosis are also reviewed by the faculty advisors and sponsoring organizations.

Phase 3 of the MAP process, solution, requires teams to engage with the issues and questions identified during the diagnostic phase in order to formulate persuasive recommendations that are presented to faculty advisors and the sponsoring organization. They consider questions such as the following: What are the biggest unresolved issues? How can we communicate the logic and thinking behind our findings in a convincing way?

During the final phase, deliverables, each team first presents its recommendations to its faculty advisors. With the benefit of the advisors' feedback, teams then submit their recommendations to the sponsoring organization in an oral presentation and a written report. At the end of the project, students have an additional opportunity for reflection in a short essay that is required of each member of the team.

The most effective way to explain what students learn from MAP is to describe an actual project: to help a company in the waste management business understand the business impact of changing attitudes and business practices with respect to the environment and develop a set of actions it might take. In the project entry phase, the team created an inventory of all the changes that could affect the business. For example, students considered how the emphasis on reducing waste and recycling and reusing waste might affect the demand for the company's services, and how the company should respond. Should it plan on slower growth? Should it invest in new technologies? Should it invest in new services? How quickly might regulations change, and what might these changes be? Should the company invest in these areas ahead of regulatory requirements? Would customers, under pressure from society or anticipating regulatory changes, be more likely to do business with the company if it invested in newer technologies, such as bioreactor landfills, that are more costly to maintain but that accelerate the decomposition of organic wastes? Would customers be willing to pay higher prices for these services? Would technologies that minimize methane emissions, extract landfill gas, and track the process of waste degradation pay off in a carbon-constrained regulatory system?

In the diagnosis phase, students interviewed management and customers and studied regulatory trends to gather data and identify the major changes that were likely to affect the company. The short time period for completing the project forced students to exercise judgment regarding the likelihood of particular developments and the extent of their impact. The team created metrics to measure these impacts and developed preliminary models to quantify and aggregate them. As it weighed different options and recommendations, the team also considered who in the organization favored certain recommended solutions and who did not. How strong would these objections be? What challenges would be involved in overcoming these objections, and how might this be done?

In the solution phase, students estimated the probability of specific changes, identified metrics to measure their impact, and developed models with variables and parameters that quantified the financial impacts on the company from the potential economic, social, and environmental trends. Students ranked these impacts based on specific assumptions and values of the variables and parameters. They tested the sensitivity of these impacts to various assumptions. Based on this analysis, the team considered actions the company could take to improve its financial and environmental performances, and the challenges of implementation.

In the final phase of the project, students recommended four high-priority actions to the company. First, they advised the company to engage in the legislative debate about climate change because it could potentially benefit from legislative efforts to limit emissions through waste gas recovery. Second, the team recommended that the company undertake a strategic review to plan for future developments using the team's analysis of trends and their potential impacts. Third, the students suggested that the company develop training activities to help employees respond to evolving customer needs. Fourth, the team recommended that the company launch an internal sustainability effort consistent with its external messaging.

In terms of Kolb's framework, the project scoping and diagnosis phases correspond to concrete experiences and reflective observations.

The solutions and deliverables phases engage students in abstract conceptualization and active experimentation. In the process, students learn to work in teams, think critically, adapt theories to practice, and apply ideas within organizational constraints.

Experiential learning poses several challenges. It requires significant commitment of faculty resources and time. Moreover, the discipline-based training of many faculty is not optimal training for advising projects that are inherently multidisciplinary. On the other hand, experiential learning offers great promise for faculty to broaden themselves while developing significant professional expertise. Moreover, team and communication coaches provide critical complementary support. The organization, planning, and coordination of experiential learning courses, particularly when done at scale, require substantial human and financial resources. Students need support as they work in teams on messy, complex, and ambiguous problems in unfamiliar, difficult, and high-pressure situations. Without proper support, teams can become dysfunctional, considerably diminishing the benefits of experiential learning.

Despite these challenges, experiential learning offers a special opportunity to narrow the knowing-doing gap. It provides a uniquely different dimension to business education by giving students the chance to define and scope problems, test ideas in practice, recognize the constraints placed by organizational realities, think innovatively, and recognize the need to reconcile multidisciplinary and sometimes conflicting perspectives. These benefits are even greater in the context of global projects that require students to apply and adapt the concepts and frameworks they have learned to countries with different cultures, institutions, markets, and business practices. Experiential learning also promotes interactions with designers, manufacturing workers, salespersons, and administrative staff, and in doing so helps students connect with the very individuals they will engage with as managers. Students also get better insight about themselves—how they interact with others, how they lead and contribute, and how they can develop personally. Despite the costs, many schools have recognized the benefits and are experimenting with a wide range of approaches to experiential learning.[25] We expect these trends to accelerate as schools develop further expertise in the area.

The Role, Responsibilities, and Purpose of Business: The Leadership and Corporate Accountability Course

Business leaders today are increasingly wrestling with the changing scope and nature of their responsibilities. Especially for large multinational corporations, the line between public and private activity has become ever more blurred and difficult to define. Executives must determine how best to balance financial and nonfinancial objectives while simultaneously juggling the demands of such diverse constituencies as shareholders, bondholders, customers, employees, regulators, legislators, NGOs, and the public at large. Walmart, for example, has become so large and pervasive that executives must consider its labor and benefits policies in light of their impact on local and state economies—so much so that some observers have proclaimed it the "New Washington."[26] Nike, prodded by consumer boycotts and lobbying by NGOs, has been actively improving the working conditions in its overseas factories. Large pharmaceutical firms, under pressure from legislators, regulators, and media critics, have had to change their pricing policies to make expensive life-saving drugs more affordable and available. Mining and petroleum companies, faced with complaints from local governments as well as international watchdogs, have begun to pay more attention to the environmental and health impacts of their digging and drilling. In the aftermath of the economic crisis, banks and financial services firms have found that legislators and regulators now hold strong views about how they should manage their balance sheets, design and sell complex financial products such as derivatives, and pay senior executives, and have had to respond accordingly.

These changes all reflect the need for MBAs, as executives in training, to broaden their scope and think more deeply about the role, responsibilities, and purpose of business. A number of business schools now offer courses that directly address these issues and have made them part of their core curriculum. Examples include New York University's Professional Responsibility: Markets, Ethics, and Law course, the Wharton School's Ethics and Responsibility course, and Harvard's Leadership and Corporate Accountability (LCA) course. Here we focus on LCA.

LCA presents students with a wide range of case studies featuring moral and ethical dilemmas, thoughtful actions by managers facing trade-offs between private profits and social gains, and questions about the limits and extent of corporate activism. It is designed to address the concerns expressed by the economist Robert Shiller that "the view of the world one gets in a modern business curriculum can lead to an ethical disconnect . . . courses often encourage a view of human nature that does not inspire high-mindedness."[27] Many of the cases describe incidents or events that are by now well known but that even today raise thorny questions about the goals and purpose of business: Johnson & Johnson's handling of the Tylenol crisis; Manville's response to a scientist's claim that its mainstay fiberglass products were likely to be carcinogenic; Royal Dutch Shell's response to environmental, community, and political problems in Nigeria; Yahoo!'s decision to provide the Chinese government with information about a local dissident who was using its e-mail services; and Aaron Feuerstein's decision, after a devastating fire, to provide ninety days of full pay to all workers at Malden Mills while rebuilding the plant in Lawrence, Massachusetts, even though it exposed the company to potential bankruptcy. Other cases describe incidents that are less well known but present students with equally difficult trade-offs and choices: a Swedish travel company's decision about how best to respond to emerging information about the tsunami in Southeast Asia, which might have struck an area where several hundred of its clients were vacationing; a Swiss mail-order company's decision about whether to cut off suppliers who might possibly be relying on child labor; and a sustainable investment firm's decision about whether to invest in a company that would raise living standards in India by providing electrical power and employment but that at the same time was certain to increase environmental pollution because of its reliance on coal-fired generators.

To help students think systematically about these questions, the course is divided into three parts.[28] Part I of the course introduces students to the distinctive responsibilities of business leaders. It does so by dividing those responsibilities among four separate modules, organized by stakeholder groups. Each group of stakeholders presents a special set of challenges. The first module addresses responsibilities to investors. There, the primary challenge is trust: investors need assurances that their interests are aligned with and well served by their agents, who may be partners, corporate officers, or members of the board. A key lesson for students is the existence of fiduciary duties and the extent to which they impose requirements that go beyond contractual terms. The second module addresses responsibilities to customers. There, the primary challenge is information asymmetries: companies often have more information about their products and the associated risks than do their customers. A key lesson for students is the need for transparency and disclosure, even when information is partial or incomplete. The third module addresses responsibilities to employees. There, the primary challenge is power asymmetries: employers have considerable power over their employees and are responsible for establishing safe and secure working conditions, employment rules, and guidelines for hiring and firing. A key lesson for students is the importance of fairness and fair treatment in ensuring harmonious, productive work environments. The fourth module is about responsibilities to society and the public at large. There, the primary challenge is market and government failures: companies often operate in settings where externalities such as pollution are not properly priced, where regulation is limited or incomplete, or where governments are corrupt. A key lesson for students is the need to consider ethical and social factors when operating in these settings and to recognize that, despite the lack of market discipline, powerful forces such as public opinion will still hold them accountable for their behavior.

Part I of the course ends with a summative session that asks students to contrast two distinct views of the corporation: the shareholder maximization perspective and the multiple stakeholder perspective. The goal of this session is not to pigeon-hole students, but rather to help them understand the strengths and weaknesses, as well as the assumptions and limitations, of each perspective. The session also underlines the importance of combining economic, legal, and ethical considerations when making business decisions, a point that we highlighted in chapter 5.

Part II of the LCA course shifts attention to issues of corporate governance and organizational design. It asks students to consider the systems that are necessary to ensure that companies and their leaders are effective in meeting the multiple responsibilities of part I. This section contrasts failure stories such as Enron and WorldCom with success stories such as Johnson & Johnson under James Burke and Salomon Brothers under Warren Buffett. In the course of discussing these cases, students learn about the power of external and internal governance systems for shaping behavior. They discuss the roles of regulators, auditors, and boards of directors on the one hand, and incentive, compliance, and values and belief systems on the other hand, as factors that influence the decision making and actions of executives.

Part III of the LCA course is about personal development. It asks students, often through reflective exercises that draw on their personal and professional experiences, to consider the ways in which leaders (and, by implication, the students themselves) are inspired to rise to the challenges of responsible, accountable leadership. This section focuses on the essential skills students must develop if they are to behave wisely, especially in the face of powerful pressures to do otherwise. Students learn the importance of having a broad repertoire of moral behaviors, including the classic trilogy of exit, voice, and loyalty, and of knowing how and when to draw on different behaviors. They learn about the need for resilience—the ability to bounce back and learn from obstacles or failures—when faced with difficult moral challenges and tests of responsibility. They learn the importance of self-command—the ability to step back from a crisis or stressful situation, keep a clear head, and avoid the temptation to micromanage or interfere with the work of others lower in the organization as they carry out their work. And they learn the necessity of having a clear set of moral commitments, personal values, and ethical principles to guide their actions in times of stress.

The reflective exercises are designed to cement these lessons by personalizing them. Students come to class with one or more paragraphs based on their own experiences but tied to the issues in that day's case: a time when they were asked to do something that they found to be ethically uncomfortable, a time when they handled an ethical challenge poorly, or a time when they witnessed or experienced someone else leading them or others to rise to meeting an ethical challenge or moral dilemma. Students share these vignettes and then try to generalize the lessons. What, for example, makes it so difficult to behave responsibly when faced with ethical challenges? What leadership behaviors seem to bring out the best in others? The course ends by pairing a discussion of Dr. Martin Luther King Jr.'s "Letter from Birmingham Jail," one of the hallmarks of the civil rights movement and a powerful piece of contemporary moral philosophy, with a written exercise that asks students to address the question of how they hope to become "leaders who make a difference in the world" (Harvard Business School's mission is to educate leaders who do just that). In the process, they continue to shift from knowing to being and further internalize the message of LCA about the many responsibilities that business leaders have to society.

Courses like LCA that help students to reflect on the role, responsibilities, and purpose of business raise several challenges for business schools and their faculty. The multidisciplinary nature of such courses requires faculty to draw on a broad array of disciplines and experiences. Developing a common language is often difficult, as is mastering the concepts, theories, and frameworks from fields as distinct as accounting, economics, law, and moral philosophy. As with many multidisciplinary courses, staffing is frequently a challenge, and senior faculty and professors of management practice are often better equipped than junior faculty to meet the teaching demands. In addition, because of the controversial nature of the topics, faculty in these courses must pay special attention to classroom climate and tone. Evenhandedness and an open, accepting stance are essential. Students must feel that the classroom is a safe, protected environment in which they can openly explore and question one another's deeply held beliefs without the need to parrot back a prescribed philosophy or point of view.

Risk, Regulation, and Restraint: Understanding the Limits of Models and Markets

The issues surrounding risk, regulation, and restraint gained much greater salience as the economic crisis unfolded in late 2008 and early 2009. Many business schools began responding to needs in the areas that were exposed at that time. Yet as of this writing, most curricular changes have been piecemeal—a few sessions spread throughout the curriculum, rather than an integrated, cohesive response. For this reason, unlike earlier sections of this chapter, this section does not feature a single, specific course. Instead, we describe a variety of approaches that business schools are employing to teach students about previously underappreciated aspects of risk, regulation, and restraint.

These topics are not new to business schools. For many years, in fact, they have been staples of the curriculum, featured in discussions of decision making under uncertainty, risk aversion and expected utility, insurance, the relationship between risk and return, and the capital asset pricing model and its implications for portfolio diversification. Now, however, schools are beginning to add courses on underrepresented aspects of risk, such as liquidity risk, credit risk, country risk, and counterparty risk.[29] At the same time, scholars are questioning whether uncertainty can always be conceptualized as "numerical probabilities [attached] to the possible outcomes of actions," in part because the world is changing so rapidly, in part because of our ignorance of "unknown unknowns," and in part because of the need to rely increasingly on intuition.[30] This view explicitly recognizes the fragility of risk models. Consistent with this theme, one new course takes the view that the key to identifying and managing strategic risk is engaging members of the organization in dialogue by asking tough questions about the range of choices, underlying assumptions, emerging patterns in the data, and evolving action plans.[31] Such questions force students to make difficult choices about customers and a company's value proposition, recognize what might cause a strategy to fail, understand major franchise and reputational risks, and assess whether controls and employee commitment to core values are in place to prevent individuals from behaving badly.

The role that regulation plays in providing an operating context for business has historically received little attention at business schools. Our analysis of MBA curricula in chapter 3 showed that in the past few schools required students to take courses with a heavy regulatory component. As a result of the economic crisis, many schools are now moving quickly to fill this gap.[32] Some courses aim to help students understand the origins of financial markets and instruments, the causes of financial crises, the behavior of financial actors and groups in the context of financial bubbles and crashes, and the role of government regulation in managing risk and externalities. Other courses focus on the interface between public policy and business; the role of business leaders in analyzing and directing public policy in areas such as environmental problems, the provision of health care, antitrust laws and enforcement, intellectual property rights, energy supply, discrimination and equal opportunity regulations; and the deregulation of industries such as airlines, communications, and electrical power. The goal is to help students understand the economic and social principles that drive regulation, including market failures, market imperfections, externalities, information asymmetries, and power asymmetries. Students also learn to make judgments about whether regulations can be designed to achieve the goals of preventing social harm and abusive practices without hampering private incentives for innovation and efficiency.

A final set of issues that business schools are now addressing can be grouped under the term *restraint*. Examples include recognizing the imperfections of models and frameworks, and studying and learning from failures. The first of these topics was already being introduced into the curriculum before the economic crisis. Courses in behavioral economics, behavioral finance, and prospect theory had begun to examine the role of mass psychology, herd behavior, and cognitive biases in the operation of markets, as well as in individual and group decision making. The housing bubble and the recent economic crisis only accelerated this trend. Still, the continued reliance of institutions on quantitative risk models (often as a substitute for good judgment) and the continued belief in rational, efficient markets on the part of many policy makers and regulators show that more needs to be done to increase awareness of the limitations of our theories and how models should be used.

Other courses focus on learning from failures. They improve students' understanding of the circumstances that raise the likelihood of failures, the sources of error that cause these failures, and strategies to avoid them.[33] For example, a number of courses now consider how discontinuous changes, such as new ventures, mergers and acquisitions, and major shifts in technologies and customers, can lead to failure. They examine such sources of errors as misleading experiences (resulting from retrievability bias or false analogies); misleading prejudgments (resulting from cognitive dissonance or overconfidence bias);

inappropriate self-interest (resulting from an inability to see opposing viewpoints or from overweighting the short term relative to the long term); and inappropriate or excessive attachments to particular businesses, family, or friends. These errors are compounded by flawed assumptions about marketplace and organizational realities and breakdowns in communication systems, often caused by arrogant leadership styles. To minimize the risk of failures, organizations can implement a wide variety of safeguards. Courses discuss such safeguards as seeking out relevant experience, presenting data and analysis on both benefits and risks, encouraging processes of group debate and challenge (such as devil's advocacy and dialectical inquiry), and instituting governance mechanisms that foster a culture where people are willing to speak up.

Whereas most of the courses discussed in other sections of this chapter were designed to develop the "doing" and "being" components of the knowing-doing-being framework, efforts to improve students' understanding of the limits of models and markets address gaps in "knowing." Because these courses are still emerging, the biggest challenges involve course content and placement. Schools need to address the question of whether these topics should be featured in new courses or incorporated in already existing courses, and if so, whether they should be part of the required or elective curriculum.

Part Two

Institutional Responses

Both part I and part II examine the challenges and opportunities confronting business schools today. They do so, however, from different vantage points, using different levels of analysis. Whereas part I provides a detailed, empirically grounded portrait of the larger environment for MBA education, part II shifts the focus from an industrywide perspective to in-depth portraits of particular institutions. Chapters 7 through 12 present rich, field-based case studies of business schools and executive programs that have responded in distinctive ways to the unmet needs identified in chapter 4. These chapters give readers the opportunity to review specific changes and initiatives in the context of institutions as a whole, allowing for an appreciation of the many reinforcing activities involved in efforts such as implementing a sweeping curriculum reform or building a program around global content.

The cases were originally written in late 2007.[1] As the global economic crisis unfolded, we reconnected with each institution in the spring of 2009 to collect follow-up information. Initial responses to the crisis, which appear as updates at the end of each case, coalesced around several themes: increased attention to the interconnectedness of global economies, markets, and organizations; greater emphasis on teaching ethics and accountability, regulation, and risk management; and the necessity and benefits of developing courses in collaboration with other parts of the university, particularly schools of public policy and law and departments of political science and economics.

The case studies show that business schools, faced with similar (precrisis) challenges and opportunities, responded in very different ways. Each case, in fact, focuses on something of an "ideal type," an institution that best embodies one of the themes or concerns that arose in our interviews. In that sense, each case is an exemplar of one or more central concepts, philosophies, or approaches: discipline-based and flexible courses at Chicago Booth, a global orientation at INSEAD, individual and small-group leadership development at the Center for Creative Leadership, general management and closeness to practice at Harvard, integration at Yale, and customization at Stanford.

The cases thus take an institutional perspective; they map out a set of choices that institutions have made across a variety of topics, curricula, courses, and pedagogies. Each of these choices can be arrayed on a spectrum, showing the range of possible approaches open to business schools as they seek to address the challenges identified in part I:

- From organic, incremental curriculum changes to planned, large-scale redesign

- From a focus on several unrelated themes to a broad unifying purpose

- From a traditional sequence of courses to a more radical repositioning of topics

- From minor variations on existing courses to novel and innovative course content

- From rigid requirements to greater flexibility and customization

- From loose integration to a tight coupling of courses

- From pedagogies based on large classroom lectures and case discussions to field work, experiential learning, small-group activities, and even one-on-one instruction

We begin in chapter 7 with an examination of the University of Chicago Booth School of Business. This case shows how core business functions such as marketing, finance, and strategy can be taught from a disciplinary perspective, and how change can be accomplished through an organic, evolutionary process. Chicago Booth places a strong emphasis on grounding functional courses in the foundational academic theories of economics, statistics, psychology, and sociology. An additional feature of the Chicago Booth MBA is the flexibility of its course structure. Beyond distribution requirements, only one course (LEAD) is mandatory. Students select from a large menu of Foundations and Breadth Requirement courses, providing them with a large array of choices varying in difficulty, teaching style, and disciplinary approach. The Chicago Booth case highlights both the advantages and disadvantages of flexibility and limited requirements, bottom-up approaches to curricular change, and basing courses on a strong disciplinary orientation.

Chapter 8 examines INSEAD and its comprehensive approach to developing leaders with a global mind-set. Among the critical elements of INSEAD's approach are two campuses, one in France, the other in Singapore; an alliance with an American business school; the opportunity to move freely across campuses; a curriculum infused with global materials; highly diverse multinational students and faculty; and a requirement that students speak two languages upon entering the program and three languages at graduation. Beyond raising questions about the most effective ways of developing global awareness and a global mind-set, the INSEAD case prompts consideration of the optimum length of an MBA program, since the school offers an MBA in only ten months.

Chapter 9 features the Center for Creative Leadership. This case provides insights into a rich, multifaceted approach to leadership development based on behavioral science research, personalized coaching, and an assessment, challenge, and support (ACS) model that relies heavily on interactive class work, group exercises and simulations, and introspection through guided reflection. Since its founding in 1970, CCL has built on its ACS model by designing and delivering an expanding set of executive programs, including the Leadership Development Program and the Looking Glass Experience. In the process, it has pioneered experiential and reflective approaches to leadership development and has created a distinctive set of assessment tools, simulations and exercises, and feedback techniques. The CCL case helps readers think more deeply about the elements of an effective, comprehensive approach to leadership development while also raising questions about the content, cost, and consistent delivery of such programs.

Chapter 10 focuses on the Harvard Business School. This case explores the general management orientation of the school's MBA program, its commitment to the case method, and the resulting closeness to practice. Changes in Harvard's MBA program have occurred every few years in a stepwise fashion as substantial new courses have been introduced into the required curriculum, most recently to address ethics and social responsibility (the Leadership and Corporate Accountability course) and entrepreneurship (the Entrepreneurial Manager course). In addition, the school has launched a number of multidisciplinary initiatives to foster research and course development in areas such as leadership, social enterprise, globalization, and health care. This chapter raises questions about how best to link the worlds of scholarship and practice; the elements that support an integrated, general management perspective; and the advantages and disadvantages of an extensive and tightly packed required curriculum.

Chapter 11 examines the Yale School of Management. This case describes a large-scale, planned curriculum change built around a single theme: integration. Yale's new curriculum replaced traditional MBA courses, organized by function, with an integrated curriculum, organized by constituencies such as the investor, the customer, and the employee. In addition, the school introduced a number of innovative courses, such as Problem Framing, which teaches students how to structure and frame business problems, and the Leadership Development Program, which helps students to align their actions with their personal values and beliefs. The Yale case raises questions about the most effective curriculum design for teaching integration, the trade-offs between depth (intense training in the functions) and breadth (offering more integrated multidisciplinary courses), and the challenge of developing in traditional, discipline-based faculty the broad knowledge required to teach integrated courses.

Chapter 12 focuses on the Stanford Graduate School of Business. Several of the themes of part I come together in this case, which describes the adoption of a broad-based new MBA curriculum through large-scale planned changes in the sequence, structure, and content of courses. The most dramatic shift was toward customization of functional and foundational courses, with students allowed to select from basic, intermediate, and advanced offerings. In addition, while the program maintained its general management perspective, it added to or expanded upon its efforts in leadership development, global management, faculty advising, and the teaching of critical thinking skills. The primary motivation behind these changes was a desire to increase the level and quality of student engagement. Questions raised by this case include the advantages and disadvantages of dividing a cohort of students into groups that take core courses at three different levels, the sustainability of intensive faculty involvement as student advisors and the leaders of intensive, small-group discussion classes, and the most effective sequence of topics and courses over the two years of the program.

Together, these case studies not only describe a range of curricular choices but also illustrate a diverse set of processes and approaches for changing MBA programs. At one extreme is Chicago Booth, a discipline-based program with a change process that is less planned than organic and evolutionary. The inherent flexibility of the program makes change relatively easy; the curriculum shifts as faculty propose and offer new courses. Both INSEAD and CCL represent a second approach, developing around a single, dominant theme that is then embellished by new ideas that enhance and reinforce the central objective (for example, INSEAD's second campus and CCL's global leadership training program). Having a dominant theme increases the urgency for each institution to adapt to changes in the business environment. Harvard, Yale, and Stanford represent a third approach: broad, diversified, general management–oriented MBA programs. Each has a large set of required courses, which creates inertia and makes change more difficult. Harvard has responded by changing in a stepwise fashion (for example, by adding new first-year courses such as Leadership and Corporate Accountability and The Entrepreneurial Manager, and by expanding its international presence through global research centers), but is just beginning to contemplate holistic, integrated changes. Both Yale and Stanford have instituted broad, large-scale planned changes in their curriculum, built around a single theme (at Yale the theme was integration, and at Stanford it was customization), a few common areas of focus (such as globalization, leadership, problem framing, and critical thinking), and simultaneous changes in the sequence, structure, and content of courses.

We see several ways in which these cases might be helpful to readers. They can be used by faculty and administrators to compare and contrast the benefits and challenges of different approaches to modifying or reforming the MBA curriculum. They can also be used to zero in on particular institutions or reforms that are most relevant or appealing to a school seeking to redesign its MBA program. At a minimum, the cases provide readers with an introduction to a few of the exciting experiments currently under way at business schools today, as well as an appreciation for the diverse approaches that schools have chosen in response to the opportunities and challenges that we described in earlier chapters.

7

University of Chicago Booth
School of Business

Flexibility and the Discipline-Based Approach

OVER THE COURSE of its history, the University of Chicago Booth School of Business had developed a discipline-based approach to business education. During the school's 2007–2008 curriculum review, Dean Edward A. (Ted) Snyder noted that although there was significant change under way at some other leading MBA programs, Chicago's existing approach was unlikely to be seriously questioned. "Neither recruiters, nor students, nor alumni are calling for curricular change," Snyder observed. "I would be shocked if the committee recommended major changes to our course requirements. We are happy with what we do, it is good for us, and it matches Chicago, our faculty, and our values." Stacey Kole, the deputy dean of the full-time MBA program, agreed. Kole explained, "I think Chicago is very well positioned in its classical approach. We consciously do not jump at the latest fads. Our approach is to teach students 'how to think' rather than 'what to think' by unraveling the foundational elements of complex problems. Our curriculum is not broken and other schools are moving toward more flexibility in their programs."

Chicago's flexible, discipline-based curriculum offered students the opportunity to choose and sequence courses to fit their educational goals. A key strength was the school's depth of offerings in functional disciplines such as accounting, statistics, psychology, sociology, and economics, and the application of these disciplines in areas such as marketing, finance, and strategy. Many theory-based courses were developed and taught by some of the world's top research-focused academics—including six Nobel laureates. According to Snyder, "Whatever courses you take, you'll leverage disciplines like economics, sociology, and psychology and diverse points of view to get to better solutions. The goal is to get ready for high-stakes moments during your career when there are no formulas or cases to guide you, and when you have to make the decision."

Chicago required its students to select courses from a range of disciplines and functional areas to ensure that each graduate received a breadth of exposure, but the only required fields were accounting, economics, and statistics. In these fields and the elective areas, students could select courses with varying degrees of difficulty, approach, and teaching style. The sole required course was one on leadership, and even that was mandated only for students in the full-time MBA program. "On a spectrum of requirements amongst top business schools," Snyder explained, "Chicago anchors the flexibility end of the scale."

Background on the Institution and Its MBA Programs

The University of Chicago founded its business school in 1898, making it the second oldest business school in the United States. Originally an undergraduate institution, the school added graduate programs in 1916 and the MBA in 1936. In 1950 it became an all-graduate institution. Long a leader in graduate business education, it had been first to initiate a PhD program in business (1920), first to grant a PhD in business to a woman (1929), first to launch an academic business journal (1928), and first to offer an executive MBA (1943). It was also the first business school to have one of its faculty members, George J. Stigler, receive a Nobel Prize in economic sciences (1982).

To help support its research, the school had several research centers and institutes. These included the Center for Decision Research, the Center for Population Economics, the Center for Research in Security

Prices, the Polsky Center for Entrepreneurship, the Kilts Center for Marketing, the Stigler Center for the Study of the Economy and the State, and the Becker Center on Chicago Price Theory.

By 2000, the school (by then known as the University of Chicago Graduate School of Business, until its 2008 renaming as Chicago Booth) operated four campuses. The main campus was located on the grounds of the University of Chicago, seven miles from downtown Chicago. It housed the faculty, the full-time MBA program, the PhD program, and various research centers. Chicago also operated a city-center campus in downtown Chicago, located close to many large employers. This campus housed the evening and weekend MBA programs and the U.S. portion of the executive MBA program. Finally, Chicago had additional campuses in London and Singapore for its executive MBA programs.

The MBA Programs

Chicago offered six ways to earn an MBA degree: a full-time, two-year MBA; an evening MBA; a weekend MBA; and three executive MBA programs. The full-time, evening, and weekend programs had almost identical requirements. The three executive MBA programs were similarly nearly identical, offering students a cohort experience with relatively few electives. Chicago faculty taught in all programs, and the school awarded the same MBA degree to students regardless of the program in which they studied. In fact, there was no wording or title on the degree that identified a student as a full-time, evening, weekend, or executive attendee.

Students applied to and were admitted into one of the six programs. Once enrolled, non-executive students in the full-time, evening, and weekend programs were free to take courses in any of these three programs. It was common, for example, for full-time students to take some evening or weekend courses to get desired professors or to get into courses that had reached capacity on the weekdays. In contrast, the executive MBA program assigned students to cohorts and followed a schedule that prohibited cross-registering for courses. Chicago enrolled approximately 1,100 full-time MBA students (550 students per class), 1,100 evening MBAs, 350 weekend MBAs, 480 executive

MBAs, and 120 PhD students. It had some 41,000 alumni in 2008. Placement data for the class of 2006 showed that nearly 52 percent had taken jobs in financial services, and 22 percent went into consulting.[1]

Students in the full-time MBA program came from around the world, with an average age of approximately twenty-seven. A significant majority were career switchers. Evening-program students came from the Chicago area and tended to be slightly older, with an average age of twenty-nine. Somewhat fewer of these were career switchers. About half of the weekend students came from outside the Chicago area. These students had an age makeup and career switcher percentage similar to the evening students. In the three executive MBA programs, students were thirty-six years old on average and had thirteen years of work experience. They came from the United States, Asia, and Europe. One other difference in program populations was that full-time students spent more time focused on their job search than did part-time students. Otherwise, several faculty members commented, in the classroom there were few apparent differences among the students in the full-time, evening, and weekend programs—in fact, because of the cross-registering opportunities, these students often sat side by side in the same classes.

Full-Time, Evening, and Weekend MBA Programs. Chicago ran courses on a quarter schedule. Despite offering students significant flexibility to choose their own courses, the program did require students to take a total of twenty courses within several areas, as specified in the following breakdown.

Foundations. The foundations courses served almost like the core courses at other MBA programs. Students were required to take one course from each of three areas (three courses):

- Financial accounting (one of five choices)

- Microeconomics (one of four choices)

- Statistics (one of thirteen choices)

Breadth Requirements. To ensure that students did not overly focus their course choices into one or two narrow subject areas, Chicago required students to take one course each from four of the six breadth areas (four courses):

- Financial management (eight choices)

- Human resource management (five choices)

- Macroeconomics (six choices)

- Managerial accounting (two choices)

- Marketing management (one choice)

- Operations management (four choices)

General Management. Students were required to take one course each from group A and group B (two courses):

- Group A: Strategic management (three choices)

- Group B: Managerial and organizational behavior (four choices)

Electives and Concentrations. Students had to take a minimum of eleven elective courses. In all, Chicago offered approximately 150 different courses. Students also had the option to choose a concentration by taking between three and six courses in one of thirteen different areas. Students could select up to three concentration areas, including finance, entrepreneurship, strategy, and operations management, among others. Students also could take up to six courses outside the business school at other parts of the University of Chicago.

LEAD. The sole distinction between the full-time, evening, and weekend MBA programs' requirements was the requirement that all full-time students take the Leadership Effectiveness and Development course (LEAD) during the fall of their first year. (See details later in this chapter.) This course was offered as an optional (tuition-free) twenty-first course for evening and weekend students.

Executive MBA. The executive MBA programs were cohorted, largely lock-step programs that lacked the flexibility for which Chicago's other MBA programs were known. Executive programs ran on their own schedules, different from the university's quarter system. They also had a required international component.

Chicago claimed it was the first MBA program to have campuses on three continents. The school had opened a European campus (first located in Barcelona and later moved to London) in 1994, and an Asian campus in Singapore in 2000. The London and Singapore campuses were used primarily for the resident executive MBA programs. Another cohort of executive MBA students was based in the downtown campus in Chicago.

Prospective executive MBA program students applied to the campus location closest to where they lived. Once in the program, students spent the majority of their time in a ninety-person cohort at their home campus. Students at the Chicago campus attended classes every other weekend for six weekends of classes each quarter. Students at the London and Singapore campuses attended class for a full week, had six weeks off, and then took another full week of classes. These two 1-week sessions made up one academic quarter of class time. Executive MBA students applied to the program on their own. Their employers often paid some or all of the cost of the program, but employer sponsorship was not a requirement.

Students from each of the three campuses gained further international exposure by studying with their counterparts from the other two campuses. For example, the Chicago-based executive MBA students spent one week in London and one week in Singapore with students from those countries. Chicago-based students also had a one-week session in Chicago with students from London and another one-week session in Chicago with students from Singapore. A similar schedule existed for London- and Singapore-based students.

The total executive MBA program consisted of fifteen required courses and two electives taken over a twenty-one-month period (table 7-1). The executive MBA courses followed essentially the same syllabi as were offered in the other Chicago MBA programs, but the coursework was condensed to fit the schedule. Further, the selection of courses was smaller because not all courses were offered in this program. The program also had a general management focus, with more breadth and less depth, although it was just as analytical as the other Chicago MBA programs. The faculty members who taught in the

TABLE 7-1

Executive MBA course listing and schedule

Course sequence for the executive MBA program on all three campuses

Quarter 1: Summer (June–September)
(Optional pre-MBA courses: Math and Accounting [in Chicago])
(Kick-Off Week [in Chicago])
Financial Accounting
Microeconomics
Essentials of Effective Management

Quarter 2: Fall (October–December)
Macroeconomics
Competitive Strategy

Quarter 3: Winter (January–March)
Statistics
Managerial Accounting

Quarter 4: Spring (March–June)
Operations Management
Investments

Quarter 5: Summer (July–September)
Decision Making and Negotiations (in London or Singapore)
Marketing (in London or Singapore)
Electives Week (in Chicago)

Quarter 6: Fall (October–December)
Corporate Finance
Strategic Leadership

Quarter 7: Winter (January–March)
Cases in Financial Analysis
Managing the Workplace

Source: School document.

program remained based in Chicago. They traveled to teach the one-week sessions in London and Singapore. This travel between campuses helped expose Chicago faculty to more international students and cultures outside the United States. In some instances, Chicago faculty became involved in international research projects because of this exposure. Because of scheduling differences, faculty members teaching in the executive MBA program generally did not teach in a full-time, evening, or weekend program during the same academic quarter.

A Discipline-Based Approach

Chicago's curriculum strongly emphasized academic theories from fields including economics, psychology, and sociology to support the more applied functions, such as marketing and finance. This approach leveraged the recognized strengths of the rest of the university: for example, its economics department was home to more Nobel laureates than any other in the world, and the field of sociology traced its origins to the university. Although Chicago courses typically included case studies, faculty members placed a heavy emphasis on lectures, textbooks, problem sets, and other materials to teach the underlying theories and concepts for each discipline. This was especially true for introductory-level courses, but also applied to many advanced courses and electives. Whereas Harvard typically used cases as points of departure for discussion and analysis, Chicago's faculty tended to use them to illustrate how frameworks could be applied to real-world situations.

The discipline-based approach played out differently in different subject areas and in individual courses. For example, one marketing course did not use a textbook popular at other leading business schools because it did not connect disciplines such as microeconomics to key marketing concepts. Teaching through microeconomic theories, the course professor believed, helped students better understand when and why to apply marketing concepts, such as pricing, in a way that other approaches to teaching marketing might not. In financial accounting, by contrast, there were relatively few opportunities to teach using basic disciplines. One financial accounting course used a leading financial accounting textbook. Students read text chapters for every class, and most class sessions included academic lecture time. For nearly all classes, students also completed problem sets from the text and prepared a short case study.

A competitive strategy course that met the group A general management requirement provided another example. This course, taught by an applied microeconomist, included economic and game theory topics. The two required course textbooks were *Economics of Strategy*, by David Besanko et al., and *Thinking Strategically*, by Avinash Dixit and Barry Nalebuff. One class session was titled "Introduction to Game Theory and Strategic Interactions"; another "Price Competition: Price Wars, Tacit Coordination and the Rules of the Game"; and a third "Wars of Attrition, Commitments and Standards." The frameworks for many of these sessions came from ideas in microeconomic theory and industrial organization.

Professor Steven Kaplan, who taught in the entrepreneurship and finance areas, confirmed the essential characteristics of the discipline-based approach: "Our students have to take microeconomics and learn microeconomics. They have to take accounting, and learn the nuts and bolts, rather than only doing cases where they probably get less in-depth knowledge. We teach the frameworks first (for example, supply and demand concepts in microeconomics) and then we have the students apply the frameworks to cases."

Faculty Life: Personal Choice in Research and Teaching

The flexibility of Chicago's MBA curriculum was as important to faculty as it was to students. Faculty members enjoyed an extraordinary amount of freedom in pursuing their professional activities. Teaching meetings were kept to a bare minimum. Even faculty members teaching the same course number and title were allowed to offer quite different versions of the course, as long as their course descriptions disclosed the essential differences.

One area in which the school expected faculty to put in time for the collective good was in recruiting new colleagues. Throughout the academic year, faculty members put huge amounts of effort into reading job market papers, attending seminars, and debating the merits of job candidates. The faculty and deans used the "best available athlete" approach to hiring. Once recruited, however, new faculty were left largely to their own devices to develop their research strategy and meet the internal market requirements for teaching, with the expectation that any course offerings would be fresh and well executed.

Research at Chicago fit well with the school's focus on the disciplines and flexibility. Research faculty—typically tenured or tenure-track professors, but also including some visiting professors—decided for themselves what research to do just as they chose what to teach in their courses. This allowed faculty to teach their passions by bringing research into the classroom and closely tying together their research and teaching interests. One marketing professor noted that he discussed his own research papers with students in several class sessions during the course. On somewhat rarer occasions, this professor brought in actual research data sets for the students to study and draw their own conclusions. Another professor explained that although not all courses included the study of research topics, many did. She stated, "Our students are capable of being exposed to academic research. Chicago is not unique in this, but I think we can do more of it because our students are a little more conditioned for it and more receptive to it."

The linkage between research and teaching exemplified the school's claim of a unified value system for faculty and students. Dean Snyder argued that the same process that generated great research generated better decision making in business—in both cases, the goal was to take the best provisional approach, evaluate it critically, and use discipline-based knowledge to make it better. The link between research and teaching also helped attract the best faculty given the disciplinary nature of the academic job market. It supported the school's culture, which emphasized discipline-based research, and created an environment favorable to such research. A previous dean, however, had hired several faculty members with more integrated, cross-disciplinary expertise, but by 2007 only one of those hires remained at the school.

Whereas some business schools tried to influence the research topics of their faculty through various funding mechanisms, Chicago did not take that approach. One faculty member described it as a decentralized institution with few "middle managers," such as research directors or associate deans sitting between the faculty and the dean, who could influence research. Accounting professor Abbie Smith commented that "being a faculty member at Chicago means having maximum flexibility to design your courses and chart your research agenda.

It is a free-wheeling place with independent thinking, very little bureaucracy, and a minimum of meetings."

Like many business schools, Chicago employed tenured professors and tenure-track professors (assistant professors and associate professors). It also had adjunct, visiting, and clinical professors. In late 2007, the school had sixty-four tenured faculty, fifty-five tenure-track faculty, thirty-five adjuncts, nineteen visiting faculty, and thirteen clinical faculty members. Clinical faculty members were granted five-year appointments on the vote of the tenured faculty. They were typically full-time faculty members who combined a practitioner background with PhD-level training.

Managing Flexibility

Students' choices in the nonelective part of the curriculum came in three basic forms: multiple course-level options, personalized course sequencing, and preferred teaching/learning style.

First, although Chicago students were not allowed to test out of courses or requirements, the program offered multiple course levels, or "entry points," from which to choose when completing both the foundations and breadth requirements. Students with little or no background in a subject area often selected the basic, broad course that introduced them to a range of elementary topics. Students with prior knowledge and experience could select a more advanced course that tended to have a narrower, specialized focus. For example, the basic course to meet the financial accounting requirement was, not surprisingly, called Financial Accounting and introduced students to financial statements and financial reporting systems. One approved substitute course was Financial Statement Analysis, and another was Taxes and Business Strategy. Each area offered courses that advanced students could substitute for a basic course to meet the area requirements. Students could also petition for faculty permission to take other substitute courses beyond the approved set. The ability to take an advanced course in place of an introductory course was regarded as valuable by a subset of students, although a large majority of students took the introductory-level courses offered by the school.

Second, students could sequence their courses in any order that suited their needs and interests. Several factors might drive their preferences. Students who were career changers, for example, with little business education background, typically loaded their first quarter with foundations courses similar to a core curriculum at other business schools. During the remainder of the first year, such students had time to determine their interests, satisfy breadth requirements, and select appropriate electives. Students looking to go into investment banking, however, might pursue a different strategy. To get an investment banking job upon graduation, it was helpful to get an investment banking internship between the first and second years of the program. To that end, students could take as many courses as possible to prepare them for investment banking during their first year and then take courses to meet their remaining degree requirements in their second year.

Third, because faculty members could structure their courses to accommodate their own preferred teaching styles, students were able to choose sections by pedagogy, with varying degrees of emphasis on elements such as the case method, intensive work in teams, or guest speakers.

Snyder summarized the argument supporting the flexible approach: "Chicago has a diverse student body, and it does not make sense to force all students to take a common set of core courses. Certain schools bring in successful people and trap them into the core. For them, it's not clear what value the core is adding. We don't have that problem. Students are able to use our flexibility to get the value they want and need. Many students indicated that they chose our school because of its flexible curriculum."

Supporting Students' Choices: The Internal Market

Through the Dean of Students' office, the school provided a support structure that included course advice and guidelines to help students decide whether they should choose basic or advanced courses. It also helped students select an appropriate mix of courses given their career interests. One faculty member explained that students often needed help beyond what these systems provided, but added, "Faculty do not do much to advise students on what classes to take. First, we don't know a great deal about what other faculty are teaching, and second we would be reluctant to push one faculty member over another. We take an SEC approach—we provide full disclosure and the students take what they want."

Students indicated that they learned a lot from each other regarding what courses and professors were considered good by their peers. They also looked at course syllabi and course evaluations to gather information. Students occasionally sought out faculty to learn more about a specific course. One professor noted, however, that a downside of the ad hoc nature of finding information to guide course selection was that small, niche courses might well be missed by students.

Students spoke positively of the flexible curriculum and the strength of the courses. The curriculum review committee surveyed members of the class of 2007 several months after they had graduated. The results showed that 92 percent of these recent graduates were very satisfied or satisfied with Chicago's curriculum. Only 3 percent were unsatisfied or very unsatisfied.

To enable students with the most intense interest in a course to gain a seat, the school employed a point-based bidding system to allocate students to courses. Students in the evening, full-time, and weekend programs could bid for and take any course in any of the three programs. Students used various bidding strategies to improve the likelihood of gaining a seat in the courses they most wanted: for example, altering the sequence in which they took courses.

Snyder explained, "There is an internal market, in which faculty members offer courses, students vote with their feet, and the faculty respond to student demand." For example, there were seven courses titled Competitive Strategy. Each of the seven had the same course number and met the group A course requirement. Seven different faculty members taught these courses, and each faculty member decided what topics to teach, what course material to use, and what combination of papers, presentations, class participation, and exams to use to grade the course. Students then opted for the version of the course that best suited their interests, and faculty with low enrollments would frequently alter their course material to draw a larger crowd. Marketing professor Sanjay Dhar provided another example: "I teach the basic course in marketing, as does my colleague. We have different backgrounds and take different approaches to teaching the same topics. I approach it more from a quantitative perspective and commonly use accounting principles, regressions and multivariate techniques in my class. My colleague brings a more psychological perspective to the course and includes attribution theory and social psychology."

Courses did follow expected norms: a competitive strategy course was indeed about competitive strategy, and faculty members teaching basic or introductory-level courses generally focused on the same, commonly accepted topics. For basic courses, most of the variance was in the selection of teaching methods and the specific articles, cases, exercises, or problem sets chosen by the faculty member. But for more advanced courses and electives, faculty faced few constraints on how or what they taught. Even for multiple sections of a course with the same course title, there was little coordination among faculty members.

Delivering the Full Curriculum

Chicago required few systems to manage its flexible curriculum. The dean's office determined the set of courses required to maintain an MBA program, particularly with regard to basic courses aimed at first-year students and high-demand electives. One or more senior faculty members served as course schedulers in each discipline area. Occasionally, the course schedulers suggested additional courses that should be offered.

Course schedulers had to find faculty members to teach each course; usually, they had little difficulty finding instructors. Occasionally, a visiting faculty member would be hired to teach a course if no tenured or tenure-track professor was available. Newer tenure-track faculty tended to teach introductory-level courses, and in their first year they generally followed an existing course syllabus passed on to them by a senior colleague. As they gained experience, some of the newer faculty moved to elective courses. A number of senior faculty, however, still chose to teach introductory-level courses.

This system worked well for the discipline-based courses that made up the majority of Chicago's offerings. Course schedulers faced a bigger challenge, however, when it came to finding faculty members to teach non-discipline-based courses in areas such as leadership, entrepreneurship, and international studies. Kaplan, who served as the course scheduler for the entrepreneurship area, explained that he first tried to find discipline-based faculty members to teach the courses where a discipline base had value. At the same time, he tried to find practitioners or clinical faculty to teach courses that did not fall neatly into a discipline-based category. He observed, "The school is built on its discipline-based faculty. The advantage of also hiring clinical faculty, however, is obvious. It allows us to teach some things we otherwise could not teach. Entrepreneurship is primarily a teaching area, and we use both practitioners and academic researchers to teach our courses." When Chicago brought in an outside teacher, a tenured faculty member provided a broad outline of the expectations of the course to be taught. Beyond that, the outside teacher had much of the same freedom to design and deliver the course as did tenured faculty.

Most of the clinical faculty members had PhDs, many of them from the University of Chicago. Some clinical faculty had been associated with the school in the past but then had nonacademic careers elsewhere before returning to the school. Chicago had relatively few ex-CEO-type instructors. One school administrator argued that many of Chicago's clinical faculty could get tenure at other schools and explained that the challenge was finding clinical faculty who could contribute while also understanding and respecting the school's values as a research-based institution.

The school had great confidence in its teaching and its faculty mix. One faculty member stated, "I don't think the students care about whether their teacher is a tenure-track or clinical faculty member. Sometimes I don't think they can tell us apart. Mostly, students look at the course content and the teaching evaluations when selecting courses, not whether the instructor is on the tenure track or not."

Chicago placed very few formal requirements on faculty members who wanted to propose and develop new courses. The key hurdle was student demand. Faculty members generally preferred to teach two or three sections of the same course to use their course development and maintenance time more efficiently. It was much easier, for example, to teach three sections of the same course in one quarter than to teach three different courses over the year. Faculty members frequently taught a course in more than one program—for example, during the day and in the evening—to get this level of demand. Typically, a course stopped being offered when a faculty member lost interest or there was low student demand. Occasionally, the dean's office would cancel a course if enrollment remained too low.

Putting Knowledge to Work

Alongside the strictly discipline-based curriculum, Chicago offered students the opportunity to develop personal leadership skills, sensitivity to international issues, and practical experience in real working teams.

The LEAD Program

Chicago launched its LEAD program in 1989 to teach leadership skills and awareness through classroom and experiential activities. LEAD was the only required element of the school's curriculum and the only cohort-based course in the full-time MBA program. LEAD's mission statement was "Through skill-based, interactive curricula and programming, we advance students' self-awareness and interpersonal effectiveness," and its goals were to "continuously improve students' abilities to motivate people, build relationships, and influence outcomes." Deputy Dean Kole stated, "The idea of LEAD is to hold a mirror up to the students to help them see how others see them, to teach them how to gather information about their own effectiveness, and to teach them how to communicate better."

For the LEAD program, Chicago assigned incoming first-year students to ten cohorts of approximately fifty-five students. Each cohort was further divided into squads of seven students. LEAD classes were taught by teams of second-year students, who acted as facilitators and mentors. These second-year students were selected in a competitive process and trained by a team of staff coaches and non-tenure-track faculty. LEAD was scheduled so that it unfolded during orientation and through the first seven weeks of the fall quarter and totaled approximately 125 hours of course time.

Students took several self-assessments, including the Myers-Briggs Type Indicator and a 360-degree evaluation, the summer before they arrived on campus. In early September, during their first two weeks on campus, all students went on a three-day Leadership Outdoor Experience designed not only to build relationships among students but also to teach team-building concepts. A number of modules and classroom sessions followed, covering topics such as leadership research, interpersonal communication, team dynamics and team conflict management, presentation skills, and ethics. LEAD concluded in mid-November.

The LEAD program provided several opportunities for students to receive individual feedback on their leadership and interpersonal skills from the second-year facilitators. In one early module, for example, students were videotaped as they worked in teams to complete an activity. Later, the students watched the videotape and discussed their group's dynamics. Students also met individually with their facilitator to discuss their performance as team members. Near the end of the LEAD program, each student again met one-on-one with his or her facilitator for feedback and coaching on individual performance during the program and to create a development plan for the future. Within a few weeks of the program's end, interested first-year students applied to be facilitators in the following year. Accepted students received training in the winter and spring quarters. The approximately forty facilitators received credit for two courses.

Chicago faculty members recognized that leadership skills were critical to the development and ultimate career success of MBA students. At the same time, many felt that theories of leadership and the practice of teaching leadership skills were not well developed fields and were difficult to deliver. One additional challenge for the school was that although it employed primarily research-based faculty, few of them were researching leadership topics. In addition, some faculty believed that the field did not have a strong research base. As one faculty member put it, "LEAD has been very useful for our students, but it is not academic."

Most students observed that LEAD was valuable for building relationships with fellow students in an otherwise flexible program and that LEAD facilitators benefited at least as much from the course as first-year students. Others had more mixed views. One student referred to LEAD as "the spinach of business school," stating, "I didn't like going through it, but looking back, I did get some insights from the course. The feedback was great." A few students noted that although LEAD taught a number of invaluable skills, they had undergone similar training in their jobs before business school.

International Options

Chicago offered several opportunities for MBA students to gain international experience or exposure to international issues. Like many other programs, it tried to create an "international" educational environment on the campus by selecting students from around the world and by considering foreign business experience or other international exposure in admissions decisions. Chicago's students came from more than fifty different countries, and 35 percent of students were not U.S. citizens. In addition, a significant fraction of U.S. students came to Chicago with work experience outside the United States. One reflection of the amount of student interest in global issues was the active participation of many U.S. and European students in the Asia student interest group. Approximately 20 percent of the class took a summer internship job outside their home country, and 20 percent took such a job upon graduation.

The school covered global issues in several courses. Some, such as International Comparative Organizations and Managing the Firm in the Global Economy, were specifically designed to address international or global topics. Other courses, not focused on international issues, often included a number of case studies or readings that covered non-U.S. issues or companies. In response to student requests, some faculty members tried to insert additional non-U.S. content in their courses. Kaplan explained that bringing international issues into the classroom was up to the individual faculty member teaching the course. He observed, "Faculty members bring international material in when they feel it is appropriate. There is nothing systematic about how it is done. Our approach is very bottom up."

Chicago offered students in the evening, full-time, and weekend programs the opportunity to study overseas in short programs (two to three weeks) and in quarter-long courses as part of the International Business Exchange Program (IBEP). Through the IBEP, Chicago partnered with thirty-three other business schools around the world. These schools were located in twenty-one different countries and taught in seven different languages. IBEP participants incurred no additional tuition costs because for each Chicago student who attended an overseas school, Chicago accepted one student from that institution. Students could only take electives through the IBEP and often reported that foreign courses were not as academically challenging as those at Chicago. Still, many concluded that the program was worthwhile because of the cultural experience and foreign business exposure they received. Nearly 10 percent of Chicago students studied abroad while earning their degree, most typically in the winter quarter of their second year.

Students most committed to learning about global business issues could enter the school's international MBA (IMBA) program. To earn this degree, students took the same nine foundations, breadth, and general management courses as other students. Then, instead of taking eleven electives in any area, the IMBA students selected five of approximately twelve Chicago courses plus courses offered in other divisions of the University of Chicago that focused on international business, banking, or policy issues. The international electives were open to all Chicago students. In addition, students in this program were required to take three courses during a study-abroad quarter at one of the IBEP partner schools. This left only three electives not related specifically to international issues. Finally, to graduate with an international MBA, students had to demonstrate proficiency in a second language.

Chicago started the international MBA program in the mid-1990s. Although roughly 20 percent of Chicago applicants expressed interest in the school's international programs (IBEP and the IMBA), the actual number that enrolled in the IMBA declined in the early 2000s. By 2007, only a dozen students were working toward the degree. Part of the reason few students chose the program was that because of the rigidity of the requirements they viewed the degree as having only limited signaling value in the marketplace. Students felt that there were too many appealing electives at the school that would be missed if they pursued the degree. Further, it was possible for any student to take international courses or study abroad without enrolling in the international MBA.

Several faculty members commented on the challenges of trying to develop internationally capable, or at least internationally aware, students. Finance professor Raghuram Rajan stated:

> There are no easy answers. Globalization is not just about learning another language, or taking a two-week trip overseas. Nor is it about attending a foreign school, or taking a few classes at one, because business schools are rarely well integrated into their societies. Globalization is about appreciating different mind-sets and different value systems. It is very important, but also very difficult, for faculty members to appreciate these differing points of view. When it comes to globalization, there is a certain amount of unreasonable expectations on the part of corporations. They want people who can succeed in any culture. Such people are very few in number; besides, you don't learn how to do this in the classroom. Perhaps we should reduce expectations around what we can produce.

Julie Morton, associate dean of career services, added, "Much of the global perspective of a student comes from their experience—in student groups, in study groups, in peer-to-peer interactions, and on student treks—in addition to what transpires in the classroom." Some faculty members believed that such approaches were difficult to do well and were outside the school's core competence of strong, discipline-based academic coursework taught by top research faculty.

Experiential Learning Labs

Chicago offered several experiential learning programs that gave students the opportunity to apply the tools they had learned in the academic courses and the skills and experience they had developed prior to coming to the school. These offerings were primarily "laboratory" courses that students could take as electives, but also included student competitions both within the school and externally.

Lab courses operated in a number of formats. In Management Labs, groups of ten to twelve students worked for a corporate client in much the same way as an outside consulting team. The client provided a problem to be solved. Students analyzed the problem, gathered data, conducted research, developed potential solutions, and made a formal presentation to the client. Problems typically involved questions of business strategy, new product development, and operational issues. Projects lasted for several months, with teams on location around the world, and were not necessarily timed to coincide with an academic quarter.

The New Venture and Small Enterprise Lab placed students in teams of three to five and gave them projects in small for-profit and not-for-profit organizations or start-ups. Topics included market research, consumer studies, and strategy development. In the Private Equity/Venture Capital Lab, students worked fifteen to twenty hours per week as interns, either alone or in small groups, at a private equity or venture capital firm, helping these companies evaluate business opportunities.

The International Entrepreneurship Lab gave students the opportunity to develop a business plan for opening a new international business venture focused on China. Students took classes at Chicago and later went on a ten-day trip to China. While in China, they spent part of their time at an existing company, learning about the culture and business environment. Most of their time, however, was spent working on their own business plan. This lab was offered in the summer quarter and was geared toward part-time students.

Each laboratory course was headed by either a tenured or a clinical faculty member and often included at least some classroom sessions. One lab course head explained that classroom sessions might include topics such as appropriate financial models, legal aspects of a business situation, or how to think about market research. The course head also coordinated the activities of various other contributors to projects. For example, most labs had several coaches who worked closely with students to help them think through business, country, or team issues specific to their project. Coaches came from both the business school and other parts of the university, and a few came from outside business organizations. Most had field experience. They might work twenty hours per week for a quarter on a lab course. The course head and coaches might also help students connect with outside experts, such as Chicago alumni willing to speak with students and provide advice.

Most lab courses required students to apply for acceptance. Students were selected in part based on their past experience to ensure there were qualified individuals serving on student teams. These courses often required one or more prerequisites. Typically, students received one course credit when taking a lab, but could earn two course credits for labs that involved significant international travel.

Chicago faculty felt that lab courses were an effective way of giving students real-world experience and a chance to quickly apply what they had learned in courses. They were, in part, a response to student demand. One faculty member explained that although students tended to come to Chicago for its academic rigor, a number of them wanted more experiential opportunities, which prompted the school to offer more of such opportunities. Others noted that getting some of the research faculty involved in the experiential courses was helpful for their own personal development.

One challenge specific to lab courses was logistics. Several faculty members argued that it was difficult to expand these types of courses to make them available to more students, because expansion meant finding and selecting additional appropriate topics as well as hiring additional qualified coaches. Finally, because of the significant work required during a lab course, the uncertain timing of that work, and the added pressure of working for an outside client, some students had difficulty meeting the demands of their other courses while taking a lab.

Looking Ahead

Chicago anchored the ends of two important and related spectrums: it offered a highly flexible curriculum to students, and faculty believed it to be the least bureaucratic of the world's top business schools. The benefits of this free-wheeling environment were not, however, without costs. Chicago relied on organic change to move its curriculum forward—course by course, section by section—as opposed to top-down and more systematic change requiring collective action. The school benefited in its recruitment of faculty and in bringing students to the forefront of academic knowledge but seldom chose to make wholesale changes in its curricula.

Snyder was aware that although Chicago scored extremely well with recruiters and in rankings by *BusinessWeek*, the *Economist*, and *U.S. News and World Report*, some continued to question whether the program provided sufficient breadth in general management or the skills needed to manage organizations effectively. From the student perspective, the school was a good fit for those who wanted a rigorous analytical program, but it rated lower with those seeking an emphasis on management and teamwork.[2] Snyder acknowledged that "one of the 'knocks' on Chicago Booth is that students get tagged as having a lack of organizational awareness."

Still, the dean recognized the complementarity of Chicago-style education and interpersonal effectiveness. Beginning in 2004–2005, his full-time admissions team revamped their evaluation processes to identify intellectually curious candidates who demonstrated effective team and communication skills. In January 2007, the school hired a new director of the LEAD program, who brought extensive industry experience coaching senior executives, to strengthen students' portfolio of leadership and management skills. Further, the curriculum committee was polling Chicago graduates about their course-taking paths through the school's flexible curriculum in an effort to identify any needed refinements.

Snyder viewed the world as coming Chicago's way, requiring leaders who combine judgment and command of complex issues. He believed that the goal of MBA education should be to ensure that students understand both markets and competition and how organizations work. "If we accomplish those goals," he stated, "our graduates can go and lead in all sectors, in all seasons." Although this more classic approach "appeals to some, scares others, and imposes some costs on students' decision making," the biggest challenge facing Chicago in Snyder's view was "narrowing the gap between how the school is positioned in terms of intellectual rigor and the everyday reality of the MBA experience for our students."

In April 2009, as the economic crisis unfolded, we obtained an update on Chicago's view of its curriculum and courses. The key responses and initiatives included the following:

- The school remained committed to rigorous, discipline-based courses with high levels of flexibility and choice for students and faculty.

- Based on the curriculum review committee's recommendations, the school added a new academic concentration in analytical management and required that all students in evening MBA and weekend MBA programs take a leadership development course.

- Faculty developed a number of new sessions in response to the crisis. Most changes arose organically and were focused at the course level. For example, Economic Analysis of Major Policy Issues, a course taught jointly by three faculty members, focused on risk and risk management, economic policy, bailouts in the financial services and automotive industries, and the U.S. stimulus program. The dean argued that the most important change needed was not new curricular materials or courses but faculty and student behaviors that encouraged deep questioning and professional communication without trading substance for deference.

INSEAD

The Credo of Globalization

WITH ONE CAMPUS right outside Paris, in Fontainebleau, another in the center of Singapore, and an alliance with the Wharton School of the University of Pennsylvania, INSEAD positioned itself as "the business school for the world," where faculty, students, and staff benefited from a highly multicultural experience.[1] Founded in 1957, just after the signing of the Treaty of Rome, the school had expanded, over the years, beyond its original pan-European focus to embrace a worldwide approach to business education. The 2000 opening of the full INSEAD campus in Singapore and the 2001 alliance with the Wharton School of the University of Pennsylvania, which included student, faculty, and research exchanges, were key steps in the school's effort to become a truly global knowledge and learning network. As the dean, Frank Brown, put it: "I want INSEAD to be seen as the world's preeminent business school for training the next generation of transcultural leaders who can step off a plane straight into effective management anywhere in the world."

In November 2003, INSEAD launched a modular executive MBA program emphasizing teamwork, leadership, and personal development. The school opened regional centers in Israel in 2006 and in Abu Dhabi in 2007 for research and executive education. In late September

2007, INSEAD opened a New York office to develop its contacts and brand in North America and also launched a dual-degree executive MBA program between its Singapore campus and Tsinghua University, a leading Chinese business school. "Globalization is a reality, and teaching about business demands attention to it," explained Professor Antonio Fatás, dean of the school's ten-month MBA program (2004 to 2008):

> INSEAD is special. We are entrepreneurial, and we do not belong to any country. This has allowed us to be very flexible and adventurous. Furthermore, in the MBA we started with a one-year intense program. This has been working better and better, and we see other schools moving in that direction. The combination of these two assets—a second campus and a short, intense MBA format—is a powerful one.

Background on the Institution and Its MBA Program

In mid-2007, INSEAD offered MBA, PhD, executive MBA, and nondegree management education programs to nearly 900 MBA students representing 71 nationalities, 64 PhD candidates representing 21 nationalities, another 59 executive MBA students, and over 8,500 executive education students in the nondegree programs, representing over 120 countries and 2,000 companies. Nondegree programs provided nearly half of INSEAD's revenues. At any given time, roughly 600 of the MBA students took classes at the European campus in France; the remainder were on the Asian campus in Singapore (a handful of students attended classes at Wharton, as explained later in this chapter). As of 2007, the school had minted about 18,000 MBAs since 1960 and counted another 19,000 alumni from 150 countries for all its other programs combined.[2]

INSEAD competed for students with Harvard, London Business School, MIT, Stanford, and Wharton.[3] The average age of INSEAD MBA participants in 2006 was twenty-nine, with ages ranging from twenty-three to thirty-five. INSEAD asked that students bring three to five years of real-world work experience. "We look at experience very carefully," Brown noted. "It matters to faculty, too. We believe that business school is valuable because our MBAs have a level of maturity that allows them to appreciate the experience they are having." Furthermore, to gain admittance, along with fluency in English, students had to have practical knowledge of a second language (implying ability to communicate on familiar matters). To graduate they needed to demonstrate basic knowledge of a third language. Students could learn new languages on their own or work with an INSEAD-approved external language provider. The most popular languages were French, Spanish, Japanese, and Mandarin.

As preparation for global management and teamwork, INSEAD assigned MBA students to highly diverse study groups, which served as their learning and preparation vehicles for the first two of five periods. The groups also did some project or team work, especially in organizational behavior–related courses; some faculty and administrators hoped to see more group work in the future. In core courses students sat together by study group in preassigned seats. In their elective courses, seating was open, and students commented that nationalities or regions tended to sit together. "There are two models of diversity," a faculty member explained. "That of the melting pot and that of the salad bowl. I am not sure which one applies here."[4]

The faculty was nearly as diverse as the students. INSEAD's standing and affiliated faculty totaled 143 from 31 countries, with 100 located in Fontainebleau. About 53 faculty members were full professors; 30, associate professors; 39, assistant professors; and 21, affiliate professors. An additional twenty countries were represented in the ranks of the school's 715 administrative and support staff across both campuses. About 80 percent of the school's core faculty held U.S. PhDs, and 20 percent were American. The school also had 84 visiting faculty. Faculty recruiting was driven by discipline; country of origin was not taken into consideration.

INSEAD faculty credited the school's success to its "One Year, Two Campuses" MBA formula, unique among leading business schools. Applicants seemed to agree. Between 40 and 50 percent of INSEAD students applied only to INSEAD and to no other programs.

The One-Year MBA

INSEAD offered students "one year to challenge your thinking, change your outlook and choose your future." The INSEAD MBA program consisted of ten intensive months, starting in September or January depending on the cohort students chose. Each class was academically identical, although the timing differed. The January cohort ended in December, and the September cohort ended in early July of the following year. The January cohort therefore had an eight-week summer break, creating time for an internship or project work. Campus exchange opportunities were the same for both cohorts.

According to faculty, INSEAD packed 85 percent of the class hours of a typical two-year MBA program into each ten-month period. Classes were taught in five 8-week periods, with very little down time during the program. Each period ended with exams and was followed by a short break. Three class sessions were held almost every day and sometimes on weekends. Many students scheduled job interviews in the early evening.

The curriculum featured thirteen required core courses and a minimum of ten and a half electives. The core courses of the second period built on those of the first. For example, the first session of period 2's Leading Organizations course opened with a video and case bridging back to period 1's Leading People and Groups course. (Table 8-1 describes the required curriculum.) During periods 1 and 2, students took classes at either the Fontainebleau or Singapore campus. During periods 3, 4, and 5 of the program, students could switch to either INSEAD campus or Wharton (for one period only), choosing from eighty electives. Electives in Singapore and Fontainebleau were similar but driven by faculty availability.

Most classes were a blend of lecture, case discussion, and exercises. Discussion typically consumed half of the class time, with the balance reserved for a lecture or further discussion. Grades were not disclosed to recruiters; the proportion of a course's grade based on class participation varied considerably. In some classes, such as Financial Accounting, class participation amounted to 25 percent of the final grade. In Managerial Accounting and Leading Organizations, however, class participation counted only 15 percent, and in Leading People and Groups, class participation was not graded.

TABLE 8-1

Core courses

Period 1 had five courses that formed the basis of INSEAD's curriculum. These courses, taught from an international perspective, provided the fundamental skills of business, including the basic concepts of microeconomics, financial reporting, statistical tools and decision heuristics, valuation and investments, managing individuals, and working in teams.

Courses

Financial Accounting

Financial Markets & Valuation

Prices and Markets

Uncertainty, Data & Judgment

Leading People and Groups

Period 2 featured six courses to provide the pillars of operating a business enterprise, building on the foundations established in period 1, and showing how integration of functions helps in managerial problem solving.

Courses

Corporate Financial Policy

Foundations of Marketing

Leading Organizations

Managerial Accounting

Process & Operations Management

Strategy

Period 3 looked at the big picture, showing the interdependence between each of the functional areas of business and how they are all affected by the turbulent, competitive, and international environmental context in which corporations operate. These courses developed cross-functional and holistic thinking in widely diverse conditions of imperfect information.

Courses

International Political Analysis

Macroeconomics in the Global Economy

Source: INSEAD, "INSEAD MBA: Core Curriculum," www.insead.edu/academics/core_courses.cfm, accessed October 11, 2007.

The Singapore Campus

INSEAD veterans explained that the Singapore campus was a clear result of classic INSEAD culture at work—a combination of research interests, entrepreneurial spirit, and potential commercial opportunity. In the mid-1970s, INSEAD had launched a program on Asian business to bring Asian companies to Fontainebleau, and in 1980 opened a

Euro-Asia Center, based on the Fontainebleau campus, to promote faculty research on Asia. It later launched an Asian Business Area academic department to deepen faculty attention to the region. In the 1990s, there was a debate about starting a second campus to get closer to Asian business practice. Professor Douglas Webber recalled:

> In this sense the opening of the Singapore campus ties in to the other big development at INSEAD: the strategic choice to expand our research activities in the 1980s. The Singapore campus was to some extent a path-dependent choice as we already had strong links to Asia. The other factor in opening the Singapore campus was the market opportunity. The Asian economy had boomed over the previous 30 years, and INSEAD saw potential for growth in both MBA students and executive education.

INSEAD delegations traveled to Malaysia and Hong Kong, and Japan was also considered. Yet Singapore, Fatás explained, was "a clear winner" as a potential site. "It is very multinational, with different religions and races. It is also small so that we did not risk being absorbed by the local culture. Furthermore, government support was enthusiastic and the location was very central." Hellmut Schutte, dean of the INSEAD Asia campus between 2002 and 2006 (a role subsequently absorbed under Brown), added, "We wanted to be part of a hub rather than be part of a large country. Obviously, China was very attractive. But we wanted to build an Asia campus, not a China campus."[5]

A number of options were debated within INSEAD. Gabriel Hawawini, dean of INSEAD at the time, explained the central challenge posed to business schools by globalization:

> It is no small challenge to encourage faculty members to marry global perspectives with their disciplinary expertise. Although there are many international students in doctoral programs, business schools face challenges in developing faculty with the right combination of global perspective, regional expertise, and the ability to conduct classes with a large number of non-local students. It is easy to make mistakes in this context. For example, one cannot assume that a new faculty member who is a native of Korea and earned a doctorate at a top U.S. university will want to become one of the school's Asian experts.

In response to these challenges, business schools could select several alternative approaches. They could, for example, choose to "bring the world to campus" and make the campus a global meeting place. Most schools successfully using the "global importer model" had been founded with an international mission. "This probably means that it is easier to create a truly international business school from scratch than turn an existing local school into a world-class international institution," Hawawini said.

Another view held that because knowledge was dispersed, it was important for business schools to be mining knowledge from various places and then integrating the knowledge into breakthrough ideas. To learn from the world, schools could use an "export model"—sending students abroad via student-exchange agreements with foreign schools, delivering programs abroad, and encouraging their faculty to visit foreign universities to teach and learn.

A third approach, the "foreign-presence model," entailed the establishment of full-fledged campuses abroad. Various multiple-campus structures could exist. The *multilocal model* consisted of opening campuses abroad to deliver a school's programs locally. The *multinational model* entailed opening campuses abroad and delivering different programs in each location, allowing students to take courses on more than one campus. The *global business school* was the most developed approach to internationalization—creating an institution with complementary and interconnected campuses in various parts of the world, ideally "the Americas, Asia, and Europe," Hawawini explained. Faculty worked at each site, and students flowed back and forth in a seamless program.

After a core group of faculty interested in building a physical presence in Asia brought the idea to the entire faculty in 1997–1998, INSEAD built on its transnational origins, its entrepreneurial culture, and the already global focus and nature of its faculty and students and elected to follow a global business school model. Fatás recalled, "The collective decision was, 'Let's open a campus there.' Some were skeptical because of the potential difficulties in finding participants and faculty, but they were convinced, and little by little a consensus emerged around the decision." Choosing to become a global business school, faculty argued, moved INSEAD away from its "Eurocentric" image. Commented Schutte, "We believe in diversity in everything we do, and don't like doing things in a mono-cultural environment."[6]

INSEAD held the opening ceremony for its MBA program in Singapore on January 6, 2000, having invested an estimated $27 million in the campus nestled in the lush greenery of Singapore's Buona Vista district, known as the country's "knowledge hub." A large new auditorium, classrooms, break-out rooms, and meeting rooms were added in 2005. By 2007, campus facilities included seven amphitheater classrooms, each with state-of-the-art telecommunications linking students and participants on each INSEAD campus in real time to lectures and discussions at the other. Residence halls and the 13,000-volume Tanoto Library filled out the campus, which boasted forty-three permanent faculty members and eighty-one administrative and research staff.[7] The school also benefited from support from the Singaporean authorities, who were eager to attract academic and research activities to the city-state.

The Student Experience

INSEAD worked hard to build momentum around the new Singapore program. At launch, there was an effort to convince MBA applicants to start their studies in Singapore. By 2007, however, such incentives were no longer necessary; most Europeans started in Asia. "With more Europeans going to Singapore and more Asians going to Fontainebleau you get cross-pollinated even if you don't move," Professor Stephen Chick noted. "When students talk about learning from each other they mean that, thanks to the second campus, they have a greater exposure to fellow participants from Asia," explained Dean of the Faculty Anil Gaba. "Just before we opened the campus in Asia, only 7 percent of our MBA participants were Asian. Today, the percentage is close to 30 percent and growing." In addition to learning from their Asian counterparts, INSEAD students believed that the campus in Singapore provided a way to explore and understand Asian markets. Geographic proximity made it easier to travel to other countries and interact with local business people in Singapore.

INSEAD ran a single, centralized admissions process. Applicants were guaranteed the opportunity to spend at least one period outside their starting campus. As long as space was available, students could also extend their campus exchange to two or three periods. All students were encouraged to transfer between campuses and spend some time in both geographies. About 70 percent of students took advantage of the cross-campus exchange each year.[8] About 20 to 25 percent of MBAs completed the entire program at one of the two campuses; 35 to 40 percent were "switchers," starting at one campus and completing the program at another. "Swingers" made up the same proportion, starting and ending at the same campus while sandwiching a period at the second campus in between. About two-thirds of the class started in Fontainebleau.

Learning Environment

Although a small number of electives, such as Comparing the World's Business Systems and Strategy for Asian Businesses, were offered only in Singapore, "the program was essentially the same across the two campuses," Brown said. "Some electives might be tailored to the region but otherwise the experience is the same." "We do not want to have an Asian version of INSEAD," Fatás added.

For all the emphasis on the similarity of the experience on either campus, students nevertheless felt that "everything on the Asia campus, including cases, simulations and events, is influenced by Asian economic, strategic, and political developments. The campus serves as a platform for the school to create knowledge sharing with institutions in Asia." Some Singapore courses included company visits. INSEAD invited many speakers to the Singapore campus and encouraged students to complete projects and internships with local companies. In several instances alumni were very involved in building those experiences and making them possible. "But we are not providing the students with the level of nuance about local East Asian culture that gets right to the nitty-gritty," a faculty member explained. "That's not the intent, because MBAs are not looking for it. Instead, we help MBAs understand different cultures sufficiently to be capable of interacting effectively. We are not aiming to make them into experts on individual countries and cultures."

Students enjoyed the intimacy that Singapore's smallness created. They mentioned that interactions and lunches with faculty were much more common in Singapore. Students also reported that it was easier to socialize with each other in Singapore, where large groups could go out together. Students traveled extensively in the region, and some reported on their blogs about their experiences.[9]

Operating in the highly diverse dual-campus environment was both exciting and challenging to students. "After you come to this program you can understand people better," a Lebanese student noted. However, this also came at a risk. "We are all misfits to a certain extent," a student observed. "Many of us are dual nationals who grew up or spent a lot of time in a third country, or even several more. So sometimes I am not sure whose opinion I am really hearing in class." In the same spirit, an Indian student who had grown up in Abu Dhabi and whose study group included an Israeli software engineer, a Lebanese banker living in London, and a Japanese woman pointed out that he ran the risk of leaving the school thinking that the Israeli, Lebanese, and Japanese in his group were somehow representative of their home countries. "It is a bit artificial," a faculty member explained. "Beyond the national differences students have some cultural similarities since most of them have been consultants or investment bankers before coming here."

Working in Asia

The second campus had radically changed post-MBA placement options. Whereas western Europe accounted for 80 percent of INSEAD's placements at the time the Singapore campus opened, only about 52 percent of the class of 2006 accepted positions in Europe after graduation. The majority of INSEAD graduates did not work in their country of origin or where they had worked before. A third of students typically went into consulting, investment banking, and industry, respectively; in recession years, industry took a slightly larger share. Recruiters received a book of résumés with no information on whether the student in question was in Fontainebleau, Singapore, or Philadelphia. Although recruitment opportunities for the two classes were comparable, investment banks recruited primarily for their summer associate program (applicable for the January cohort) as an entry point for full-time positions.

A British student argued that a stint in Singapore was invaluable for students wishing to work in Asia, especially because recruitment there was driven by relationships. "The campus allows people to go to industry meetings and gatherings," she explained, "and also to meet entrepreneurs and guest speakers who come to visit." "A year or two ago, 20 percent of MBA graduates got their first job in Asia," Gaba said. "The fact that these people took their first job in Asia reflects their interaction with people at the Asia campus. It is increasing exponentially from year to year—more recruiters and more people are coming to the campus."

However, the percentage of MBAs who took up positions in Asia was significantly smaller than those who took positions in the West, in part because of salaries: few Asian companies could afford to employ MBAs from top schools. Nevertheless, in 2007, 20 percent of INSEAD graduates found jobs in Asia, although it appeared that more Asians took jobs in Asia and more Europeans took jobs in Europe. To reach this level of placement in Asia, INSEAD had engaged in extensive market development activities and outreach. "The MBA market in Asia is small," Fatás explained, "so we basically opened it up by ourselves."

The Faculty Perspective

In the early 2000s, while keeping salaries the same across both campuses, INSEAD provided faculty with incentives to move to and stay in Singapore (not including Singapore's 15 percent income tax rate versus France's 35 percent). Families with children faced greater challenges. "From a cost and logistics point of view it is not easy," Professor Charles Galunic observed. However, Fatás said, "We did not have to buy people. Some faculty wanted to go to Asia and some were very flexible." Most faculty had already uprooted at least twice before, first to obtain their PhD and then to move to Fontainebleau. Fatás noted, "Most of us had already taken the risk of relocating and leaving our academic network by coming to Fontainebleau, so Singapore is like déjà vu."

Nevertheless, Webber explained, "There was risk involved in going to Singapore. The campus was small and geographically isolated, so links with colleagues were restricted. Singapore itself was not a vibrant academic environment." Here, too, Fatás felt that prior experience helped. "In Fontainebleau, we have always been a bit isolated, so we have overcome that by traveling and making an extra effort to remain connected. Singapore was no different in that respect."

By 2007, the Singapore campus had become very popular. Faculty, students, and staff all commented that the atmosphere in Singapore was more relaxed. A smaller organization bred tighter ties. "It is a little bit like Fontainebleau used to be," an old timer said. Faculty saw value in having the possibility of teaching in Singapore for a period. The dual-campus structure had not posed teaching challenges for INSEAD because the MBA was structured in identical two-month modules on each campus. "Once you are in the classroom there are no differences," a faculty member reported. Another added, "Singapore can seem to be more fun. It is a smaller, more cohesive group right in the middle of a city, sunny and hot. Fontainebleau is a stoic, rustic pastoral setting more conducive to deep thinking, more like a traditional campus." "Having Singapore means more clearly that we are not bound to a certain country. If you are a truly international business school, then you should not be bound to one place," Galunic explained. "From a branding point of view this means that we are from the world. Internally it solidifies our identity as multicultural."

Faculty felt that the Singapore campus had "its own momentum" and was "attractive enough on its own." "Quite a few faculty members have moved from Fontainebleau to Singapore. In fact, some faculty members are now more at home culturally in Singapore than in France." "Being half the size and in one building," a junior faculty member in Singapore commented, "allows for more cross-area and cross-tenure mixing across faculty."

"There is high demand to move to Singapore," Professor Ilian Mihov explained. "It is more innovative and relaxed, the quality of life is high, and there are fewer administrative duties. My own research productivity increased tremendously during my time there." His colleague Douglas Webber agreed: "I did research and wrote cases on topics that I probably would not have written on if I had not been in Singapore."[10] Webber continued:

> Even the core courses have flexibility in content to allow for regional differences. For example, in the International Political Analysis course I teach in Fontainebleau and Singapore there are

12 one-and-a-half-hour classes, and topics vary by campus. In Fontainebleau there will be one more class on European integration, and in Singapore there is more emphasis on Korean reunification and on the relationship between China and Taiwan. The analytical frameworks remain the same, but there is scope for tailoring.

INSEAD's departments included faculty on both campuses. The school's deans were split across the two locations (in 2007–2008, Fatás was dividing his time equally between the two campuses). Dean of Faculty Anil Gaba was based in Singapore, as was the dean of executive education, whereas others sat in Fontainebleau. Dean Brown was based in Fontainebleau, but like his peers spent extensive time in Singapore. By 2007–2008, about 70 percent of the faculty taught on both campuses in any given academic year.

The dual-campus structure had changed daily rhythms and habits. A program chair explained that he had a three-hour window each day to interact with staff in Singapore (an hour less in the winter because of daylight savings time in Europe). By 11 a.m. Paris time, the Singapore campus was winding down. The campuses were connected by state-of-the-art telecommunication and data links. Unit meetings, seminars, and faculty meetings were held in the morning in Fontainebleau so as to allow for videoconferencing. A faculty member could deliver a course to audiences on both campuses, with live interaction from both sides. INSEAD was also a leader in the creation and development of business simulations, a format that pitted students against others, often in teams, and was well suited to distance learning.[11]

Professor Gianpiero Petriglieri, a self-professed fan of face-to-face interaction, explained his adaptation: "At first I wondered how I would strike up meaningful relationships with colleagues halfway across the world. But it is incredible how quickly you learn and how openly you can interact. It becomes so natural that it is almost dangerous. You can fall into the illusion that this is daily life for everyone and that it is the way the world works."

For incoming faculty members, however, moving campuses could add to the stress of integration. They were encouraged to get their teaching established and their research fully functional. "If a cross-campus trip helps a junior faculty member get their research supported, then this is encouraged. Some faculty members have crossed campuses for periods in order to complete their teaching load, and trips are combined for research and teaching when possible," Chick explained. "Otherwise, trips for research alone could potentially be supported too. If you have a preference to live in France but you are studying a phenomenon in East Asia, then it might make sense, or the other way around—you might want to visit the other campus for potential collaboration." Two junior faculty members from Singapore came to Fontainebleau recently on different occasions, for example, to spend time with more-senior colleagues who were experts in a topic of common research interest. Several PhD students based in Fontainebleau had also traveled to Singapore for a few months to work on research projects with faculty. "However," Mihov said, "the physical distance from Fontainebleau and from the U.S. can be a problem, especially for junior faculty. For research productivity, the people around you matter. We try to overcome the problem by encouraging regular attendance of conferences in Europe and the U.S., longer research trips to top business schools, and also by increasing the number of visits to INSEAD of high-profile academics from all over the world."

As of the fall of 2008, the new class of doctoral students would be given the same choice MBAs had in terms of starting campus. "While the doctoral program used to be based in Fontainebleau, going forward there will be no home for the doctoral program either," Fatás explained. At some point all members of the cohort would rejoin to spend some time in Fontainebleau. INSEAD had about twelve doctoral students per year and was hoping to increase the number to eighteen.

The Wharton Alliance

INSEAD's alliance with Wharton was a further example of INSEAD's commitment to an MBA curriculum that reflected and engaged with the global business economy. In 2006–2007, fifty-eight INSEAD students studied at Wharton and forty-four Wharton students attended INSEAD; twenty-four of these studied at the Singapore campus.[12] Students also engaged in the MGEC Markets Games, a computer simulation that allowed teams from Wharton and INSEAD to build companies and compete against each other, with the goal of maximizing profits while at the same time fostering cooperative business relationships.[13]

The alliance was also designed to stimulate faculty research. Via the INSEAD/Wharton Center for Global Research and Education, the two schools promoted faculty and doctoral student exchanges, the establishment of joint dissertation committees, and the use of technology-supported learning. Together the schools' faculties and doctoral students worked to publish articles, books, and cases on globalization addressing entrepreneurship, marketing, strategy, management, and finance. In addition to the forty faculty and six doctoral students who collaborated on research, twenty-three faculty members from INSEAD and Wharton had taught at the partnering school, and a series of books and articles had come out of trans-Atlantic collaborations. The alliance also offered global-centered customizable executive education and open-enrollment programs at the schools' combined four campuses in the United States (including Wharton's San Francisco facility), Europe, and Asia. A general management program for high-potential managers was offered at all four campuses, using a modular design with the specific needs of multinationals in mind.[14]

Teaching and Learning in a Hyperdiverse Classroom

INSEAD's global mission and its multicultural student body brought challenges in the classroom. In electives, students brought different experiences into the room—some had been to Singapore or Wharton, whereas others had not. All classes were conducted in English, the native language of just 20 percent of INSEAD students. Within the MBA program, there was no dominant culture among students, with the largest nationality representing around 10 percent. "Even if you are the only representative of a country, your voice will not be drowned out by the larger majority," Brown explained. "I enjoy being on a campus where there is no dominant nationality," a faculty member observed. "Getting rid of that minority feeling really opens people up."

One week per month both campuses held a "national week," a popular way for students to share their culture and local business practices.

Such weeks featured a wide variety of events and displays. To show-case Morocco, for example, tents were set up housing water (smoking) pipes, or hookahs. Sauerkraut was served in the cafeteria for German week, yodelers amused lunchers during Swiss week, and a London taxi and double-decker bus graced the campus lawns for U.K. week. "We try to show what is real about our culture, dispel the myths, and show that, 'Yes we are different but we are also very similar,'" a student ex-plained. "People want to show that their cultures are more than stereo-types," a peer added.

All courses were taught from an international perspective. There were no core "global" courses per se. Fatás observed, "I don't chase faculty around and tell them to be more global." "Globalization," Brown noted, "is infused throughout the curriculum," although he preferred to de-scribe it as "developing a worldly perspective." INSEAD did have a core course on international political issues, but otherwise very few courses even featured the word *global* or *international*. In fact, one of the early MBA rankings attempted to measure globalization in busi-ness schools and ranked INSEAD at the bottom of the table. "The journalists had counted the number of appearances of the word 'inter-national,' which was so ubiquitous that it never arose in our course de-scriptions," Fatás explained.

Teaching at INSEAD required using examples and cases from a mul-titude of geographies. Some faculty reported avoiding U.S.-centered cases. "The students simply require global content and materials," Pro-fessor William Maddux explained. "INSEAD has always been quite an international place," noted Galunic, "but in the old days that meant Greek, Italian, Spanish, and German. Today different parts of the world that did not interact much—Russia, China, parts of Africa, Latin America—are getting used to doing so. The tough part from a faculty point of view comes in addressing the class and creating a productive learning atmosphere. For example, we often use humor to set the scene or bond the class, but using humor with thirty different nationalities is very hard; blank, puzzled stares are crystal clear signals, though." Cul-tural figures that might be widely known in a U.S. business school class-room, such as Malcolm X, were also confusing in INSEAD classrooms.

Cultural relativism was a challenge. "For every example you use, you have to expect a culturally based response," Maddux explained, particularly in soft courses such as leadership in which there are no correct answers. "So if you present a strategy as effective, students sometimes respond that, 'Where I am from this will not work.' I try to get them to think about what might need to be adapted to make the approach work in that particular culture." In a discussion about delivering feedback, for example, a faculty member explained, "Germans and Norwegians may have a point of view that differs from that of Chinese students, who may caution their fellow classmates that 'you cannot do that in China.' Then again, if an Italian from Naples makes a comment, someone from Milan might say 'but you cannot do that in Milan!'" In such circumstances, "we encourage people to adapt rather than adopt," Galunic explained. "In some instances I will say that things are universally desirable, say, honesty and integrity from their leaders. Others may be more culturally determined, for example, the level of directness in communications. You cannot be forcing a universal approach." Another faculty member explained, "The interesting thing is that topics like overconfidence can be discussed from various perspectives but all students tend to have the same biases. There is a common human experience."

Another challenge was fostering productive open debate. "The political diversity can lead to difficulty in mediating discussions," explained a faculty member. "Sometimes this can be extremely challenging, as political passions are ignited." Another noted, "We allow a lively atmosphere and more freedom in the way we conduct things, but we come down quite strongly if there is any overt bigotry. That is very INSEAD." To Petriglieri, classes were "extraordinarily exciting and extremely international, which means that they do not always display the norms that you might expect if you are used to a U.S. classroom." He elaborated:

> Students are not all familiar with the same forms of political correctness, which is both refreshing and delicate. It gives people opportunities to talk openly to each other, to stumble into real relationships. However, you need to be sure that the conversation is fruitful and not divisive, that it goes beyond stereotypes and first impressions. The faculty need sensitivity and experience in managing dialogue and orchestrating a learning and development process. It is great to have seventy-five individuals with incredible stories and talents in the same room, but that is

not enough. We are all trying to figure out ways to maximize a sort of "return on experience," to transform these intense, condensed experiences into meaningful learning.

Finally, faculty members had to manage varying expectations concerning classroom norms and deadlines. "It is not easy to teach in an environment where entry norms differ," Galunic explained, "but the richness from the diversity far outweighs the costs." "Student engagement overall is a growing problem among the MBA population," a faculty member noted. Furthermore, socialization in respective national educational and political systems meant that Americans and northern Europeans spoke up much more than their East Asian and southern European counterparts. A faculty member explained, "It is difficult to ensure that all national voices get almost equal air time. It also takes people longer to express themselves or for others to understand what they are saying." Cultural origins also affected faculty evaluations, with some students being highly complimentary whereas others never consider rating a faculty member more than a 4 (of 5).

For all these reasons, teaching at INSEAD was reputed to be very challenging yet was also a key to faculty success. "This is part of the schizophrenia," Galunic explained. "We love getting out there and seeing people learn and getting them engaged. If your performance is poor you will be devastated." A junior professor reported, "Students are tough and standards are high. There is also a lot of demand for senior faculty time given all the executive education, so this is not a hand-holding kind of place. The entrepreneurial spirit is still strong. In fact, my PhD advisor recommended against my coming here, fearing that teaching would take too much time." To help new faculty members, INSEAD instituted a formal mentoring program in 2006 in which faculty members in their third year were assigned one mentor for teaching and one for research. Several faculty members felt that the focus on research excellence had increased in recent years.[15]

Looking Ahead

In late fall 2007, school leaders were proud of a sharp increase in MBA applications, which they saw as proof that their approach to training global leaders was effective despite a significant increase in other schools offering one-year MBAs. Brown nevertheless felt that INSEAD had not really communicated its distinctiveness, especially in the United States, where he had spent time talking about INSEAD with CEOs. Brown, who had taken office in July 2006, was the second American dean in the school's history, and although he had lived in the United States all his life, he had worked in all parts of the globe. "We really need to communicate better," Fatás agreed. "Some folks still ask, 'Can I go to INSEAD if I don't speak French?'" He continued, "What we say is, 'If you want a global career, come to INSEAD.' We try to understand the world. That invites the question: 'Are we achieving that?' Are both campuses helping us understand Asia better? I think they are because the faculty is integrated across the campuses and now move back and forth."

According to Brown, INSEAD would consider another campus when it ran out of room on existing ones. "The operations side of running two locations with two time zones is not easy," he said, "but we do it extremely well." INSEAD leadership believed that the launch of the Asia campus in Singapore and the school's increasing presence in other countries had been important aspects of INSEAD's success. They also knew that INSEAD would need to maintain its unique entrepreneurial culture while growing in operational complexity, which included having faculty spread across different continents. Finally, it would need to grow its €65 million endowment.[16] Doing so, INSEAD faculty members explained, required staying close to practice while at the same time producing impactful research. "This is a tension," Galunic explained. "It means that we have to continue to focus on managers' needs while publishing in top journals. We see it as a challenge to be relevant but published. This is like capital markets; market pressures can make us better."

In March 2009, as the economic crisis unfolded, we obtained an update on INSEAD's view of its curriculum and courses. The key responses and initiatives included the following:

- The school reaffirmed its commitment to globalization through multicultural and multilocation experiences.

- Electives were added to improve students' understanding of risk management, corporate governance, compensation, and regulation. New courses on corporate governance and project finance were in development, and a course on regulation—Business Law and Government Regulations—was revised to include material relevant to the crisis.

- INSEAD faculty wrote several new cases that focused on critical aspects of the economic crisis, such as risk analysis and management.

- Opportunities to study the relationship between the private sector and public policy were expanded beyond established electives, such as Business and Public Policy. INSEAD was in the process of launching a dual MBA/MPA degree in partnership with leading public policy schools in Europe, North America, and East Asia.

- A course on ethics was expanded, resulting in four half-day modules, each one embedded in a different part of the program: orientation week, period 1, period 2, and period 3 courses.

- A capstone course, comprising eight sessions, was to be introduced to bring together the entire MBA program. Taught by some of the most experienced faculty at the end of the program, the course would draw on cases that wove together multiple topics (marketing, accounting, finance, strategy, leadership, etc.) and business simulations.

- With applications to the MBA program rising, INSEAD decided to grow its Singapore program by opening a third section comprising sixty-five students. The number of students starting the program in Fontainebleau remained the same. Simultaneously, new processes were to be introduced to better manage the flow of students across campuses and to ensure a balance of students in Fontainebleau and Singapore throughout the year.

9

The Center for Creative Leadership

Leadership Development at the Core

THE CENTER FOR Creative Leadership (CCL) was founded in North Carolina in 1970 on the premise that leadership was not innate but could be learned. The nonprofit educational institute specialized in developing the leadership skills of midcareer executives in the private and public sector while also catering to up-and-coming managers and C-suite executives via a portfolio of leadership development programs. Some programs were developed specifically for organizations (custom programs), whereas others were designed internally for open enrollment.

CCL helped clients worldwide cultivate creative leadership, defined as "the capacity to achieve more than imagined by thinking and acting beyond boundaries."[1] CCL founder H. Smith Richardson believed that leadership meant responding creatively to change to avoid or overcome pitfalls typically faced by leaders. As heir to the Vick Chemical Company that his father had founded, Smith Richardson had observed that new leaders often failed, and recognized the need for leadership training if a firm was to sustain its growth. With this in mind, the Richardson Family Foundation began in 1957 to fund research by behavioral scientists on leadership and creativity.[2]

By 2007, CCL had evolved into one of the world's top leadership development organizations, involved in both research and program design and delivery. Over 400,000 participants had graduated from CCL programs.[3] The organization described itself as a unique center for business education that combined behavioral science research and practical business applications, one that integrated cutting-edge knowledge about leadership with innovative training, coaching, assessment, and publishing.[4] "People come to CCL because they are facing complex challenges that demand creative solutions," said David Altman, senior vice president for research and innovation.

In all of its programs, CCL believed that being engaged in a developmental experience could enhance individuals' abilities to learn, which in turn helped participants extract more from their subsequent set of experiences.[5] CCL had a specific model for leadership development, centered on assessment, challenge, and support, or ACS. ACS was a combination model—one that sought to encourage practice and reflection on the part of participants.[6] *Assessment* tools, designed to collect information on a participant's style, personality, and approaches to problem solving, were sent to participants as well as their workplace colleagues several weeks before programs began. "The days of a person registering for a course and then coming the next week have long gone," a CCL group manager said.[7] The second aspect of ACS was *challenge*. Exercises or simulations of work environments pushed participants out of their comfort zones, prompting reexamination of their abilities, approaches, and effectiveness. Breaking with habitual ways of thinking required participants to develop new capacities and adapt their ways of understanding.[8] Finally, *support* through an empathetic climate provided security in the face of a new challenge. Participants appreciated the reassurance that breaking ingrained habits would lead to a new and more constructive equilibrium on the other side of change.[9] During programs, support came from facilitators, coaches, and peers. After programs concluded, participants were encouraged to build support networks to continue their leadership development.

The effectiveness of its approach had earned CCL the respect of scholars and executives alike, as represented by its competitive position among the rankings of executive leadership programs worldwide. The 2009 *Financial Times* worldwide survey of executive education ranked CCL sixth overall.[10] The *Financial Times* ranked CCL seventh for open-enrollment programs and fourteenth for custom programs, and *BusinessWeek* ranked CCL eighth for custom programs in its 2007 survey. Its open-enrollment programs placed among the top ten in aims achieved, course design, teaching materials, follow-up, and faculty, and its custom programs were rated among the top ten in future use and teaching materials.[11]

Background on the Institution

In 2008, CCL employed about five hundred staff across its Greensboro, North Carolina headquarters and four campuses: Colorado Springs, Colorado; San Diego, California; Brussels, Belgium; and Singapore. In addition, fourteen network associates—CCL-certified satellite organizations—delivered CCL programs in many other geographies, including Australia, Japan, and Mexico. CCL began licensing its programs and technology in the early 1980s, training associate organizations to expand its global reach.[12] In 2008, CCL reported $88 million in operating revenues.[13] Of that total, tuition, program, and coaching fees accounted for 86 percent, followed by products and publications (6 percent), licensee royalties and fees (3 percent), donations and other income (3 percent), and grants and research contracts (2 percent).[14]

In 2008, over 20,000 individuals participated in a CCL program, representing over 3,000 different organizations across the public, private, nonprofit, and education sectors. About 84 percent of participants came from the private sector, 7 percent from education, 5 percent from the public sector, and 4 percent from nonprofits.[15] About 76 percent of program participants hailed from the United States (10 percent came from Europe).[16] Approximately 27 percent of participants were top- and senior-level executives, 56 percent were middle- and upper-middle-level managers, and the remaining 17 percent were first-level managers or did not fit the aforementioned classifications.[17] The gender breakout was 65 percent men and 35 percent women. Two-thirds of CCL graduates participated in custom programs (although custom programs accounted for about 40 percent of revenues), 22 percent in open-enrollment programs, and 11 percent in programs offered by network associates. CCL also reached practitioners via its research and publications, including general-use and custom case studies.

Recognizing the need for on-the-ground leadership research outside the United States, CCL established the Brussels-based Center for Creative Leadership–Europe in 1990, employing many associates fluent in English and at least one major European language. (In 2007, the Brussels staff spoke seventeen languages.) As in CCL's North American work, CCL-Europe featured a pre-program interview with the participant's boss or manager in order to maximize that individual's support.[18]

In the mid-2000s, CCL leaders realized that CCL needed to expand its research and program delivery outside the United States and Europe. Consequently, the organization established CCL-Asia, based in Singapore, in 2003. By 2007, CCL-Asia had twenty-three full-time staff and delivered programs in Australia, China, Hong Kong, India, Japan, Korea, Malaysia, Singapore, and Thailand. To understand more about the differences between leaders in Asia and their western counterparts, CCL-Asia, with the support of the Singapore Economic Development Board, established an Asia Research unit in 2005. Two years later, eight researchers were working on several major research studies. CCL started to systematically collect data with a global focus and work on cross-cultural teams. In 2005, CCL partnered with Tata Management Training Centre (TMTC), one of India's leading management training institutes, and developed a research partnership dedicated to leadership issues in India and eventually created a series of leadership education initiatives.

Although CCL's global locations taught varying numbers of courses, the CCL philosophy of leadership development remained consistent across all locations. As more research was conducted on the similarities and differences in leadership across the globe, CCL expected that both global offerings and regional or country offerings would be developed. The U.S. open-enrollment program portfolio offered the full spectrum of CCL's products and services, whereas the European campus included a subset of the U.S. offerings. In Europe, six of the fifteen open-enrollment courses taught in the United States were available, although the large majority of business in Europe was in custom programs. In Asia, CCL's open-enrollment program was even more tailored to specific client needs, with just two of the fifteen U.S.

courses offered. The organization's core Leadership Development Program (LDP) was taught at all locations. Interestingly, gender ratios among LDP participants differed: in the United States, 70 percent of participants were male, compared with 43 percent in Europe.

Leadership development needs differed significantly across geographies. For example, organizations located in northern Europe tended to deploy very sophisticated talent management systems. To serve that market, CCL recruited more faculty and associates with industry experience to manage its programs there. Another complication was regional and national views on leadership per se. For example, leadership in some eastern European countries still held a totalitarian connotation. Creative leadership in Asia might suggest illegal activities. In March 2007, CCL launched a Chinese-language Web site that provided information about CCL products and services offered in China and Asia. CCL also provided Chinese companies with customized programs and considered the possibility of opening a campus in the country. "In Asia," a CCL coach noted, "we talk more about management education. But everywhere the needs are great, and leadership does have common traits around the world."

Teaching and Research: Ideas into Action, Action into Ideas

CCL's programs and research were designed and driven by the organization's eighty-five core faculty members, half of whom held doctorates. About a dozen were industrial or organizational psychologists, or both. "Most of our faculty members are eclectic and trained in one discipline but upon coming to CCL work on the fringe of their discipline," explained Lily Kelly, former executive vice president of global leadership development. "We encourage bridging the boundary of traditions." Some faculty were involved in teaching, others in research; some did both. About twenty-four were research-only faculty. "Over time," Altman explained, "we should be able to compete for talent with academic institutions."

CCL researchers were organized into five primary groups: Individual Leader Development; Global Leadership and Diversity; Groups, Teams, and Organizations; Design and Evaluation Center; and Knowledge and Innovation Resources. Teaching faculty had skills in individual leader development and organizational leadership development. In addition to key long-term research projects, CCL faculty conducted smaller, short-term studies for organizations and institutions.

By using research as the basis for programs as well as assessing the impact of programs to further test and refine their research, CCL staff and faculty were not only putting "ideas into action" but also "actions into ideas," by taking back to the "laboratory" observations made about practicing leaders. At CCL, research discoveries were incorporated into leadership courses and assessment tools. In turn, classroom experiences and assessment data informed or initiated research projects— CCL's portfolio was both built on research and was an essential component of that research.[19]

CCL claimed that its programs helped it "access and understand real-life practicing leaders and managers, as opposed to university students who traditionally [were] used as subjects for academic research."[20] Altman noted, "The main difference is that we are studying real people. We have over 400,000 observations in our databases." In addition to observing leaders in its "program laboratories," CCL conducted research through interviews, surveys, and observations, using both traditional and more innovative methods. "We want research that gets into books and peer-reviewed journals but also into practice," Altman noted.

Senior researcher Marian Ruderman explained what this meant for CCL's research and teaching staff: "All CCL research is done with applications in mind. We are always asking ourselves: 'What is the leadership challenge out there? What is the up and coming issue? What is good science around this topic? What do we know? Is there enough content to create a product, program, or service?'" Research could be proactive as well. "When the need for more global content in our programs became acute, the Global Leadership and Diversity Group already had content from their ongoing research program that could be integrated," explained senior researcher Jennifer Martineau.

"Basically, the center sees development of our products as something of a relay race," Ruderman explained. "We are all on the same team but have expertise in different aspects of the development process. We develop products on the basis of research, and then pass the work to a curriculum design team, which passes it to the faculty. As an R&D group we try to provide new ideas and content. As such, we apply for grants, do research, write publications, create programs that flow out of this research, and also give back to the field."

Each new CCL program was observed by an evaluator from the design team tasked with thinking about outcomes and potential impact evaluation. The design and evaluation team reviewed all iterations of each program. CCL also ran focus groups in addition to gathering participant feedback. Other feedback came from the coaches working with participants after classroom sessions and from the results of 360-degree assessments completed after participants had attended a program. "The theory in leadership development is still weak," explained senior fellow Ellen Van Velsor, "so most of the research is around evaluating the impact of leadership development initiatives and looking at how people develop leadership skills." Using post-program 360-degree results to gauge impact was an imperfect tool, however. A CCL manager explained: "Some personality types, perhaps the one who might benefit the most from greater self-awareness, don't fill out the assessment form and don't go through that process."

CCL faculty members were not completely free to study whatever they chose. CCL researchers worked with a balanced scorecard, and their research goals and tasks related to those of the group to which they belonged. Deliverables included contributions to new programs and new publications. Group leader deliverables were related to CCL objectives. Research was applied rather than basic and for the most part was conducted with future programs in mind; teaching and research were synergistic and mutually supportive. "There is a creative tension between gazing at our navel and looking at the outside world," said Altman. "We monitor the world and competitors and seek feedback from participants and their organizations." From such interactions CCL defined nine core themes (e.g., strategic leadership, corporate social responsibility, talent management, and globalization) against which CCL portfolio directors and marketing, program, and research directors assessed annual group and individual research plans. CCL had also set up an "Innovation Incubator," Altman explained, "to make it organizationally acceptable to pursue the fuzzy front end of innovation. In the past, despite our strategic planning, there was a lot of 'under the radar work' going on that didn't really fit with the plan, but was diverting our attention and we were missing opportunities."

Coaching for Individual and Team Development

In addition to its staff and faculty, CCL deployed over four hundred leadership coaches worldwide, most of them independently contracted professionals. Since the early 1970s, CCL's open-enrollment and custom leadership development programs had employed highly trained professional coaches to provide a personalized element to the experience of participants through individual meetings during programs. Coaches were all deeply versed in the use of assessment instruments and other data sources for focused personal and professional development. Through the years, CCL broadened the range of services these coaches provided beyond interpretation and application of individual assessment data to include team coaching, coaching workshops, and specialized coaching services for very senior leaders. Additionally, as CCL expanded the locations in which it worked, the coaching pool broadened to meet client needs. As of 2007, CCL leadership coaches were located in twenty-four countries and spoke twenty-eight languages.

A distinctive element of CCL coaching was its emphasis on increasing the learning capacity of the person being coached. The process relied on elicitation by coaches rather than advice giving or direct interpretation. CCL coaches established healthy, trusting relationships with clients, carefully encouraging them to extend their own assessment of the factors affecting their leadership effectiveness, clarify and take on their own challenges, and create the necessary resources for support. At the same time, CCL coaches were expected to help clients maintain an awareness of the connection between their own development and the business objectives of their organizations.

These requirements demanded that CCL invest significant resources in the recruitment, selection, training, approval, and quality management of its coaches. Chief assessor Johan Naudé was in charge of these functions at the Greensboro campus. Coaches were required to have an advanced degree in the behavioral sciences or a closely related field or else an MBA and at least five years of coaching-related experience. Coaches were expected to become part of the learning community, and Naudé created multiple opportunities for professional development (for example, in 2007, CCL coaches associated with the Brussels office were given access to 120 hours of continuing education organized by

CCL). Coaches were deployed with clients only after significant training and direct observation by senior professionals and were continuously evaluated by clients and colleagues. "Because we contract upfront on what success looks like, we can gauge our coaching effectiveness," Naudé explained.

In parts of the world where emerging economies rapidly promoted young managers in large numbers, CCL was exploring alternative delivery methods and coaching models. Lyndon Rego, a manager in the Research and Innovation Group, explained: "While most coaching tends to be for senior-level people, India presents a different challenge because of its large number of young managers. It forces us to ask, 'Can coaching be democratized? Can it be scaled? Can it be available any time you need it? Could call centers, for example, be manned by coaches available around the clock?' While a lot of what we do at the center is face-to-face, we may be able to reach more people through technology. Some of what we're looking at includes social networking [sites], Second Life, gaming, phone SMS messages, and online simulations."

Building Blocks: The ACS Model

Behavioral science research provided the foundation for CCL's programs, approaches, and tools. Although the center used many methods to accommodate different learning styles and perspectives across wide age and experience levels, interactivity and introspection were the consistent themes and building blocks of the assessment, challenge, and support model. The interactive part came through classroom work, exercises, and simulations. The introspective part involved some form of guided reflection, drawing on surveys as well as participating in activities. Altman explained, "Each individual component may not be that novel but the way that we put all this together is to produce synergistic impact so that the total impact is bigger than the sum of its parts."

Assessment

In the early 1970s, leadership development was a relatively new and poorly understood concept. According to CCL staff, the organization's belief that leaders could be made (not simply born) contributed an important insight to the then-new field of leadership development. Based on that assumption, CCL researchers proposed "assessment for development" as the key first step to professional and personal growth. This notion too went against the trend of the times, where assessment was used mostly for executive selection, promotion, and performance review. CCL researchers believed that for any assessment to be useful developmentally, it had to be confidential, enabling those assessed to save face while also improving reviewers' candor.

In 2007 CCL continued to place a strong emphasis on the correlation between self-knowledge and leadership. CCL philosophy was centered on helping leaders "learn how to learn," a practice allowing individuals to gain a comprehensive view of themselves through open and extensive feedback. This feedback provided individuals with greater self-knowledge and personal insight, information upon which personal development goals could be devised and achieved. Using the language of Kurt Lewin, the well-known social psychologist, CCL faculty referred to the process of becoming aware of one's strengths and weaknesses "as a type of 'unfreezing.'"

Assessment addressed the current state of the participant—his or her effectiveness as a leader, behavioral patterns, skill levels, and so forth. Assessment was basically information, presented formally or informally, that told participants where they stood, what were their current strengths, what development needs were important for their current situation, and what was their current level of effectiveness. The assessment data not only placed the participant within a current context, but also provided an opportunity to formulate future goals. Participants could ask themselves, "This is where I am, but where do I want to be?" enabling them to focus on desired developmental objectives.

Although CCL used a set of assessment tools, 360-degree feedback was at its core. In fact, in the 1980s, CCL had been instrumental in creating the 360-degree assessment tool that later became popular in all types of organizations. CCL described 360-degree feedback as a "method of systematically collecting opinions about a manager's performance from a wide range of coworkers. This could include peers, direct subordinates, the boss and the boss's peers, along with people outside the organization, such as customers and in some cases family members."[21] Surveys were completed by coworkers or "raters" to evaluate the participant's skill level and effectiveness as a leader in the organization. Once the surveys were processed, a coach sat down with the participant to discuss the results and establish a plan to meet the newly recognized goals set for leadership development. The 360-degree feedback model used by CCL forced "managers to examine the perspectives other people hold of them."[22] Some managers were "jarred to attention about their shortcomings by agreement among their raters."[23] "People cannot change by themselves," Ruderman explained. "The 360 sends the message to folks around you that you are trying to change."

The extensive use of 360-degree assessments gave CCL a database that it described as the "envy of organizational researchers:" the largest pool of "normal" working adults ever psychologically assessed.[24] Although the data were mostly about males located in North America, this was changing as CCL expanded globally. Nevertheless, the information helped CCL identify two key differentiators affecting how individuals developed as leaders: personality and job experience. With this knowledge, CCL focused its training on these two factors. By 2007, CCL was processing more than 39,000 participant assessments each year.

Challenge

The challenge piece of the CCL model provided elements of an experience that was new to participants and that often required skills and perspectives not currently mastered or acquired. It was designed to create an imbalance in the participant and provide an opportunity to question established ways of thinking and acting. Martineau observed, "We don't want people to complete our programs or services having only learned new content. We want them to be 'unfrozen,' made aware, and able to experiment with new approaches at such a deep level that they are fundamentally understanding something differently and doing something different as a result."

The genesis for the challenge piece came from a late-1980s CCL research project to interview executives who were succeeding and others who had "derailed." This research on "success and derailment" led to the development of the Job Challenge Profile assessment tool, which helped managers to see and use their job assignments as valuable learning opportunities while avoiding demotions or career plateaus. CCL research concluded that although most leadership development tasks took place on the job through developmental assignments, hands-on, action-based exercises and simulations could be designed to mimic these challenges and achieve similar developmental aims. They would do so by taking participants out of their day-to-day work life and placing them in situations that exposed the limitations of their management styles or perceived "winning formulas." Armed with feedback from the assessment phase, participants were invited to practice their leadership as facilitators and peers watched and engaged with them. CCL facilitators provided feedback during these exercises that challenged participants to act differently and help each other. This phase, Mary Hollingsworth, regional director of business development, explained, had multiple objectives: "We are also teaching people to be behavioral observers of each other. We do not simply tell people *this* is a good leader, we say this is what good leadership *looks like*. We get specific about the behaviors shown by our research to be critical for success as a leader."

Support

To ensure that lessons learned from the assessment and challenge pieces of the ACS model inspired and stimulated rather than depressed and demotivated participants, CCL encouraged participants to establish a network of relationships that would provide reinforcement and help them to gauge progress. The support piece provided elements of an experience that enhanced self-confidence and reassured a person about his or her strengths, skills, and established way of thinking or acting. Faced with overwhelming challenges, participants might be tempted to deny that the challenges existed at all. With support, CCL research had found, participants were more likely to take positive action.

The support piece had two major components. The first was ensuring a positive learning climate within CCL classes, which gave participants the trust to experiment and take risks. The second component was a supportive coach who laid the foundation for a support network once participants left the program. CCL encouraged participants to gather support and chart their progress against development goals by drawing on coworkers, bosses, friends, family, and mentors via communication and the use of 360-degree assessments. This approach also reminded a manager's peers, employees, and supervisors—all those completing the post-program assessments—of the manager's interest in and commitment to positive change, hopefully enrolling them in helping the manager achieve positive transformation.

The ACS model was the basis for two of CCL's most popular programs, the Leadership Development Program (LDP) and the Looking Glass Experience. More recently, CCL launched a program targeted to leadership challenges in an international context.

The Leadership Development Program

As early as 1974, CCL staff began building programs to test their theories and techniques. The first eventually became LDP. Each year, more than 2,000 leaders worldwide went through LDP in groups of twenty-four at a time. By 2006, there were 47,000 LDP alumni worldwide. The majority of participants were sent to the program by their organizations, often because they had been identified as high-potential managers or as a prelude to a potential promotion. In some instances, personal work done at CCL made participants realize that a new career or organization might be a better fit. In other instances, small changes in leadership skills had big impacts. Altman observed, "If you are flying an airplane from San Francisco to the East Coast and are off by 5 percent, you could land totally off target in Boston rather than Washington. In the same way, small changes in leadership, perhaps a tool that helps you correct course a little, can pay huge dividends." In fiscal year 2007 the average LDP participant was thirty-eight years old, and 42 percent reported being in upper-middle management. About 40 percent held a bachelors degree and 37 percent an advanced degree; about a third worked for organizations with more than ten thousand employees.

LDP focused on how a leader's actions affected leaders and those around them. By using self-awareness tools and activities to enhance leadership abilities, LDP taught strategies for continuous self-development. Through extensive assessment, group discussions, self-reflection, small-group activities, and personal coaching, individuals were expected to learn to give and receive feedback more effectively, lead change in their organization, build more productive relationships, develop others, leverage differences in other people, and set clear, attainable goals. "It is a top gun philosophy," explained a senior faculty member and manager of the LDP in Greensboro. "We tell participants: 'You are good now, but we want to make you better.'"

The Program and Process

Day 1 of the five-day program shined a spotlight on each participant's personality, behavioral strengths, and areas for development. Participants also viewed and commented on a videotaped group activity. Day 2 focused on helping participants understand the unintended consequences of their actions by focusing on the results of a 360-degree assessment and by engaging in group activities that involved stress and how to best leverage differences. One such activity had the group of twenty-four split into two and sit in a circle blindfolded. A set of plastic pieces in five different shapes and five different colors were distributed to participants. Participants described their shapes to each other and sought further information from a facilitator regarding the color of pieces. Participants were limited in the information they could provide or solicit. The team that honed in fastest on the number of shapes and colors during this twenty-minute exercise was declared the winner. The exercise encouraged participants to work on potentially unproductive team and leadership behaviors identified in day 1.

On day 3, participants practiced purposeful leadership behaviors that they selected, based on feedback from their benchmarks and 360-degree assessment data, in a set of exercises and simulations. On day 4 participants received peer feedback and one-on-one feedback from their coaches. Day 5 was reserved for planning ahead and putting lessons into practice. LDP alumni also participated in "Friday 5s" as part of a ten-week follow-up process in which they submitted two or three goals for the coming week (the goals were set jointly with their coaches) every other Friday at 5 p.m. Coaches then followed up with participants, who shared their achievements and challenges. Finally, about three months after the conclusion of LDP, colleagues who knew the participant before the course provided feedback on changes seen in the participant's behavior.

In most LDP iterations, two facilitators and twelve coaches worked with twenty-four participants. The facilitators stayed with the group for the duration of the program, either in the room with participants or observing from behind one-way mirrors. Coaches delivered assessment feedback in a half-day session and then worked with participants to maintain their momentum once they were back at work. Participants formally evaluated each one-on-one session with their coach and used CCL's assessment tools to gauge their progress against personal goals. They also took part in a ten-week, Web-based follow-up goal management system that helped them discuss progress on their goals with a CCL feedback coach or other LDP participants, or both.

The Looking Glass Experience

Another core CCL offering, the Looking Glass Experience (LGE), immersed participants in a simulated work environment. Like the LDP, this course encouraged participants to become more aware of their automatic patterns of behavior and provided opportunities for adjustment.

As they interacted with practitioners, some CCL researchers grew increasingly interested in managerial information sharing and decision making. In 1979, with start-up funding from the U.S. Office of Naval Research and under the influence of management scholar Henry Mintzberg, they created the Looking Glass, Inc. (LGI), a simulated, fictitious glass manufacturing company, and organized LGE around it. The simulation was designed to replicate a day in a manager's work life and to provide participants with feedback on their individual and relative performance in the simulation. From 1979 through 2007, more than 300,000 managers tried their hand at running the fictitious company. LGI and LGE had both been updated several times over the years, most recently in July 2006 with the addition of three new positions, more international elements, and more emphasis on leading in complex situations.

The course taught individuals how to lead and influence others in an organization. It placed emphasis on the effects of leadership style on colleagues and the workplace environment, as well as the individual's own leadership successes and failures. LGE gave participants tools to approach complex decision-making situations that paralleled real life. Through management activities designed to mirror performance behaviors at home organizations, the simulation provided participants with a more complete view of themselves associated with a heightened self-awareness. Participant outcomes also included the ability to recognize opportunities and avoid pitfalls, balance tactical concerns with strategic possibilities, and become better at making decisions. It was filled with the kind of unexpected twists and turns executives typically faced in their jobs. Staff members and peers in the class all took part in assessing each participant's skills and behaviors.

The Program and Process

The day before the five-day course, students learned about the simulation in a short session designed to familiarize them with the company, its top management positions, and each other. Ground rules were set, and a glossy LGI "annual report" was handed out. The company, whose 5,250 employees generated $1.4 billion in sales, had three operating divisions, each with different internal and external operating environments. Participants became members of the top management team, with positions ranging from president to plant manager. They selected their positions in accordance with their individual learning needs. Once the roles were selected, all participants received hard-copy e-mails and reports to review, including division history, product information, and financial data—for a total of over 172 problems and opportunities ranging from strategic investments and production capacity problems to soaring energy costs and personnel issues.[25]

At "work" the next day, participants found their own office area, complete with desks, intercom phones, in- and out-baskets, and meeting tables. The company opened for business, meetings were scheduled, phones rang, memos flew, and participants interacted while faculty observed from behind one-way mirrors. "At first participants glance at the mirror once in a while," a facilitator explained, "but soon they totally forget and immerse themselves in the business at hand."

Interactions were not scripted. Instead, participants moved freely from their desks to meetings and informal discussions and interacted with anyone within or beyond the company by memo, by phone, or in person. The simulation was behavioral and therefore deliberately low-tech. Providing participants with e-mail access would encourage them to manage by e-mail rather than through personal interaction. The pace made it easier for participants to fall into their normal management style and behavior. The six-hour simulation ended with an all-hands meeting chaired by the company president. Participants then filled out a Process and Issues Questionnaire (PIQ) documenting what they knew and had decided upon, the issues they had addressed, and the perceived influence and effectiveness of their peers in their division and the overall organization. This information was aggregated and compared with norms from the CCL database for use in the debriefing process.[26]

Three separate debriefing sessions followed, unpacking the exercise to allow participants to see the strengths, weaknesses, and impact of their behavior. The first debriefing captured participants' immediate reactions to the simulation. The second addressed division (team) effectiveness. The third debriefing was a peer feedback process by facilitators and peers that helped each participant set goals for improvement.[27] In debrief 2, participants examined the results of the PIQ. This debrief used their own data, along with the observations of the trainer/facilitator working with their group/division. Participants reviewed the information they had selected as important enough to focus on during the day, what other related information they sought out, how they communicated this information, and the decisions it led them to make. Debrief 2 also prepared participants for feedback they were likely to hear in debrief 3 by examining how their co-participants rated them in influence and effectiveness. Debrief 3 involved participants providing each other with feedback in an open, round-robin fashion.

Advancing Global Leadership

As LDP and LGE grew in popularity, CCL developed a number of other open-enrollment programs. By the 1990s, globalization and technology were transforming the practice of leadership; CCL researchers therefore launched a stream of research on the experiences of expatriates and the requirements for leading globally. Whereas CCL and other leadership development experts had until the late 1990s focused on what "leaders do"—implying that the quality of leadership hinged primarily on the traits, skills, and style of individuals—the new research focused on connections and practices. Cross-geography leadership required particular attention to relationship management and local practices. A member of the open-enrollment department realized that CCL could play a role in helping managers address these challenges, resulting, in February 2008, in the launch of the Advancing Global Leadership (AGL) course. Its goal was to make managers aware of cultural norms and the impact cultural systems had on both the workplace environment and the functioning of the organization itself. Students learned leadership tools for dealing with global challenges. The AGL ran in three locations at the same time but was managed as one program. Participants, who typically held global roles or were coming into them shortly, were teamed with a cross-continent learning partner—a participant in another geography. Students then completed assignments before, during, and after the program.

Collectively, the two-person learning teams simulated the running of a cross-border shipping organization, testing new behaviors and approaches on the basis of their self-reflection work. The program revolved around a simulated meeting of regional vice presidents and human resource representatives grappling with major events that should cause the organization to rethink "who they are and what they want to be" and learn to operate as a global organization and not simply a collection of regional units. The simulated day's work started in Singapore. Participants' work there was fed to participants in Brussels, then on to participants in the United States, and finally back to participants in Singapore at the end of the day. Interactions were via Skype and e-mail. In total, the simulation consumed half of the three AGL program days.

AGL highlighted the importance of understanding one's social identity and memberships in multiple social groups defined by categories such as gender, race, nationality, socioeconomic status, and religion, among others. "In a global world, people react to you on the basis of your social identity," Ruderman explained. "We wanted to create a sense of awareness. At CCL, we provide tools for assessment for development—know thyself. And now we say 'know yourself in terms of your social identity.'" For this reason, AGL contained an exercise designed to help participants map out their "social identity." Ruderman and her team were now working on new assessment tools to help global leaders evaluate behaviors concerning participation, autonomy, and face-saving, among many others, as well as regional expectations of effective leadership.

Expanding Impact, Increasing Competition

Since its inception, CCL had evolved in tandem with the growing field of leadership development. When CCL started in 1970, a CCL manager explained, there was only one card in the New York public library system under the heading "Leadership." By 2007 there were over two thousand. Googling "leadership development" yielded nearly 1.7 million hits. "We were pioneers," explained a CCL manager. "Now competitor offerings are pretty much the same as ours. But our instruments are grounded in how managers talk, and they are based on what participants tell us." CCL was no longer the predominant provider of leadership training, a market it estimated at $4 billion per year. For a typical custom initiative at CCL, which usually covered three days with twenty-four participants per program, an average fee would be $90,000. A three-day initiative for two hundred participants would require nine programs and total about $825,000. On the assessment side, twenty-four participants for the usual one-and-a-half-day feedback workshop ran about $28,000. Covering two hundred participants would require nine workshops at a price of about $250,000.

"We are in an all-out war," explained a staff member. "Today we need more innovative design capabilities. We believe we're the best in the world at individual leadership development, but we've only been growing at 6 percent a year," noted John Ryan, CCL president since the summer of 2007. "That's largely because we have not yet moved fully into the custom and organizational leadership development arenas."

Greater demand for leadership development attracted competition from a wide range of players. CCL counted as its competition specialized training providers such as DDI, an organization focused on assessments, as well as consulting companies moving into organizational development work, and business school offerings. "Because of the growth and interest in leadership and low barriers to entry, anyone can set up shop in this arena. It is hard for clients to tell who is legitimate and good," explained Kelly.

Several major business schools had recently supplemented their core programs with experiential leadership development training and, in some instances, such as at Stanford and MIT's Sloan School, hired specialized resources. Sloan, for example, had replaced its traditional thirteen-week semester with a new rhythm of six-one-six, featuring six weeks of coursework on either side of an intense week of experiential leadership training.[28] "Business school offerings are different because they are less hands-on and high touch than our programs are, but the average participant might not get that difference," Altman said. "To do what we do in an MBA program you need to have people with facilitation skills. That requires a very different skill set for faculty members," a CCL manager added. "Our approach might not be particularly scalable or transferable."

Looking Ahead

Beyond the scalability of the approach, Ryan raised the issue of fundamental interest in business schools. "Why are people going to top business schools? How many students really want to be leaders? In contrast, when I visit the Naval Academy, my alma mater, and ask 'Who wants to be a leader?' all hands shoot up." Altman nevertheless saw various topics of relevance regarding leadership and business schools:

> The first is the leadership implication of being a manager in a "flat world." Second, MBAs need to learn how to work across boundaries in ways that optimize interdependence and connectivity. Third, they need to learn how to deal with complexity. MBA students can hone in on issues very quickly, but are not always able to understand how to solve complex challenges with appropriate solutions. Fourth, given what we know about why executives derail, by not adapting to change and not managing interpersonal relationships, it might be possible to begin the process of inoculating MBAs against these problems in business school. And finally, anyone can benefit from greater self

awareness. We make the case that "soft skills" are the hard or more difficult skills; they become differentiators in the success of leaders.

More globally, Ryan was confident about the need for continued attention to leadership development. "Every day there is something in the paper about our need for more leadership. Even being generous, the world deserves a C-minus in leadership." Ryan argued that CCL needed to help improve this situation. The organization's tools had been translated into a number of different languages, with more translations planned. CCL was committed to furthering leadership development in emerging markets and creating affordable programs for countries such as Russia and Ukraine. Altman explained, "What top management schools do in terms of executive education and leadership development reaches the top, but we've collectively failed to address issues faced by people at the middle and bottom of the socioeconomic pyramid. We are now working with many NGOs, so we're not just in the classroom or working with a small segment of privileged leaders." He continued:

> We do a lot of good for 20,000 participants each year. But there are seven billion people on earth, and we now ask ourselves how to engage in leadership development for the rest of the world. It's not by working with 25 participants at a time and charging $8,000 for five days. How can you improve the human condition through the lever of leadership development in a way that is high quality, delivered in a way that is culturally relevant and scalable? How do you democratize leadership development? The field ought to be embarrassed that we have not taken research and application to more people throughout the world.

In March 2009, as the economic crisis unfolded, we obtained an update on the Center for Creative Leadership's view of its programs. The key responses and initiatives included the following:

- The client base was broadened to include companies in the legal, government, and healthcare sectors. CCL now reached underserved populations through its Leadership Beyond Boundaries initiative, which provided leadership training for public health officials in the Caribbean; nongovernment and community leaders in Ethiopia, Kenya, Uganda, and Ghana; and young adults in Sri Lanka and the United States.

- CCL expanded its geographical reach by opening an office in Russia in January 2009 and had begun planning for a new office in India.

- CCL's new approach to delivery was exemplified by the launch of a product line called In-House Solutions that helped companies deliver CCL-branded training themselves.

- CCL introduced cost-cutting initiatives to leverage offerings so that lessons could be provided at lower costs. For example, through the Leadership Beyond Boundaries initiative, a Train-the-Trainer program for nongovernment leaders throughout the world was offered at deeply discounted prices through grant support.

- After piloting the Advancing Global Leadership program, CCL decided to remove it from its portfolio for the time being, and instead redeploy the program's content and assessments for use in other offerings.

10

Harvard Business School

General Management and the Focus
on Practice

2008 MARKED THE 100th anniversary of the Boston-based Harvard Business School (HBS). Planning for the centennial had provided an opportunity to reflect on the past and, more important, look ahead to the future. Noted Dean Jay Light:

> The strategy for our MBA program has, by some accounts, looked remarkably consistent: offer a two-year program with a focus on general management taught primarily via the active engagement of our students in classroom discussions of complex, ambiguous, business cases. Yet fundamental elements of the program have been changing dramatically: our students are more diverse, our faculty members are coming from a wider range of disciplinary backgrounds, and our classrooms are using technology in ways unimagined even a few decades ago. Moreover, the curriculum has evolved substantially, with new cases and new courses being introduced each year in a deliberate strategy of continuous improvement. Indeed, even the pedagogical materials we call "cases" have changed—many are multimedia, and all are richer and more complex teaching vehicles than they were just a few years ago. We are mindful that the world, and our peer

schools, are changing in significant ways. Undoubtedly there are "disruptive technologies" on the horizon. How should we adapt to embrace new forces in business education while retaining the elements we think make HBS distinctive and successful?

Thus, throughout the centennial year, the HBS community and leadership reflected on how the school might continue to fulfill its mission of "educating leaders who make a difference in the world." HBS offered "education and training for management practice," or as noted case method teacher C. Roland Christensen had put it, "mating knowledge and practice."[1] The case method was a central and distinguishing feature of the school's pedagogical approach, and was employed throughout the MBA program's two years. Indeed, HBS faculty generated 80 percent of the world's total case output and were known for their field-based research. Professor Joe Badaracco explained the centrality of the case method to the HBS formula: "It is not just a few instructors who teach via the case method, it is almost everyone. With the case method at the center of the curriculum you have to remain relevant and close to practice. Students expect us to be able to understand and discuss current managerial problems. If we moved away from the case method, we would be like everyone else."

Two other distinguishing features of the HBS MBA program were its required year-long core curriculum and the breadth of its elective curriculum. All students spent their first academic year in sections of roughly ninety students, building a broad foundation of general management concepts and skills across key disciplines. (Term 1 courses focused on the internal functional operations of business enterprise, and term 2 courses covered the relationship of the organization to larger economic, governmental, and social environments.) During their second year, students chose from a wide array of elective courses and field studies, enabling them to integrate the skills learned in the first year and go deeper into areas of particular interest. Although HBS had not pursued partnerships with other business schools within the United States or abroad, many students cross-registered for courses elsewhere within Harvard or at MIT and Tufts. In recent years, increasing numbers of students enrolled in new joint-degree programs with the university's schools of government, law, and medicine.

Background on the Institution and Its MBA Program

Harvard Business School opened its doors in October 1908 with fifteen faculty members (including its dean), a new degree (the Master in Business Administration), thirty regular students, forty-seven "special" students (those taking one course or more), and borrowed quarters. Its required curriculum comprised courses in economic resources, commercial law, and principles of accounting, and the school was given five years by the president and fellows of Harvard College to establish and prove itself.

From the outset, HBS had a twofold mission: to define a curriculum that would educate and produce business leaders, and to make clear and significant contributions to business theory and practice. The Bureau of Business Research was founded in 1911 to facilitate curriculum development. Initially, the bureau gathered pricing data on a variety of retail products and reported its findings in a monthly public bulletin.[2] Later, it focused on developing a large number of field-based cases. The case method—brought to HBS by its second dean and Harvard Law School graduate Wallace P. Donham—was introduced in 1920; by the mid-1930s it had become the primary method of instruction.[3] The method was originally referred to as the "laboratory method" or "problem method." Early on, class materials were anything that faculty members considered to be a good basis for a dynamic discussion: legal documents, a report, or a particular business problem. The method spread rapidly, both within HBS and among other business schools, and by 1922 casebooks had been adopted by eighty-five institutions.[4]

In 1924, a gift from George F. Baker, president of the New York National Bank, provided the capital to build a much-needed campus in Boston, across the Charles River from Harvard's Cambridge campus. The first doctoral degree, in commercial science, was awarded the following year, and executive education—initially called retraining—was launched during 1943 to support the war effort and later the commercial reintegration of veterans.

Over the next six decades the physical campus expanded, and a series of innovations helped broaden and shape HBS offerings. The school opened enrollment in the MBA program to women in 1963. Ten years later, the school held its first executive education program outside the United States, when it initiated its Senior Managers' program in Switzerland. The program was brought back to the HBS campus in 1984 and was eventually folded into the Advanced Management Program (AMP) as part of the school's growing executive education offerings. To bolster the case publication and distribution functions that had existed for many years and to extend HBS's reach beyond campus-based programs, the school established Harvard Business School Publishing (HBSP) in 1993 as a wholly owned subsidiary. In 2007, HBSP sold nearly eight million case studies and two million books, and had a circulation of 248,000 for the *Harvard Business Review*.

MBA Students and the Core Section Experience

From its inception, Harvard Business School considered admission to be an invitation to intellectual and cultural engagement. Students were expected to undergo a transformational experience that would challenge their current perspectives and assumptions, foster innovation in thinking and leadership, establish new skills and talents, develop judgment, and instill a greater sense of responsibility for their place in the world. "I came here because I wanted to figure out what I wanted to do with the rest of my life," one student explained. "Now I find that I can step outside myself, reflect on how I think and work, and articulate what is important to me. At the end of two years, being able to answer some of these questions is very valuable."

Of the 901 students in the HBS MBA class of 2009, 36 percent were women, 24 percent U.S. ethnic minorities, and 33 percent international. Applications were up 10.5 percent over the prior year, reaching 7,424. Typically, nearly 90 percent of students accepted by HBS chose to attend the program. By graduation, about 97 percent of the MBA class of 2007 had received a job offer, and 94 percent had accepted one. According to 2006 placement data, 42 percent went into financial services and 21 percent into consulting. About 10 percent of students were sponsored by firms that paid most of the expenses associated with undertaking the MBA; these firms expected graduates to return to work after commencement. Of the 2003 graduating class, approximately 3 percent launched their own enterprises before or immediately after graduation. Recent alumni surveys revealed that about one-third of graduates who had been out of HBS for at least fifteen years started their own business.[5]

A central element of the MBA student's first year was the section experience. Sections were the core unit of interaction and learning in the first year, and comprised about ninety students carefully selected for their varying cultural and business backgrounds, interests, and goals. The section experience was designed to be intimate and encouraged students to bond as they supported one another's learning and growth and developed communication, decision making, and interpersonal skills. In addition to being the venue for all first-year classes, sections elected officers, governed themselves, and socialized together. Section mates frequently became lifelong friends and contacts. Alumni typically identified themselves, first and foremost, by their section—even decades after graduation. As one student observed, recalling the section experience, "We can't succeed alone."[6]

The Required Curriculum

The required curriculum (RC) covered the main functional disciplines, such as accounting, marketing, operations, and strategy; two semesters of finance; leadership and organizational behavior; a course on business, government, and the international economy; and courses titled Leadership and Corporate Accountability and The Entrepreneurial Manager. (Table 10-1 describes each of the core courses.)

The general management perspective infused the first year. As a result, most RC class discussions were not just about frameworks, theories, or tools but about the broader organizational context for their use and their implications for the general manager. Functional knowledge was placed in context even in finance courses. Although tools and techniques were provided, classes revolved around using these tools to make decisions. Even more specialized functional courses, such as Technology and Operations Management, held greater general management content than they might at other schools, faculty members believed.

Thus, the RC strategy course often challenged students to consider the impact of their strategy recommendations on distribution, finance,

TABLE 10-1

Harvard Business School's required curriculum for the MBA

Term 1 Course Titles	Term 1 Course Descriptions
Finance I	This course examines the role of finance in supporting the functional areas of a firm, and fosters an understanding of how financial decisions themselves can create value.
Financial Reporting and Control	Recognizing that accounting is the primary channel for communicating information about the economics of a business, this course provides a broad view of how accounting contributes to an organization.
Leadership and Organizational Behavior	This course focuses on how managers become effective leaders by addressing the human side of enterprise.
Marketing	The objectives of this course are to demonstrate the role of marketing in the company; to explore the relationship of marketing to other functions; and to show how effective marketing builds on a thorough understanding of buyer behavior to create value for customers.
Technology and Operations Management	This course enables students to develop the skills and concepts needed to ensure the ongoing contribution of a firm's operations to its competitive position. It helps them to understand the complex processes underlying the development and manufacture of products as well as the creation and delivery of services.

Term 2 Course Titles	Term 2 Course Descriptions
Business, Government, and the International Economy (BGIE)	This course introduces tools for studying the economic environment of business to help managers understand the implications for their companies.
Finance II	This course builds on the foundation developed in Finance I, focusing on three sets of managerial decisions: how to evaluate complex investments; how to set and execute financial policies within a firm; how to integrate the many financial decisions faced by firms.
Leadership and Corporate Accountability	In this course, students learn about the complex responsibilities facing business leaders today. Through cases about difficult managerial decisions, the course examines the legal, ethical, and economic responsibilities of corporate leaders. It also teaches students about management and governance systems leaders can use to promote responsible conduct by companies and their employees and shows how personal values can play a critical role in effective leadership.
Negotiation	This course focuses on developing negotiation skills and analysis. At its core are carefully structured negotiation exercises.
Strategy	The objective of this course is to help students develop the skills for formulating strategy.

| The Entrepreneurial Manager | This course addresses the issues faced by managers who wish to turn opportunity into viable organizations that create value, and empowers students to develop their own approaches, guidelines, and skills for being entrepreneurial managers. |

Source: HBS documents.

and human resources, for example. The same held for marketing. "We ask 'What is the problem facing the company?' and marketing is where the customer enters the equation. We look at the whole enterprise, and offer a framework for marketing that's about creating, capturing, and sustaining value for the firm," Professor John Gourville explained. "So we're offering a broad management perspective. You can think of it in terms of the 'little m' and 'big m' approach to marketing. The 'little m' approach deals with the tactical aspects of marketing—pricing, promotion, product development. The 'big m' looks at the bigger picture—how marketing feeds into managerial decisions. We take the 'big m' approach."

HBS faculty credited two relatively recent RC course additions for significantly shaping the first year and helping integrate the various tools and approaches into an even more holistic view: The Entrepreneurial Manager (TEM) and Leadership and Corporate Accountability (LCA).

The Entrepreneurial Manager. In 2000, HBS replaced its General Management course with TEM in the first-year curriculum.[7] By providing students with the skills needed to successfully establish and grow an entrepreneurial organization while creating value for stakeholders, the course aimed to prepare students for entrepreneurial roles in organizations both large and small, and both new and established. The course paid close attention to the challenges and issues that start-up managers faced, including identifying potentially valuable opportunities, obtaining capital to fund these opportunities, managing the organization once it was founded, and achieving sustainable growth for the business.[8] Professor Richard Hamermesh, who taught the course, summarized: "We can't guarantee that every HBS graduate is going to be a great entrepreneur, but we can teach a body of knowledge that focuses on the practical problems they'll face."[9]

Fundamentally, however, TEM was about getting students to think holistically about multiple functional domains within a business. As such, it drew on many first-semester RC courses and was scheduled in the second semester. Students drew on their fresh knowledge of accounting, finance, strategy, and operations, and all TEM cases provided a multifunctional perspective. In addition to teaching general management, TEM faculty felt that the course addressed leadership at different types of organizations—nonprofits, small companies, and large corporations. "We do a good job of teaching leadership without consciously attempting to teach it," said one professor.

Leadership and Corporate Accountability. Ethics and social responsibility had been a part of the HBS curriculum from the time of its founding. In 2003, however, following a multiyear process to approve and design a full-semester offering and in the wake of a series of very public governance failures, the Leadership and Corporate Accountability (LCA) course was launched. The course used three disciplinary lenses through which to view accountability: economics, law, and ethics. In thirty sessions spread over fifteen weeks, the course examined challenges ranging from customer privacy to environmental trade-offs to the unfettered pursuit of shareholder value. Students explored personal dilemmas and decisions, specifically, the challenges that can occur when personal values collide with those of the company or superiors.[10] The course was consciously designed to be managerial and realistic, opening with cases involving hostile takeovers and high-stakes financial matters, so that students could easily see its relevance to their post-HBS careers.

Part 1 of the course focused on managerial choices or challenges that concerned the corporation's responsibilities to investors, customers, suppliers and employees, and the public. Part 2 centered on governing the corporation and had students consider the roles and impact of external forces (e.g., laws and regulations, NGOs, and the media), boards of directors, and internal forces (e.g., organizational design, compensation systems, and corporate culture) in shaping management and employee behavior. The course concluded with a module on personal development.

As a key LCA architect, Professor Lynn Sharp Paine, explained, "Business leaders have multiple responsibilities, and to deliver on them you need a grasp of the basic tools of general management. The emphasis in this course, however, is not so much on mastering the tools themselves or on general management functions. It is about delivering on essential responsibilities." "We are training future practitioners," Paine continued. "We focus not on rare events or abstract issues in moral philosophy, but on decisions that students will have to make in their careers. The course gives them an analytical framework for thinking about issues, not a prescribed set of solutions."

LCA was designed by a team of faculty members representing nearly every unit of the school. In its initial years, LCA teaching faculty tended to be relatively senior. Although sustainability is generally a challenge for any cross-disciplinary course, LCA had little trouble recruiting new faculty. The topics were those faculty liked to debate anyway, an LCA faculty member explained. In 2008, three lecturers with extensive professional experience joined the teaching group.

The Elective Curriculum

The elective curriculum, or EC, comprised nearly one hundred courses (including half-courses) in about a dozen different areas. A small subset of these were large-enrollment, multisection offerings, but many more were specialized courses that emerged from faculty research. By combining EC courses with independent field studies, research projects and papers, and participation in the annual business plan contest, EC students tailored their program of study to their individual interests and career goals. In effect, whereas the RC provided students broad exposure to a range of topics and tools, the EC allowed them to drill down deep into one or more specialized areas of interest.

Innovation in the EC was rapid and continuous, particularly as half-courses were developed that allowed faculty to launch new offerings without the lead time required to develop materials for a full course. In 1998, for example, 47 percent of all elective courses had been introduced in the prior three years, and in the five-year period between 2002 and 2006, fifty-six new courses were created and launched. As was true at many leading business schools, some courses were perennially oversubscribed, either because of the subject covered (e.g., corporate strategy), the reputation of the faculty member, or both.

Immersion Programs

In the winter break between the first and second semesters, students (primarily those in their second year) could participate in faculty-led immersion programs—one- to two-week programs that combined educational, career, cultural, and social activities for groups of forty to sixty students. Immersion programs in 2007 focused on health care (Boston), social enterprise (post–Hurricane Katrina New Orleans), China/Vietnam, India, Europe, and the Middle East. More than a third of the class, over three hundred students, participated in immersion programs in the 2007–2008 academic year.

The China/Vietnam immersion program, for example, included readings, discussion groups, and other preparation before students departed, a series of visits with business and government leaders, company tours, and sightseeing. Many of the students who participated in the program then signed up for a spring elective course entitled Doing Business in China in the 21st Century. Eventually it was hoped that students might choose from an even larger portfolio of such programs, some in the Boston area and others that might be industry as well as geographically focused.

Recent Changes

Other innovations in the MBA curriculum over the past decade included the launch and growth of online pre-matriculation modules in topics such as accounting, quantitative methods, and information technology to reduce disparities in knowledge before classes began. Moreover, in addition to the introduction of TEM and LCA in the first year, the Finance course had been expanded and redesigned, and a new module on information technology management was developed for the Technology and Operations Management course.

In 2005, the school introduced learning teams. Because the case method required significant student preparation, HBS had long encouraged students to work both individually and in groups. Historically, students formed their own study groups to help with class and discussion preparation. Many of these groups, however, were relatively homogeneous and consisted of students of similar cultural or business backgrounds. In 2005, HBS moved to formalize these groups but to do so with a more diverse combination of students. The result was pre-assigned learning teams, groups of five or six students of mixed backgrounds who worked together over the course of the first year on both team-based, graded projects and individual class preparation.

In 2007, HBS launched the 2+2 program to reach potential MBA candidates who either might not be considering an MBA as an option or might otherwise decide against pursuing an MBA once engaged in a career. The program deferred MBA admissions for two years, giving undergraduates a guaranteed place in a future HBS MBA class, provided they graduated from college and then successfully completed two years of work experience at approved organizations. Undergraduates applied to the HBS 2+2 program during the summer after their junior year and were notified of acceptance during the fall of their senior year. Students would spend two years working, while attending a short academic program on campus each summer. HBS expected the 2+2 program to account for just a small portion of the MBA class enrollment each year.

On the outbound side, the school had initiated a supplemental fellowship program to provide debt reductions to graduating students taking jobs in regions or industries with salaries well below the MBA average. Combined with the Leadership Fellows program (a one-year fellowship enabling recent MBA graduates to work on high-impact projects with the senior management of social enterprise and public sector organizations) and significant increases in financial aid, the aim was to enable students to pursue careers based on interest rather than financial necessity.

Looking ahead, Harvard University recently had adopted a "common calendar," scheduled to take effect in the 2009–2010 academic year. By requiring all schools within the university to start and end their semesters at roughly the same time, the purpose of the calendar reform was to enhance opportunities for cross-registration by students and for teaching in other schools by faculty. A key element of the new calendar was the January term. Faculty at HBS had begun planning how existing immersion programs might be expanded during the new term, and considering what other courses might be delivered. "January offers a real possibility to experiment with ideas we have been examining for many years," noted Deputy Dean Carl Kester. "We might think about smaller class sizes, intensive simulation exercises, short specialized classes, or other types of courses that would further complement both the required and elective curricula."

The Case Method

HBS was known for its commitment to discussion-based learning using cases drawn from real-life business situations and decisions. Virtually all courses, including those in technical fields such as accounting, were taught by the case method. Because HBS faculty members wrote most of the cases they taught, instructors often knew the material intimately. HBS faculty members developed about 250 new field cases each year, as well as numerous supplements, technical notes, simulations, teaching notes, and multimedia products. Roughly one-third of the cases MBA students analyzed during their two years were new. Field cases required about six full weeks of research and writing, although the elapsed time from start to finish was often significantly longer. Faculty wrote cases alone, with colleagues, or with the support of research assistants. Typically, they spent two to three days in interviews at the host organization, collecting qualitative and quantitative information; they complemented the field research with information from published sources. Drafts were reviewed and released (authorized for publication) by the organization's officers before being taught. Without a formal release, HBS could not use the case studies in which it had invested.

The typical HBS case study placed students in the shoes of high-level managers and CEOs and called for the holistic consideration of business problems. This perspective helped HBS MBA graduates earn a reputation, according to a number of recruiters, for being especially "well-rounded " and skilled at problem solving. "HBS graduates can quickly identify problems, a thesis, and holes in an argument. They can think on their feet better than others," one recruiter explained. "I think that's because of the case study method." The MBA program staff and HBS faculty argued that repeatedly forming and articulating one's own opinions promoted self-knowledge, self-confidence, clarity of thought, and communication skills. Recruiters often commented that the case method did a "great job of simulating the job environment." Professor Tom Piper noted that a steady diet of cases, which placed students repeatedly in the shoes of decision makers, promoted in graduates "the courage to act."

Cases and case discussions served three distinct roles. First, they helped students develop diagnostic skills in a world where markets and technologies were constantly changing. Second, they helped students develop persuasive skills, an important aspect of management as a social art that required working with and through others. Third, they shaped the way students thought and acted. Faculty members believed that case discussions helped students develop not just their communications but also their leadership skills: the case method was partly about learning how to influence peers through well-crafted arguments and communicating complex concepts clearly, and partly about learning to listen and absorb others' ideas. "Even though I have a bachelor's in finance and worked in financial services," a student explained, "I like helping to train people, which I will have to do at work. In the future, I will have to work with non-experts too." Another student observed, "The case method forces you to use both logical and associative thinking. As you're exposed to alternative arguments, your thinking evolves. Your point of view can change dramatically over eighty minutes."[11]

The primary objective of a case method teacher was to encourage student-to-student dialogue. To that end, HBS classrooms were all tiered amphitheaters holding 62 to 102 students; they were designed to minimize the physical distance between the instructor and students, encourage student-to-student interaction, and promote physical closeness and trust. To maximize student input, individual faculty often called on students with work or personal experience with the organization, industry, region, or issue under discussion. They also worked hard to frame issues in ways that would stimulate students to engage directly with one another.

The case method conferred several important benefits for the faculty and institution: It was intellectually stimulating for faculty members, providing them with ongoing "opportunities for continuous education." Field cases—conducted with the participation of a host company or organization—connected faculty directly with practice. Further, the method placed value on innovation and review—frameworks being taught via cases were continuously refined and challenged as the situation in the case was reviewed in the context of current events and management thinking. "To help advance your research," Professor Joshua Margolis explained, "you need to consider questions that arise in the classroom for which you do not have good responses. That is prime material to explore theoretically and in the field." At the same time, teaching by the case method was challenging for instructors. It required both a mastery of case details and the ability to effectively lead a discussion whose direction was always partly unpredictable because it was driven by students' expertise, preparation, and passions.

The Faculty

To meet its distinctive teaching and research goals, HBS needed an equally distinctive faculty.

Bridging Theory and Practice

Organized into ten units, the HBS faculty grew from 167 in 1996 to 206 in August 2007. In an average year, a dozen individuals were recruited to join the faculty at the tenure-track or tenured level; others also were brought in to fulfill specific teaching needs or as visitors. The total included eighty-three tenured faculty, thirty-three associate professors, and fifty-four assistant professors.

Since 2000, two other categories of faculty had become increasingly important in fulfilling the work and activities of the school: Professors of Management Practice, who joined HBS following successful careers in business and brought significant management experience into the classroom, and Baker Foundation Professors, recently retired faculty who remained at the school with significant teaching and mentoring assignments. Rounding out the faculty were lecturers, senior lecturers, postdoctoral fellows, and various research fellows with shorter appointments.

A further major change was in the mix of faculty educational credentials and countries of origin. In 1980, 30 percent of the faculty held a Harvard MBA, and 36 percent held an HBS/Harvard University doctorate. By 1999, these figures had fallen to 20 percent and 30 percent, respectively, and continued to fall thereafter. Increasing numbers of incoming faculty arrived from discipline-based PhD programs. They also came from around the world: over 20 percent of HBS faculty hailed from outside the United States, and more than half conducted research overseas. At any given time, HBS researchers were active in more than forty countries.

A conventional distinction was often drawn between business school faculty who were discipline based—schooled in and attached to classic academic research—and faculty who had a more managerial focus in their research and pedagogy. At HBS, faculty from both groups were expected to take a problem-focused approach. This could create a stiff challenge and a difficult balancing act, especially for junior faculty striving to publish their work in academic journals. Most journals prized research that spoke to theory and demonstrated methodological sophistication; they often placed less value on the applicability of that research. In contrast, managers cared about theory only to the extent that it contributed to their understanding and ability to resolve day-to-day practical problems.

In the HBS classroom, faculty members sought to hit the sweet spot accommodating both these views, building course materials around research that was both academically rigorous and relevant to practice. This required a distinctive temperament and approach to scholarship. "If you are succeeding in the disciplines but you have no interest in affecting or understanding what goes on in the real world," Professor Jan Rivkin noted, "then HBS is probably not the ideal place for you." And once at HBS, he explained, "If you pursue a research agenda that gives you world-class standing in your discipline while carrying out an unrelated program of course development, your odds of success are very low. You simply run out of time. But if you can use cases to explore research topics, to illustrate ideas in your research papers, and to disseminate ideas from your papers, then you get two for the price of one. Colleagues at other schools sometimes ask me how much of my time I spend on research and how much on course development. I joke that I spend about 60 percent of my time on each. That's not because I work 120 percent of the time but because the two activities overlap intensely."

The pursuit of these dual, complementary objectives helped unify the faculty. "Even though our faculty is now big and diverse," Badaracco noted, "we basically are like-minded. There are different, thoughtful perspectives on the rigor–relevance continuum, but no sectarian strife. That is impressive for 200 people." Many faculty members worked across units to engage in interdisciplinary research. For example, a corporate governance project involved faculty from the Accounting and Management, Organizational Behavior, Finance, and Strategy units.

Faculty generally spent half their time on research and half on teaching and administration. In the latter category, they spent 65 percent of their time on the MBA program, 17 percent on executive education, 11 percent on school administration, and 7 percent on the doctoral programs.

Faculty Development

The school had various formal and informal mechanisms for bringing incoming faculty up to speed on teaching, field research, and case writing. A central mechanism was the mandatory teaching group for faculty teaching in the required curriculum, which brought together the entire faculty teaching a particular class, usually seven to ten instructors including the course head. With a mix of new and veteran faculty, teaching groups facilitated information transfer and provided a forum to discuss the teaching plan for each upcoming class session. Many teaching groups also debriefed after each class. These activities allowed more seasoned faculty to help newcomers—particularly those with less experience and less expertise in the subject matter—adapt to case method teaching. They were also regarded as beneficial for faculty members at later stages of their careers. "In teaching group meetings, faculty share best practices and teaching plans and help distill the key ideas of each case," explained Professor Michael Toffel. "We couldn't do without them. They promote continuous refinement and improvement. My teaching group at HBS has been key to my development as a general management–oriented instructor using the case method."

Other mechanisms to encourage faculty to share best practices included course development research seminars. In these forums, faculty shared and discussed their approaches to course development, including the use of cases and field research to develop concepts and theoretical frameworks, and solicited feedback from their peers. "These seminars are an example of faculty development activities connected to the mission of the school and the MBA program," a faculty member explained. "Each seminar emphasizes intellectual activities other than research published in academic journals."

To augment the school's traditional system of faculty-to-faculty mentoring and help faculty develop as teachers, the C. Roland Christensen Center for Teaching and Learning (CCTL) opened its doors in 2004. "The biggest change," noted Willis Emmons, the center's director, "was creating an institutional focus on faculty teaching development when it used to be more ad hoc and informal within faculty units. The center was created to support the process of identifying and sharing best practices with the purpose of complementing rather than replacing the work of the faculty unit."

The center's offerings and initiatives fell into four main areas: coaching faculty, communicating best practices, convening colloquia and workshops on case-based teaching, and conducting applied research on various subjects pertinent to management teaching and education. Ongoing projects included research on the special challenges of case method teaching, teaching effectiveness and evaluation, pedagogical innovations, gender and diversity issues, and teaching styles and techniques. Although the center's work focused on incoming faculty, tenured faculty also solicited its advice. Finally, through its Web site, outreach, and on-campus "teach the teachers" programs, the center provided leadership and expertise about case method teaching and participant-centered learning for instructors at other institutions in the United States and abroad.

In addition, the center ran an annual colloquium attended by some forty to sixty HBS faculty members. The first dealt with transitioning from teaching in the MBA program to executive education, the second with grading and feedback in the MBA program, and the most recent with teaching groups. Finally, the CCTL was involved in START, a four-day program attended by all incoming faculty (whether freshly minted PhDs or highly experienced lateral hires). In addition to providing a general introduction to school processes and policies, the program included practicums on case method teaching. Incoming faculty were videotaped in a practice teaching round delivered to their peers. "We don't have a flight simulator," Emmons explained, "so this is the next best opportunity."

In January 2008, the school relaunched the faculty teaching seminar, which had been quite popular in the 1980s and 1990s. Faculty gathered monthly or semimonthly to discuss topics such as how best to use the blackboard and how to craft powerful class openings and closings.

Multidisciplinary Initiatives

Although the faculty was organized by units to facilitate recruiting, mentoring, development, planning, and other activities, HBS had launched and continued to support a handful of cross-disciplinary initiatives. These initiatives typically fostered integrative research and course development projects (often collaborative), generated executive education programs, mobilized alumni, and connected current MBA students to internships, job offerings, and conferences.

Leadership Initiative

Launched in the late 1990s, the Leadership Initiative devoted its resources to developing cutting-edge scholarship and research that focused on individual leadership and the effects leaders had on their organizations and communities. The new knowledge created by the initiative had been used to develop courses at HBS and advance the scholarship of leadership. According to Tony Mayo, lecturer in the Organizational Behavior unit and initiative director, the Leadership Initiative supported three streams of research: legacy leadership, emerging leadership, and global leadership.[12] Legacy leadership research sought to understand the lessons of past leaders. It attempted to uncover the ways in which those leaders had either successfully or unsuccessfully executed their power. Emerging leadership focused on leaders in the twenty-first century and the practices and strategies they employed to run organizations. Global leadership research explored the essential skills of leading an organization in a global context. In 2001, the initiative began to compile background materials on one thousand twentieth-century business leaders. The research resulted in the creation of the Great American Business Leaders database. The database was designed as a learning tool, chronicling the legacies of great business leaders to better teach the leaders of tomorrow.

Social Enterprise Initiative

In 1993, in recognition of the increasing scope of the nonprofit sector in both the U.S. economy and the HBS student body, then-Dean John McArthur launched the Social Enterprise Initiative (SEI) with initial support from John C. Whitehead (MBA '47). "When we began the Social Enterprise Initiative, the opportunity that motivated us was how to mobilize the talent and capacity of HBS to enhance the leadership, managerial competency, and organizational capacity of social-purpose institutions and undertakings," commented Professor Emeritus James Austin. "Generating new intellectual capital and then developing it into transformational learning experiences for practitioners is how we will add significant value to the world. Our collective process now is to generate that intellectual agenda."[13]

The SEI became a lens with which to focus the research and teaching of over forty faculty, who contributed cases and working papers on topics such as the strategy and management of social enterprises, governance of nonprofit organizations, and social and financial resources. One stream of faculty research, for example, led to the 2005 Conference on Global Poverty: Business Solutions and Approaches, which in turn resulted in the 2007 publication of *Business Solutions for the Global Poor: Creating Social and Economic Value*, a book that brought together a variety of perspectives on how serving the poor could be a profitable business proposition and help improve the lives of the world's impoverished people.

A handful of core executive education programs, including Governing for Nonprofit Excellence and Strategic Perspectives in Nonprofit Management, had also been developed and delivered to over twenty-five hundred leaders since 1993.

In 2004, HBS faculty joined with faculty from Harvard's Graduate School of Education and nine urban school districts to launch the Public Education Leadership Program (PELP). PELP aimed to create knowledge and frameworks grounded in educational practice through comprehensive research, courses and programs, the dissemination of teaching materials, and engagement with school districts.

Global Initiative

Launched in the mid-1990s, the Global Initiative sought to achieve a broad range of objectives by establishing regional research centers that facilitated faculty research and case development. HBS was unique among its peers in approaching globalization through an emphasis on faculty learning and development rather than via educational programs or partnerships. The initiative also helped the school build stronger relationships with alumni, practitioners, and other educational institutions abroad. By 2008, there were five international research centers: the Asia-Pacific Research Center (established in Hong Kong in 1999), the Latin America Research Center (established in Buenos Aires, with additional researchers based in Brazil and Mexico, in 2000), the Japan Research Center (established in Tokyo in 2002), the Europe Research Center (established in Paris in 2003), and the India Research Center (established in Mumbai in 2006).

All of the research centers focused on creating links among business leaders, governments, and researchers in their regions. For example, Professor Regina Abrami worked with the Asia-Pacific Research Center to develop a case on the U.S.-Cambodia Bilateral Textile Trade Agreement, focused on Cambodia's decision to enter into the agreement and the potential repercussions of the agreement once the international textile quota regime was overturned in 2004. On the other side of the world, Professor Mihir Desai worked with the Latin America Research Center to explore Dow Chemical's bid for an Argentine petrochemical complex that was being privatized. "It's extremely difficult to get this kind of up-close, fine-grained perspective on multinational investment decision-making," Desai noted, "and the case wouldn't have happened without the center's hard work and knowledge of the region and the companies involved.[14]

To build relationships with academics around the world, the school sponsored the Colloquium on Participant-Centered Learning (CPCL), a ten-day program targeted at top business schools in emerging economies that trained faculty in case method teaching. Participants included deans, department chairs, and senior faculty with five or more years of teaching experience. The program included sessions on case writing to help schools develop their own field-based research. It also enabled foreign academics to network with HBS faculty with the goal of fostering joint research opportunities. CPCL's success led the school to develop additional, region-specific versions for faculty from eastern Europe and Asia.

Healthcare Initiative

Launched in 2005, the Healthcare Initiative brought together HBS faculty with an interest in the business and management of health care. Its mission was to improve the performance of the global healthcare system by creating and disseminating knowledge that increased the effectiveness of the leadership of the full range of healthcare organizations. Although the initiative itself was relatively new, the school's interest in health care was long-standing, with about 20 percent of HBS faculty conducting healthcare research and more than four hundred healthcare cases currently available through HBSP. The number of health-care-related cases had grown steadily over time to 10 percent of all RC cases in 2006. More than three hundred students were enrolled in the three healthcare-related courses offered in the EC, and about ninety students each year accepted healthcare jobs upon graduation, a dramatic increase over the prior decade. January 2008 saw the inaugural healthcare immersion program, designed to give MBA students with little or no background in health care a foundation for future exploration and learning.

The initiative supported a number of seminars and conferences for faculty. For example, HBS cosponsored an annual conference with the Partners Healthcare Center for Genetics and Genomics. It also launched a new focused program in executive education and several custom programs. HBS faculty were both responding to strong market demand for healthcare-related educational offerings and eager to share and test their research and concepts with high-level industry practitioners. Doing more in this arena, explained faculty chair Professor Richard Hamermesh, "allows us to deliver valuable education, encourage faculty collaboration, and drive intellectual development while building our brand in healthcare." The initiative also set up an alumni mentoring program and established monthly faculty meetings to discuss research and the initiative's plans. In 2007, about fifteen faculty members attended these meetings, about one-fifth of the faculty engaged in some form of healthcare research, and eight to twelve faculty members cited health care as a primary research interest.

Looking Ahead

As HBS looked ahead to its second century, it was clear that the world of management was changing rapidly, as was what was required of leaders—including a greater understanding of the impact of globalization, technology, and diversity in the workplace. Some faculty reflected on whether HBS should be pushing its global agenda further, doing more to develop leadership skills in the MBA program, or increasing the role of experiential learning.

Some worried that the school was moving away from its commitment to and focus on field research. Deputy Dean Carl Kester was concerned that some cases were becoming more like problem sets, narrowly designed to teach technical skills instead of teaching those technical skills in a broader company and industry context. "These kinds of cases have a methodological line of attack and a single preferred right answer. Some boil down to being mathematical exercises, pure and simple." For him, maintaining the power of the curriculum required that the HBS case method remain thriving and vibrant. Increasingly, the case method was being used to teach sophisticated techniques such as valuation, forecasting, and competitive analysis—putting less focus on diagnosis, decision making, and implementation, the action skills for which it was originally designed. Case length had also increased over the years, leading to concerns about the burden on students and the quality of their class preparation.

The broader question was whether the HBS teaching and learning model would remain relevant, and how it might be expanded or enhanced to match the current environment. Was a general management curriculum still suitable for students who increasingly gravitated to jobs in financial services and management consulting immediately after receiving their MBA?

Finally, a central challenge for HBS—like most of its peers—was growing its faculty. The number of tenured HBS faculty had remained stable at about eighty-five in the past decade. Dean Light explained, "The opportunities for HBS and the market's demand for what we do are expanding dramatically. But it's hard to expand activities without expanding the faculty. If we can find a way around that problem, the opportunities are just amazing."

In April 2009, as the economic crisis unfolded, we obtained an update on Harvard Business School's view of its curriculum and courses. The key responses and initiatives included the following:

- HBS reaffirmed its commitment to a broad, general management education delivered predominantly through cases and the case method.

- The school was considering expanding its offerings in critical areas such as globalization, leadership development, critical thinking, and experiential learning, and task forces were reviewing options in each of these areas.

- The introduction of a university-wide January term in 2010 provided greater flexibility for new initiatives and experiential learning, including field projects, immersions, and short, intensive courses. Planning was well underway for a range of new offerings.

- Greater attention was expected to be devoted to business-government relationships generally, and regulation, risk management, and internal governance systems in particular. A number of new cases had already been added to the curriculum in these areas, including an integrative case on J.P. Morgan Chase Bear Stearns taught jointly in the first year by finance and LCA faculty. New second-year courses were being offered in 2009–2010 on a number of these topics.

- The school was considering developing new courses in conjunction with other parts of the university, such as Harvard Law School and Harvard Kennedy School.

Yale School of Management

Integration and Large-Scale Change

THE YALE SCHOOL OF MANAGEMENT (SOM) undertook a major review of its MBA core curriculum in 2005 and 2006. The review led to a new curriculum—unanimously approved by the senior faculty in March 2006, developed that summer, and then launched in the fall of the same year—that eliminated traditional discipline-based courses such as finance and marketing and replaced them with courses that sought to integrate teaching and learning across functions by presenting information from the perspective of the constituents with whom leaders typically interacted, such as customers, competitors, and investors.

The new curriculum did more than just integrate across functions. It also strengthened the school's efforts to develop the leadership skills of its students, added new components that looked at, among other things, careers and innovation, and required an international experience that was woven into the core curriculum. To make room for these new subjects and approaches, the school moved some material out of the core and into electives in a way that it believed would not reduce student understanding of key disciplinary concepts.

Several interrelated factors drove the introduction of the new curriculum. First were concerns about the growing disconnect between the traditional MBA curriculum and the demands of management and leadership in modern organizations. Second, when the Yale faculty sought the advice of executives about how to bring the MBA curriculum into better alignment with the demands of modern management, they received feedback that resonated with the mission and culture of the school, both of which put a tremendous emphasis on developing leaders who were capable of drawing together diverse constituencies in the pursuit of meaningful aspirations. Third, there was a strong desire on the part of many of the faculty to establish SOM as a distinctive role model in management education, and the new curriculum—if well executed—seemed to offer that possibility.

Background on the Institution and Its MBA Program

Yale offered a two-year MBA program, a PhD program, an executive MBA for leaders in health care, and assorted executive education programs. It had 208 students in its 2008 MBA class and just over 5,000 alumni. The school employed thirty-six tenured professors, eight associate professors, sixteen assistant professors, eighteen "secondary appointment" faculty, eight adjunct faculty, five visiting faculty, and thirty-three lecturers and other faculty. Roughly 80 percent of its students came from North America and 15 percent from Asia. Some 46 percent of its 2006 graduates had taken jobs in financial services, 15 percent in consulting, and 10 percent in the nonprofit sector.[1]

Yale University founded the School of Organization and Management in 1974 with the goal of preparing students for government, nonprofit, and for-profit leadership careers. The school believed that managers often changed sectors during their working lives and that leaders in one sector needed to understand and be able to work effectively with their peers in other sectors. Although close to 95 percent of its graduates worked in the for-profit sector in their first job after graduation, the school historically attracted students with an interest in making a positive contribution to society whatever their career pursuits.

From its beginnings, the school prided itself on being different from traditional business schools. Although it had offered the usual core courses in fields such as finance, marketing, and accounting, unlike most schools nearly all courses included a mix of cases and other materials dealing with nonprofit and public sector organizations. The school had included politics as a required course, and it selected almost one-third of its students from the nonprofit or public sectors. In a further signal of its uniqueness, students in the early days had earned a Masters in Public and Private Management degree rather than an MBA.

In the 1990s, however, competing business schools began offering more courses that focused on nonprofit, public sector, and other leadership activities that benefited society. This made Yale's approach to management education less unique. Yale also understood that its positioning had at times led to confusion for both applicants and recruiters. Although Yale considered itself to be an MBA program and increasingly hired faculty members with functional expertise in finance, marketing, and economics, this was not always recognized in the marketplace. In response, the school changed its name to the Yale School of Management; about five years later, it also changed its degree to the more widely known MBA.

In spring 2005, Yale named Joel Podolny as its new dean, effective July 1. Podolny had earned a PhD in sociology from Harvard and had held tenured faculty positions at Stanford and Harvard business schools before joining Yale. When he arrived, SOM's first-year curriculum was based on functional disciplines. Core courses included Financial Accounting; Financial Reporting I or Managerial Controls I; Data I (Probability Modeling and Statistical Estimation); Data II (Hypothesis Testing and Regression); Economic Analysis; Decision Analysis and Game Theory; The Strategic Environment of Management; Leadership; Managing Organizational Politics or Designing and Managing Organizations; Marketing Management; Operations Management I; and Financial Management.

A Mandate for Change

The desire to revamp the school's curriculum began before Podolny's arrival. Faculty, students, and staff had all expressed some degree of dissatisfaction with the existing program. Nevertheless, an attempt at reform—which was ultimately more modest in its aims than the curriculum design of 2006—failed to receive a majority vote from the senior faculty. Significant changes were viewed as necessary, but there was not clear agreement on where they should be focused. Podolny, however, believed that the curriculum was ultimately the essence of the school's offering to applicants and that any changes had to begin there. He often repeated a quote that he first heard from his deputy dean, Stan Garstka: "You can't brand air." Podolny used the phrase to make the point that any changes in perceptions of Yale would have to be grounded in the reality of the school experience, and that reassessing and revamping the curriculum was the most encompassing way to address those perceptions.

Podolny led a number of faculty meetings in fall 2005 at which he presented memos that sought to connect the school's distinctive mission of educating leaders for business and society with a distinctive pedagogy. Although the curriculum that eventually emerged was far more radical than the ideas articulated in those early memos—which did little more than affirm the need for a strong emphasis on teamwork and group learning as well as more "doing" and "being" courses to complement the "knowing" courses—these memos at least got the conversation about the curriculum started.

In these discussions, considerations of mission were intertwined with considerations of strategy. Although the degree change of the 1990s had helped to establish the school as an MBA program like many others, SOM remained significantly smaller than most top MBA programs, which benefited from scale economies. Larger schools could offer more electives and could amortize the costs of MBA services across more students. Although small size made coordination across functions easier, the traditional MBA curriculum required little or no coordination across functions. Except for the ability to claim more of a community-like atmosphere, there was little to no benefit associated with being small. How to turn Yale's small size into an advantage therefore became a central concern in the early discussions.

Developing a New Curriculum

Podolny did not have a specific framework in mind for a new curriculum when he joined SOM. He and several senior faculty members, including Garstka and accounting and finance professor Jake Thomas, began by spending four or five months getting the faculty comfortable with the idea of undertaking curriculum reform. They felt that it was not necessary to get everyone on board immediately, but that it would take the commitment and energy of a diverse group of senior people to both design and deliver a new core curriculum. Garstka explained that the early work was done somewhat quietly:

> We did not want to announce a process early on because we did not know what we were going to do. We spent a lot of time thinking about the faculty and what they might gain and lose. We then identified a few opinion leaders in the faculty, the people we thought that if we don't get them on board it will be difficult to succeed. A few of them initially were dead set against this; some were among the best teachers at the school. We eventually got these individuals to see that even though their course might be the greatest thing and was being delivered marvelously well, it was in the context of the wrong model.

In November 2005, Podolny set up a steering committee and six subcommittees to coordinate the design of a new curriculum. The steering committee consisted of eight faculty and two students; each of the subcommittees consisted of six faculty and two students, although additional faculty could be brought onto a committee if Podolny and Garstka felt that doing so would help increase overall buy-in. More than two-thirds of the senior faculty members were involved in at least one committee. Everyone knew that the subcommittee focused on the core curriculum would, in Podolny's words, generate the most heat, and Podolny selected Professor Jake Thomas to be its head.

As they began their work, Podolny repeatedly reminded the various committees about the school's mission. "The mission at SOM is about training leaders," he observed, "not technocrats. Yale University's mission is to train leaders in the service of society, and it is the same for the Business School, the Law School, and the Divinity School." Meanwhile, Thomas spent significant time in late 2005 and early 2006 interviewing other faculty members, students, alumni, and recruiters to get their input on both the current curriculum and on what a new curriculum might look like. His subcommittee also analyzed the curricula of eleven other leading business schools in the United States.

One early idea was to build the core curriculum around careers. This approach would address a key concern with the old functional curriculum by making it easier to teach across fields to enable students to think more broadly when solving business problems. Unfortunately, it would be very difficult to deliver because it required having similar courses aimed at people pursuing different careers. It also did not address individuals who moved across disciplines and industries throughout their careers.

The idea of focusing on careers, however, initiated a two-week period of intense brainstorming that moved the idea from careers to roles (later called "perspectives"). In this approach, the new core curriculum would consist of courses developed around the perspectives of various internal and external stakeholders. It would examine how these stakeholders drew upon multiple disciplines simultaneously. The courses, which together became known as Organizational Perspectives, ultimately formed the heart of Yale's new core curriculum.

To design the new courses, Podolny began with a series of faculty meetings. At the meetings were the eight senior faculty who would be designing the new courses as well as all faculty involved in teaching the old core curriculum. The purpose was to go through the old curriculum, course by course, and identify the key topics that were being taught so they could begin organizing the content for the new courses. Garstka described some of the benefits that came out of this process: "We made these long lists on the blackboard to show what we were doing in the current core. We found out that there was tremendous duplication in parts of the curriculum. For example, we were talking about agency theory in different ways in several courses in the core, but we never really nailed it in any one place. The new curriculum gave us the opportunity to become more efficient in the ways we delivered things because we were eliminating the old core and starting a new one from a zero base."

To gain buy-in, Thomas, Garstka, and Podolny met personally with those faculty members who expressed concern about how the design was unfolding. In March 2006, the faculty unanimously voted in the new curriculum based on an eleven-page document that presented the rationale both in terms of changes in the world of management and the need to deliver on the school's mission. Although the document included an appendix with the list of topics that would be included in the new courses, there were no syllabi and no references to particular cases or reading materials. Considerable design work needed to be done to flesh out the proposal. After the faculty approved the curriculum in a morning vote, Podolny presented the curriculum to the student government in the afternoon and to a packed town hall in the evening.

For Podolny, two conversations stood out from that day. One occurred when he bumped into professor of marketing Ravi Dhar, who, after the vote, said with a smile, "Congratulations. I guess the reputation of the school is now riding on this, and, of course, your reputation is really riding on this." The other was a question from a student during the town hall. The student asked, "What are your worries?" Podolny replied, "Execution and communication." His deepest concern was that the changes to the core would not be significant enough.

To help ensure the new courses were integrated and not just old courses that had been renamed, SOM had the same eight senior faculty members work in teams of two to design the eight Organizational Perspectives courses. Each faculty member was charged with leading the design of one course and also with backing up a faculty member designing another course. The lead faculty member on each team of two was from a discipline other than the primary discipline of the course. For example, the team that designed the Investor course was not headed by a finance professor. Podolny felt that this was necessary at the design stage to break old habits; once the new curriculum was up and running, however, he expected that a faculty member from the closest appropriate area would lead each course. One of the faculty members involved in the course design process recalled, "It is a lot harder to think out of the box than you might think, so we did not do it alone." Podolny had a formal role on two of the eight course design teams, and he offered informal assistance to a few others. Staffing was complicated by the need to retain a strong second year. A number of the school's most experienced, talented teachers were part of the design teams. At the same time, Podolny and Garstka recognized that they could not "gut" the electives by removing all of the school's strongest teachers from their courses.

Aligning Curriculum and Institution: Mission, Faculty, and Size

Podolny believed that the new curriculum fit the distinctive aspects of the school. Because the central courses were structured around the constituencies and stakeholders that a leader had to engage to be effective, the focus on leadership became central to the curriculum. Other aspects of the core curriculum, such as a leadership development program and a new course on Individual Problem Framing, were complementary.

Professor Jonathan Feinstein believed that the integrated curriculum fit well with the school's mission. He explained:

> The mission of the school is contributing to business and contributing to society in the best way you can. That is pretty broad. We want students to grasp the way organizations work, the way markets work, and the way non-market forces work, and to do so well enough that in the very diverse range of circumstances where they are going to want to make a difference, they will have the necessary traction and skills to tackle the problem. If we were training people just to go out and be financial investors or marketing people, this kind of a curriculum might not fit as well with the mission.

Garstka explained that SOM chose an integrated curriculum because it not only was the way the business world operated, but also the way SOM operated. He stated:

> Some faculty members come to us precisely because of their breadth of interests. They don't want to go to lunch with forty other professors just like themselves. If they are in finance, they likely want to go to lunch with someone in marketing or organizational behavior. It is a mind-set that many of us share. In fact, we might be the only school whose faculty lunch seminar every week is one seminar for the entire faculty. We can do it because we are small. Anyone from any group on the faculty can come and talk about their research, and about 60 percent of the faculty show up every week.

In addition, the school's small size facilitated its ability to design and deliver an integrated curriculum. Integrated courses work best when they involve faculty from more than one discipline working together to develop and teach the course. To that end, faculty must know and be willing to work with colleagues in other areas. Smaller size means far fewer faculty members need to collaborate; fewer students means one professor can teach all sections—and all students—of a core course. Marketing professor K. Sudhir stated, "Being small has helped us. I have the entire responsibility for designing and teaching the Customer class across all three sections. To get inputs from other areas, I spoke to professors in accounting, organizational behavior, economics, and other areas. We had some vigorous debates, but were able to integrate very quickly. Had there been three or four professors teaching the course, as at larger schools, the number of interactions required would have been too many to make integration feasible."

However, even SOM's typical class size—between 225 and 240 students before the new curriculum—seemed too large for a successful early transition. Under the old curriculum, each core course had four sections of between 55 and 60 students per section, and SOM's largest classrooms were physically limited to a maximum of 70 students. To ensure top-quality course delivery, SOM decided to have the senior professors who helped design the courses teach all of the sections of each course. However, an individual professor could not teach four sections at a time. As a result, SOM decided to temporarily reduce its MBA class size to 180 students and lower the number of sections from four to three, with 60 students in each.

To get to the smaller class size, SOM reduced the number of students accepted into its first entering class with the new curriculum. The process created a number of complications. After announcing the new curriculum, SOM's class yield increased from 37 percent for the class of 2007 to 43 percent for the class of 2008, which left it with an entering class just as large as in previous years. To reduce its size, SOM offered a tuition discount to any student willing to defer to the next year; this reduced the class to 208 students. For the class of 2009, the number of prospective students who applied to Yale increased by 25 percent. SOM therefore reduced the number of students it accepted to get its class size closer to 180. SOM believed that class size was only a transitional difficulty. Within a few years, it planned to involve more faculty members in the core and return to having four sections of students.

The New First-Year Curriculum

SOM's program ran on a semester basis, and second-year courses remained on this schedule. The new first-year schedule, however, followed a different format because the new core curriculum consisted of three main segments: Orientation to Management, Organizational Perspectives, and Integrated Leadership Perspectives. First-year students arrived in late August for a brief orientation period. The rest of the year was divided into four quarters: Fall I, Fall II, Spring I, and Spring II. Following orientation, the Orientation to Management segment ran from the end of August to mid-October (Fall I). These courses varied in length and had different start and end dates within the period. The Organizational Perspectives courses ran in two parts: from late October to mid-December (Fall II) and from the third week in January to the end of February (Spring I). These courses all started and ended at about the same time. Following a spring break, the Integrated Leadership Perspectives segment started in late March and ran to early May (Spring II). Because the Integrated Leadership Perspectives segment did not fully occupy a student's time, the school also offered several half-semester electives during this time period.

Orientation to Management

The Orientation to Management segment consisted of seven courses designed to focus students on their longer-term career aspirations, understand what it means to frame a problem, become familiar with some of the foundational quantitative language of management, and begin to develop some of the interpersonal skills that would help them work in group settings. Most of these courses, including Basics of Accounting, Data and Decision Analysis, Basics of Economics, Managing Groups and Teams, and Interpersonal Dynamics, involved material taught in the school's former core program. The segment also included two all-new courses: Individual Problem Framing and Careers.

Quantitative Courses. The goal for the quantitative courses in this segment was to familiarize the students with the concepts and language of management so that additional quantitative tools could be more easily presented in the integrated, multidisciplinary context of the perspectives courses. A few concepts or tools taught in the old core curriculum were removed from the new core and placed into electives.

The teams designing the courses in the Organizational Perspectives segment frequently asked the faculty members designing the Orientation to Management courses what material they planned to teach. One faculty member explained, "I am aware of what other people are teaching at the same time as me and I am aware of what they are going to be teaching down the road. So when I am teaching a concept in my class, I am also thinking about how it is going to show up later in the curriculum. The new curriculum is much more coordinated."

Individual Problem Framing. The Individual Problem Framing course was new to the SOM curriculum and perhaps to business education as well. Professor Nathan Novemsky, who helped develop the course, explained its importance:

> We searched around the country and we could not find another
> instance of a course aimed at teaching people how to structure
> unstructured problems. When new graduates go out and take
> a job, they face real-world problems. They are not always well
> defined. There isn't a title at the top that says "Economics 101,
> apply these tools." For example, say your business has some
> irate customers, who are complaining loudly. Is it the fault of
> your employees, is there a structural problem in the way you
> deliver services, or are these just a few bad customers? We have
> tried to design a course that helps students think through these
> unstructured problems.

The course taught a variety of tools and techniques for structuring and framing business problems. It helped students examine their assumptions, recognize that there were often multiple ways to frame a problem, and appreciate that the first approach chosen to solve a problem might not be the correct one.

Instruction methods for the thirteen-session course included lectures and readings, but also a significant number of small-group exercises. In one exercise, students were given a description of an airline passenger traveling with his family. The passenger had been promised when he purchased the tickets that his family could sit together, but upon arrival at the gate he found they could not. The passenger described what happened in a letter to the airline president. In the exercise, some groups of students received this letter under the title "irate customer," whereas other groups received it under the title "informant." The groups worked separately to develop possible solutions or approaches for this problem. Back in class, the students discussed how problem framing influenced their responses.

Careers. The Careers course was also new to the SOM curriculum. Feinstein explained that the purpose of the course was to help students think about their careers as a long-term proposition:

> I really believe that most students coming into business school have very little knowledge about business careers. Historically, this has been left to the career development office, to gossip among the students, and to the firms that are interviewing. This course is a way to say, "Look, this is very important. Let's bring this into the classroom where we can reflect upon it a bit more, teach some frameworks, and look at related research." Careers unfold over time, and choices that students make at the very beginning can have repercussions for a long time to come.

The Careers course consisted of six class sessions and used a combination of lectures, readings, and exercises. Readings included the autobiographies of Sam Walton and Gandhi, a biography of Warren Buffett, and a chapter in Herminia Ibarra's book on changing careers, *Working Identity*. The school also hired a professional video crew to tape three-hour interviews of a dozen alumni about their careers. These videos were used to highlight the challenges and decision points of careers. Finally, all students interviewed someone else to learn about that person's career. Feinstein felt the course was especially important at Yale because a high proportion of its students were career changers. He added, "We are trying to help students realize their potential, whatever it might be. In many cases, that potential involves leadership because that is what they need to get a group of people organized in a way to get things done."

Organizational Perspectives

Much of what the new curriculum set out to do—break out of the silos of functional courses to integrate teaching and learning across disciplines—occurred in the eight Organizational Perspectives courses. (Table 11-1 lists the courses and the array of traditional academic disciplines covered in each one.) The curriculum recognized that managers needed to "engage, motivate, and lead" the individuals in the internal and external roles that these perspective courses represented.

TABLE 11-1

Disciplines for perspective courses

Organizational Perspectives	Traditional Disciplines Drawn From	Representative Topics
Investor	Finance, accounting, economics, psychology	Different types of investors: primary investors (households, endowments, pension plans), intermediary investors (mutual funds, hedge funds); tools for primary investors: risk-reward analysis; tools for intermediary investors: valuation, CAPM; bond market investing, international investing; efficient markets; tools for hedging: options and futures
Competitor	Economics, organizational behavior, political science, marketing, accounting	Identifying competition; product differentiation; competitor motivations; simulation and dynamic games; antitrust/business ethics/competitive tactics; complementors; identity-based constraints on competitors; alliances and associations; social and environmental responsibility as competitive advantage; sustainability
Customer	Marketing, accounting, finance, organizational behavior, politics and regulation, operations	Going to market, creating a value proposition, consumer behavior, organizational behavior, global marketing, market segmentation, positioning, customer relationship management, customer costing, customer privacy, customer satisfaction and loyalty, customer-focused organizations
State and Society	Politics, economics, organizational behavior, finance	Functions of states and other public institutions, motivations of elected and unelected officials, identifying formal and informal power relations, legal environment, macroeconomic considerations, demographic considerations, discrimination, political activities of business leaders, patterns of influence by interest groups, public decision making, operations issues in the public sector, NGOs

(Continued)

TABLE 11-1 (*continued*)

Organizational Perspectives	Traditional Disciplines Drawn From	Representative Topics
Innovator	Strategy, marketing, creativity and innovation studies, organizational behavior	Creativity and innovation processes, managing innovation groups and teams, customer-based insights, social innovations, organizational obstacles to innovation and how to address them, financing R&D, long-term trends
Operations Engine	Operations, accounting, economics, organizational behavior, marketing	Global manufacturing strategy; process analysis/reengineering—bottleneck analysis, queuing models; supply chain management—inventory models, just-in-time/lean manufacturing; cost accounting—relevant costs, transfer pricing; quality management—manufacturing and service quality
Employee	Organizational behavior, economics, political science, accounting	Motivation (intrinsic and extrinsic); incentives (including performance evaluation); power and authority; negotiations (including salaries); unions; employee rights; screening and signaling (including recruitment); culture, values, and diversity; organizational culture; agency costs
Sourcing and Managing Funds/CFO	Corporate finance, managerial accounting, marketing, economics, organizational behavior	Capital structure, capital and cash budgets, mergers and acquisitions, financial planning, evaluation and control, investor relations, risk management, taxation, and alternative measures of profitability such as economic value-added and activity-based costing

Source: Yale School of Management.

When SOM launched the new curriculum in the 2006–2007 academic year, it offered the four "external" perspectives courses (Competitor, Customer, Investor, and State and Society) in the fall, and the four "internal" perspectives courses (Employee, Innovator, Operations Engine, and Sourcing and Managing Funds) in the spring. In the 2007–2008 academic year, it switched the Sourcing and Managing Funds course with the State and Society course.

Some new courses were quite similar in content to their predecessors in the old curriculum; others changed significantly. For example, the Investor class was built closely on the old Finance class. This was because there were many standard and important financial tools that had to be covered in any MBA curriculum. In general, new courses that were "tool heavy"—that is, that taught specific techniques—tended to be more similar to the old courses than new courses that taught fewer tools.

Courses were not fully integrated in all aspects. Instead, they taught some of the critical discipline-based material in depth, without integration, while integrating across disciplines on a broad level with less depth for other material. Podolny referred to these as "T-shaped courses." Garstka added:

> There are very few deep dives in the perspectives courses. Most of the material is integrative, how things fit together. I recently taught the Sourcing and Managing Funds course. I am more of an accounting person, and I co-taught the course with a finance professor. We covered some managerial accounting topics and some traditional finance topics, but we also covered some organizational behavior material such as how organizational structure impacts valuations. There is even some State and Society material because we looked at funding issues in multinational settings. We did do a deep dive to teach beta and EVA because you can't go very far in finance or accounting without knowing those topics, but we quickly came back to a broader, integrative context.

Organizational Perspectives classes were taught primarily by the lead faculty member for the course, coupled with other faculty members and guests who participated to varying degrees. In some courses the lead faculty member was in every class and a secondary faculty member was in many or nearly all classes. In other courses, there were a greater number of secondary faculty members and guests involved. Two Organizational Perspective courses had two lead faculty members, whereas a third course had three lead faculty members. Although all Organizational Perspectives courses were led by senior faculty, in some cases a junior faculty member might be asked to drop into one class to teach a subject. In such cases, the integration piece of the lesson was still done by the lead faculty member.

Customer Course. The Customer course provides an example. This course consisted of fourteen class sessions, taught by a mix of faculty.

Sudhir taught eight class sessions alone. He co-taught three classes with another senior professor, and one class with a junior faculty member. Two classes were taught by other senior faculty, drawn from accounting, organizational behavior, politics, and strategy.

The course consisted of two seven-class modules. The first module, "Understanding Customers and Creating a Superior Value Proposition," covered traditional concepts that might be found in any MBA core marketing class. The second module, "Creating and Maintaining a Customer-Aligned Organization," discussed how to align functions to a strategy. Each module included four case studies (some written specifically by SOM for the course), assorted readings, and lectures. Examples of readings included two chapters from a marketing textbook, a chapter in a strategy book, and various articles from the *McKinsey Quarterly*. The course also included an exercise on measuring customers' preferences using conjoint analysis.

In describing his course, Sudhir first explained the underlying philosophy: that you cannot think about marketing without thinking about the entire organization. He stated:

> I tell my students that an organization is a tool to execute against a strategy. In many organizations, people think of the customer as something that is owned by marketing. But if the marketing group develops a customer-centric strategy while other functions of the organization have their own plans, the firm cannot succeed. The operations people, the HR systems, the accounting people, the finance people, and everyone else must be aligned with the same strategy. And if that means changing the organizational structure to create the alignment, top management will have to do that.

Innovator Course. The Innovator course was an entirely new addition to the curriculum. Feinstein, who helped develop the course, explained its importance:

> Innovation is absolutely fundamental to organizations. Organizations that innovate will survive and grow; those that do not will get run over. Traditionally, innovation has not been taught in the core curriculum because it does not fit neatly into one of the functional silos. There is no faculty champion speaking up

and saying we should be teaching this. Offering a course on the topic is also important because creative thinking is so different, so orthogonal to other ways of thinking. So many other classes pile on top of each other in ways of thinking that are consistent. This class is different.

The Innovator course explored how new ideas could be generated, evaluated, and developed and the challenges that innovators face within organizations. Three senior faculty members served as lead instructors for the course, which used a combination of lectures, case studies, and exercises. Readings included materials on disruptive technologies and techniques for creative problem solving. Three SOM faculty members co-taught the course. The course also had occasional visitors, including a media designer and several executives.

Integrated Leadership Perspectives

The concluding Integrated Leadership Perspectives segment of the first year consisted of a single course designed to tie together the material students had learned in the first two segments of the program. The course featured complex interdisciplinary cases that required students to apply the multiple perspectives featured throughout the integrated curriculum. It was similar to a general management course. It also took a leadership perspective in that it asked students to think through how to make change happen and how to lead. When the course was offered in spring 2007, it met twice a week, three hours per class. Although the course was viewed as very effective, the workload for both the faculty and the students was deemed too high, so for spring 2008, SOM planned to have the course meet once per week for three hours.

The course began with cases on small, entrepreneurial organizations and moved gradually to larger and more complex organizations. Professor Sharon Oster, who developed the course and served as its first head, explained that the cases tended to feature current, often ongoing topics. They were described by faculty as "big messy cases." For example, one case described the development of Governors Island in New York harbor. New York City had acquired the 172-acre island in 2003 from the federal government with the goal of developing it for the benefit of the public and the city. In advance of class, students received details on the island, requests for proposals documents, Internet links that provided information on real estate and development costs in New York, statistics on parkland usage, population data, and other data. Students worked in small teams and came to class prepared to describe their proposals for developing the island. Class guests included the woman who headed the redevelopment effort for the city as well as several developers. During the first half of the class, Oster lectured on city economies and how cities worked. In the second half, the students presented and discussed their proposals and were grilled by the guests.

Although one senior professor headed the course, each class involved at least two professors as well as frequent outside guests. At least twenty-three faculty members taught in the course, and students frequently saw two of their Organizational Perspectives professors working together to teach a case.

First-Year "Platform" Electives

SOM offered several half-semester "platform" electives to first-year students during the second half of the spring semester. First-year students could take up to three of these courses. Platform electives were offered in each functional discipline traditionally taught in MBA programs, including accounting, finance, marketing, organizational behavior, operations, and strategy. The courses covered topics in a depth not possible in the Organizational Perspectives courses; they also taught material in a discipline-focused, nonintegrative manner. They were aimed at students planning to begin careers, or apply for summer internships, that required additional functional depth. As one faculty member explained, a student planning to work in investment banking did not need to know marketing's four P's in the same depth as a student planning a marketing career. The platform electives were also offered to help dispel concerns that the new curriculum would reduce learning in key disciplines. During this same time period, the school also offered a number of other, non-platform electives. Some of these courses served as prerequisites for second-year electives.

International Experience

The new first-year curriculum required an international component for all students. (A small number of students stayed in the United States because of visa, health, or other impediments.) Students traveled in faculty-led groups of about twenty-five students each to one of approximately eight countries to study the local business environment, visit companies, and meet with the leaders of organizations.

The trips ran in January and lasted for approximately ten days. However, students were involved in some aspect of the experience for most of their first year, and the program was integrated into several of the Organizational Perspectives courses. When students arrived on campus in August, they were asked to rank their preferences for a trip destination. Most trips focused on a country or location; a minority concentrated on a particular industry. In the fall, there were six sessions devoted to trip-related activities. In some weeks, the faculty member lectured or led a discussion on the country or the focus of the trip. In other weeks, outside presenters provided additional perspectives or discussed trip logistics. Students also worked in small groups to research selected aspects of the trip, such as a particular industry, the political situation, or general economic issues. Each small group then gave a presentation on its research to other students in advance of the trip.

Before and after the trips, the perspectives courses highlighted issues to look for while traveling abroad and explored the lessons learned, especially in the Innovator and the State and Society courses. For example, the Innovator course encouraged students to think about products or services that they had observed on their trips that could be introduced as innovations in the United States, and the Integrated Leadership Perspective course developed and presented two cases based on 2007 trips.

Leadership Development Program

SOM introduced the Leadership Development Program (LDP) in fall 2007 to provide an opportunity for students to think and learn more about leadership. The previous year, SOM had a shorter program focused on aspirations, which the school modified and expanded to create LDP. Students went through LDP in the same groups that were used for the classes and trips of the international experience program.

LDP sought to help students be successful over the long term by aligning their actions with their personal values and beliefs. The program worked under the assumption that students would feel a greater sense of accomplishment in their careers if they were doing work that was meaningful and fulfilling to them, that had an impact on other people, and that yielded results that mattered. The LDP was based in part on the work of James G. March that described the difference between action based on a "logic of consequence" (rooted in cost-benefit analysis) and that based on a "logic of commitment" (rooted in values or beliefs).[2] It was designed to assist students in converting their values into commitments. Heidi Brooks, head of the LDP program, stated:

> Leaders are most authentically engaged in their pursuits *and* most inspiring to others when they are working in alignment with deeply held values. Our students come to SOM with impressive ambitions. They seek to meaningfully impact business and society over the course of their careers. Leadership development at SOM builds on this simple premise: if what you aspire to accomplish is related to what you most deeply value, you will be most compelling to others. They will witness what matters to you, and that by itself is inspiring.

The LDP program began with a brief summer assignment, followed by several activities during the orientation period. After the orientation sessions, LDP classes consisted of six meetings: three in the fall and three in the spring. Meetings were held in the evening, roughly once per month, and lasted for three hours each. Each LDP group was led by a SOM faculty member and two second-year students who served as advisors. In addition to class meetings, students met one-on-one with their LDP faculty member and also with their advisor to further explore their personal commitments. Outside professional coaching was also available for students.

In fall 2007, the program focused on self-awareness. In one session, students participated in a values clarification exercise in which they looked at a list of values and reflected on their own. All students then told a story to the group about a time when they felt they were at their best. Other students provided feedback. The idea was to help students understand their own values and the importance of being able to articulate them in order to better understand their personal motivations but also to motivate others.

In spring 2008, the program focused on actions. In one session, students examined the leadership that emerged within their group on their international trips. In another, students reviewed how they had spent their time at SOM, examining the electives they had chosen, the speakers they had seen, and their job-search experiences. They then compared their actions with their intentions to see whether the two were aligned.

In early 2008, SOM was considering whether to expand the LDP program further to include sessions for second-year students.

Making It Work

Although there was great optimism for the new curriculum at the time of its launch, SOM faculty members, as well as as the school's advisory board and alumni, were concerned that students taking the new curriculum might not learn the basic disciplinary skills expected of traditional MBA students. To address this issue, SOM decided to test students in the last class of the old curriculum and compare their results with those of students taking the new curriculum. SOM created a test by drawing questions from the exemption exams previously used to determine whether students were already knowledgeable enough to be exempted from required core courses in the old curriculum. The test included calculating net present values and internal rates of return, reading financial statements, and understanding accounting methods, statistical significance testing, and other basic topics. Yale administered the test to student volunteers from the old curriculum after they returned from their summer jobs in August 2006. These exams were not graded until August 2007, when student volunteers from the new curriculum took the same test after returning from their summer jobs. After grading, SOM found no statistical differences between the two classes. However, SOM planned to continue to test learning and comprehension of the basic concepts in subsequent years, as part of a more general approach to continuing feedback and assessment on numerous aspects of the curriculum.

Case Development: Broad Perspectives, Raw Source Materials

SOM had long used cases in several parts of its curriculum. A few of these cases had been written at Yale, but most came from outside sources. Podolny recognized, however, that most traditional cases focused on a single issue and provided information primarily related to a single function. The types of cases required by the new curriculum were not generally available.

To address this need, SOM started a five-person case-writing group in summer 2006. This group consisted of a highly experienced casewriter, others with writing and journalism backgrounds, and one individual with regulatory and government expertise. Casewriters worked with the faculty to create cases that were generally broader than those used previously, that presented information from several disciplines, and that required integrated solutions based on an understanding of multiple disciplines. For example, one professor was developing a case study on General Motors and one of its unions regarding an agreement whereby GM would pay the union to take over funding responsibility for the health care of retired workers. The case, which would be used in the Sourcing and Managing Funds course, would discuss the present value of future healthcare payments, as well as the financial and political risks for the union assuming this obligation. It would include elements from finance, politics, and labor relations.

Cases were used most extensively in the Organizational Perspectives and Integrated Leadership Perspectives segments of the curriculum. New cases carried the Yale brand, and the school hoped to ultimately begin selling these cases to other schools. Some of the cases involved multimedia. A multimedia case was delivered via the Internet. One such case involved the leveraged buyout of Equity Office Properties by the Blackstone Group. It began with a short introduction and then had links to other data, including other written sections; videotaped interviews of key players, regulators, customers, or other related individuals;

video clips from news broadcasts; links to company Web sites; and links to SEC filings, analyst reports, and other data sources.

Oster noted that another difference with SOM cases was the ratio of "raw" to "cooked" data. Whereas a traditional case might provide a company's income statement (cooked), a SOM case might include a link to the company's entire 10-K filing (raw). The purpose was to expose students to more original source data, the kind of data they would have to seek out when they made decisions after leaving the school. Exposing students to more raw data and having them do their own research made for more demanding teaching. Oster explained:

> This kind of teaching can be a little scarier. When you rely on a traditional case, you get to know every which way you can slice the data. When a student says "I divided X by Y" you think to yourself, "Yes, and you got 2.3, and suppose you multiply it by Z? What else did you find?" The students think you are great. We all have, for every case, three or four little tricks or clever things that we know how to do, and we just trot them out every year.
>
> But when you include raw data, a student might bring in a piece of data that seems to contradict one of your main themes. Then you have to adjust on the fly. One of the things we emphasize with our students is that we want them to not just bring in a fact, but rather bring in a piece of analysis. When someone comes in with a different way to look at the data, I ask her to come up and show us what she got. We learn from each other.

Faculty Involvement

The development and implementation of the new integrated curriculum affected the faculty in a variety of ways. Most of this impact fell on senior faculty members. It was senior faculty who served on the curriculum committee that designed the overall curriculum framework, and it was senior faculty who designed and served as the lead instructors for all but one of the core courses. In fact, members of the senior faculty worked hard to minimize the involvement of junior faculty because they deemed it unfair to expect nontenured faculty to expend significant effort on school-specific activities that might not have value to them if they were not offered tenure at Yale.

Everyone involved in the curriculum redesign spoke about the large amount of time and effort it required. One faculty member observed, "This has been a ton of work." Another added, "It just about killed us." Not all senior faculty members were extensively involved, however, because the majority of the work fell to a core group of about eight professors. Much of their time was spent designing new courses and teaching them for the first time. During the second year that the new curriculum was offered, the workload decreased somewhat, but was still high because various aspects of courses were redesigned based on what did and did not work well the first time through.

On an ongoing basis, the faculty expected the workload would decrease further. Nevertheless, an integrated curriculum, they believed, would always require more work than a traditional curriculum because of the larger number of people, coordination, and perspectives involved. SOM gave double teaching credit to faculty the first time they taught one of the new courses. Faculty also received double course credit the second time they taught a course if they developed new teaching material for it.

In addition to the extra work required, the faculty found themselves working a bit differently than previously. There was considerable co-teaching, with two, and sometimes three, faculty regularly involved in each course. In addition, many times another faculty member or outside person (an alum or other business leader) would sit in on a single class. For many courses, there were two or more faculty members in the classroom almost every day. To help coordinate across the program, the Organization Perspectives faculty met each week to talk about what they were going to teach in their classes. These informal meetings were meant to keep faculty informed about what was happening in each class and to bring to light any potential conflicts or problems.

For the most part, junior faculty members were not involved in the new core curriculum. Several noted that they were not concerned about the effect the new curriculum would have on them. One junior faculty member stated, "Very few of us teach at all in the core. Those of us who do aren't doing strange new things; we're teaching standard material." When junior faculty members were involved in the core, they typically taught one class in a course on a topic in their area of expertise. This occurred most frequently in the Orientation to Management courses. Despite the curriculum change, SOM had not altered hiring or promotion standards for faculty.

The Research Agenda

The impact of the new curriculum on research at the school was less clear. Although it provided opportunities for some faculty members to pursue "integrative research," there was some question as to their interest in doing so and in their ability to get published or promoted if they did. Feinstein explained, "We are a research institution and we don't want to interfere with the ability of people, especially junior people, to pursue research. But at the same time, we are an interdisciplinary school. There's a lot of pushback on different angles around that, but for this school the strategy is that we're a great institution with a distinctive multidisciplinary openness or focus. I think scholars with that orientation are probably going to be a little happier here."

Sudhir explained that the new curriculum had broadened the horizons of his own teaching and his research. He described one research paper he had written with SOM colleague Jiwoong Shin:

> I have been interested in research on CRM [customer relationship management] for some time now. In marketing, we have traditionally looked at the demand side for CRM, and we never found a strong justification for why one might want to offer a better price to one's own customers. The logic essentially was: existing customers have revealed they like our products, so why offer them a better deal? However, as I worked with Jake Thomas, an accounting professor, on this new course [Customer], the importance of differential customer costs became more apparent to me. Because of customer-based cost accounting systems, the actual costs of serving customers are known to the firms that the customer does business with, but not to other firms. Firms can now exploit this customer information to give better deals to retain their best (least costly) customers, but competitors cannot react to this because they do not possess this information. Jiwoong and

I have a new paper where we explain the rationale for low retention prices for a firm's best customers.

Despite such examples, integrative research was not viewed as necessary for the new curriculum to work. Garstka explained:

It is difficult to get tenure if you are too broad too soon. You have to get published in narrower, more technical journals. That is why we use the senior people to teach the perspectives courses. They are the ones who have the luxury of thinking about integrative topics. Our senior people are very good at their own technical specialties, but are also entrepreneurial, broad minded, integrative thinkers. Even though they might not do integrative research, they are mature enough, have done enough consulting, and have had enough exposure to the real world to realize how things fit together.

Staff Responsibilities and Financial Implications

SOM hired approximately ten new full-time-equivalent administrators for the new curriculum. Five of these worked in the case development group, three in information technology, and three in Student and Academic Services. This latter group was responsible for curriculum coordination, organizing the leadership program, and the many activities associated with students' required international trips.

Podolny noted that the new program required extra effort from virtually every staff member at the school. Many of their job activities changed: mailroom staff delivered cases completed just hours before class, student services professionals found tutors for classes never taught before, and media relations, faculty support staff, and many others saw a significant increase in workload. Although SOM staff had risen to the occasion, the senior administration of the school worried that the prospect for burnout was real. To avoid it, the administration, in addition to hiring more staff, also stepped up internal communications and included staff in initiatives whenever possible to build a shared sense of ownership in the new curriculum.

The total cost for implementing the new curriculum was somewhere between $2 million and $5 million. These costs represented a combination of one-time charges and ongoing costs such as the salaries of additional staff. The class-size reduction from 220-plus to 180 also had significant budgetary implications. Eventually, the school planned to grow the class size as it hired new faculty and trained more of the existing faculty to deliver the new curriculum; meanwhile, each year with a smaller class translated into $4 million in foregone tuition.

Student Reactions

In the fall of 2007, SOM students showed strong support, excitement, and enthusiasm for the new curriculum. Nearly everyone in a focus group made up of ten students who had completed the first year of the curriculum spoke positively of the change and of their experience in the program. One student explained that he was excited to be a part of something new and felt better about his decision to come to SOM because the school had shown a willingness to change. Another added, "I was very excited that senior faculty would be more involved in teaching."

Students also liked the integrated nature of the curriculum and the stakeholder approach. In particular, some students mentioned how it was closer to what happened in the business world and how it gave them an edge over students from competing schools. One student stated, "Looking across functions is important. I had seen this in my work before coming to Yale." She went on to explain that many of her classmates came back from their summer internship positions talking about the multiple-stakeholder perspective they had seen on the job. Another student agreed, adding, "I did not find that my peers from other MBA schools had the same perspective."

In addition to their generally positive comments, a few students also noted that the integrated approach was not always as effective as it might be. One student in the focus group commented that integration worked better in some courses than others; another student felt that it might be more valuable in some careers than in others. A third student thought the integration should be saved for late in the first year, perhaps in a capstone course, rather than "watering down" the Organizational Perspectives courses. Students also differed on whether there was any loss of depth in the academic disciplines. One student explained that she thought that "this concern is overblown." Another agreed and added,

"In my summer job, I found my peers from other schools were not better prepared than I was." A third student, however, questioned the importance of some of the new additions to the curriculum and stated, "The trade-off is that macroeconomics is not taught in the core, and some accounting is lost."

Garstka believed that the integrated curriculum had another benefit for SOM students: it seemed to build their confidence. He stated, "I think the perspectives approach really builds confidence in the students that go through it. A lot of them, if they went through a traditional functional course, would say they understand the finance, they can do net present values, they can plug in the numbers, but they don't understand why they are doing it or what it means. They have no context. With the new curriculum, they feel a lot better about it and they come across as more confident. They also represent themselves to potential employers better than they did before."

Looking Ahead

SOM was pleased with the first eighteen months of its new curriculum. Application rates and alumni donations had increased in the two years following its announcement, and student and faculty enthusiasm remained strong. Feedback from recruiters was somewhat limited because the first class had yet to graduate; however, early feedback indicated that recruiters felt SOM students were stronger under the new curriculum. SOM noted that twenty-two students in the first class took summer internship positions in investment banking; in a first for the school, all twenty-two had received job offers by the end of the summer. A few faculty members had even begun to develop electives using the integrative approach for second-year students.

The key challenge faced by the school was sustainability. The current senior faculty could not continue their level of commitment indefinitely. Although several additional faculty began teaching the second time through, some faculty were still working very hard. Garstka stated, "It is a race against the clock. Can we bring into the core enough new people and really convince them this is the way forward? Or will we burn out the people who believe in it now?"

Podolny recognized this challenge when he prepared a draft white paper discussing the new curriculum in late 2007. He wrote:

> We are cognizant of . . . the possibility of "backsliding" into comfortable old functional disciplinary habits. Despite the interdisciplinary predispositions of the Yale SOM faculty identified earlier, like most scholars, our professors all came up in a single discipline, and, for years, taught primarily in a single discipline. As such, we have found that the somewhat instinctive tendency to revert to disciplinary affinities and approaches is still present. To fully establish and incorporate a cultural (as well as professional, social, and pedagogical) shift of the magnitude of our new multidisciplinary focus will likely take several years, and several rounds of correction and adjustment.[3]

In March 2009, as the economic crisis unfolded, we obtained an update on the Yale School of Management's view of its curriculum and courses. The key responses and initiatives included the following:

- The school reaffirmed its commitment to an integrated curriculum built around multiple stakeholders and constituencies.

- Responses to the economic crisis were incorporated into the curriculum, often utilizing Web-based "raw" cases that contained large amounts of up-to-date, unprocessed data. For example, the content of the Integrated Leadership Perspective course was adapted to include cases dealing with the subprime housing crisis, credit default swaps, and Brandeis University's Rose Art Museum.

- The Leadership Development Program intensified its focus on values, devoting several sessions to the topic.

- A proposal to introduce a course on macroeconomics into the core curriculum was under consideration.

- Existing courses placed more emphasis on the regulation of financial institutions, business and the environment, and the political economic perspective.

Stanford Graduate School of Business

Customization and Large-Scale Change

N FALL 2007, the Stanford Graduate School of Business (GSB) adopted a new curriculum that it heralded as a "revolutionary change in management education."[1] The curriculum was the school's most far-reaching change in thirty years, emphasizing customization, general management, and leadership development, and featured faculty advising and student coaching. Students entering the school's two-year MBA program would now start off not with a quarter of highly analytical core courses but with a set of integrative Management Perspectives, followed by Management Foundations—courses that focused on specific areas and were offered in three or more varieties at different levels to challenge students across the spectrum of background, skills, and abilities.

Stanford, like many other top U.S. business schools, noted that students were spending an increasing amount of time on extracurricular, job-search, and networking activities, at the expense of academics. Additionally, whereas the pre-MBA preparation of the least prepared students had remained constant, the preparation and experience of the most prepared students had increased markedly. This widened the heterogeneity of the incoming class's academic and professional background and made it harder to challenge the most experienced students without confusing the least experienced students in a one-size-fits-all class. Accordingly, students overall attributed less value to academics in the "value proposition" of their programs.

In the GSB newspaper, Dean Robert Joss reminded incoming students that "the 'S' in GSB stands for school." "We wanted to move the program in ways that would pull, not push, students back toward academics," said Senior Associate Dean David Kreps. He explained, "The new program aimed at accomplishing this pull by starting students off, in the Perspectives courses, with a better sense of how the curriculum connected to their past and anticipated work experiences; allowing students, especially the most advanced students in any subject, to begin their study at a level appropriate to their background and ambitions; increasing student-faculty interaction; and increasing the emphasis on subjects—especially leadership and global management—of particular relevance and appeal to students."

The world was also changing. GSB alumni noted the rapid pace of globalization and the increasing challenge of leaders to work with multiple constituencies and lead diverse workforces. Besides increasing student engagement in academics, the new curriculum aimed to increase the preparedness of GSB graduates to work in businesses and organizations throughout the world and to provide more experiential leadership learning.

Background on the Institution and Its MBA Program

In 1924, at the request of Herbert Hoover, a group of business leaders gathered at the Bohemian Grove, an executive retreat north of San Francisco, to discuss the creation of a graduate business school on the West Coast. Hoover, a Stanford alumnus, trustee, and future U.S. president, wanted to counter the outflow of business talent from the west as promising local students headed east to go to business schools. He enlisted 125 West Coast business leaders to fund the school, and in the fall of 1925 the Stanford Graduate School of Business was launched, with sixteen students enrolled in a two-year MBA program.[2]

Over its first three decades, the school built a reputation as a strong regional presence. Then, in 1958, Stanford President Wallace Sterling and Provost Fred Terman, who were determined to build Stanford into a world-class university, appointed businessman Ernie Arbuckle as the third dean of the school, with a charge to make GSB into "the best business school in the world." Arbuckle raided the faculties of a number of leading business schools, and GSB moved quickly into the ranks of the leading business schools. Successive deans continued to improve the school. In excellent academic and financial shape, GSB celebrated its seventy-fifth anniversary in 2000 under the newly installed dean Robert Joss, who looked for new initiatives and directions, including building much stronger ties with the broader Stanford community.

Students

In the 2007–2008 academic year, GSB's first- and second-year MBA enrollment totaled 740 students (38 percent were women, 24 percent minorities, and 34 percent international students). Only 21 percent of the 379 anticipated 2008 graduates had majored in business as undergraduates; 43 percent had majored in the humanities or social sciences, and 36 percent majored in math, the natural sciences, or engineering. The median work experience was four years. Upon graduation from the MBA program, members of the class of 2007 earned a median base salary of $115,500.[3] Some 37 percent of 2007 graduates took jobs in the financial services and investment sector, 29 percent in consulting, and 12 percent in high-tech companies.[4]

Faculty, Research, and Teaching

In 2007–2008, the school had ninety-one tenure-line faculty members, of whom 73 percent were tenured, and 43 percent had origins outside the United States. (Among assistant professors, the percentage of foreign-born faculty was 64 percent.) The school also employed about fifty adjunct faculty members, five of whom worked full time. The faculty was not organized by formal departments or units; instead, each tenure-line faculty member was attached to an academic "area."

However, some belonged to more than one; movement across areas was not uncommon, and important management fields such as Strategic Management, Global Management, Entrepreneurship, and Human Resource Management were served by faculty members from a number of academic areas. Stanford's MBA program had a seven-to-one student-to-faculty ratio that the school believed offered students early exposure to the latest faculty research.

The school claimed to put equal weight on teaching and research in its activities, beginning with its mission statement, "To create ideas that deepen and advance our understanding of management and with those ideas to develop innovative, principled, and insightful leaders who change the world." The faculty (including emeriti) had three Nobel laureates, three members of the National Academy of Sciences, fifteen members of the American Academy of Arts and Sciences, and two recipients of the John Bates Clark Medal in Economics.

GSB believed that no single teaching approach satisfied the needs of students or the challenges they would face in the complex business world. Consequently, instruction included participation in case studies, theoretical overviews, discussions, simulations, problem-solving sessions, role plays, and team projects.

Four centers supported the faculty's research and curriculum development and helped organize speaker programs, workshops, conferences, and clubs to further career opportunities for MBAs. The first, launched in 1996, was the Center for Entrepreneurial Studies (CES), which explored issues related to entrepreneurship for both companies and individuals. CES supported research, MBA course development, and programs for students such as internships, panels, and speakers. The Center for Social Innovation, a crossroads of business and social innovation, was established in 2000 to strengthen the capacity of individuals to address social problems. The Center for Leadership Development and Research, established in 2003, spearheaded advanced scholarship in organizational leadership, in the belief that leadership was something acquired and mastered through experience. In 2004, GSB launched the Center for Global Business and the Economy to develop and disseminate curriculum materials, research, and conceptual frameworks on global issues.

TABLE 12-1

The 2006–2007 first-year curriculum prior to the curriculum review

Autumn: Working in Groups and Teams, Microeconomics, Financial Accounting,
           Statistics, Organizational Behavior, Modeling

Winter: Finance, Marketing, Operations, Strategy

Spring: Managerial Accounting, Human Resources, Information Management,
           Non-Market Strategy (including Ethics), Organizational Design

Source: Stanford Graduate School of Business documents.

The Old Curriculum and Factors for Change

Prior to the 2007 curricular reform, students began their GSB program
with a set of "tools" courses. (Table 12-1 lists the specific courses.) Students could place out of up to nine core classes with passing grades on
placement tests. Students who did not take or prepare for the placement
tests sometimes wound up in classes below their background or ability.
The old curriculum offered accelerated classes, but many students
found it challenging to gauge accurately the appropriate level of difficulty for them. Kreps estimated that 5 to 10 percent of students were
misplaced, either because they lacked the information needed to make
these choices or because they did not realize that, with a little review,
they could place out of basic courses. When placed in a class below their
level of preparation, students would either turn off from academics or, in
some cases, side-track discussions with advanced questions that flew
over the heads of students who were struggling in the class. A larger problem was that students did not always understand why they were taking
these courses. Dean Joss used to call it "the 'trust me' core:" students
would ask, "Why am I taking all this? I want to be a general manager," to
which instructors would often say, "Trust me. You'll see why in later
quarters." Professor Garth Saloner related that when teaching Strategic Management in the winter he would hear from students that now,
finally, they understood the point of learning microeconomics in the fall.

   Joss articulated four main problems with the old curriculum:

> First, it did not address student diversity in terms of background
> and knowledge base. Second, the best-prepared MBA students

were not intellectually engaged; one-third of students said that their undergraduate degree was more intellectually challenging. Third, we were not addressing their global future well enough. We needed to do more to address multicultural and multinational issues. Fourth, while we were strong on the analytics, we were not helping our students move from knowing to doing.

"Too many graduates told us: 'You could have pushed us harder,'" Joss added. "That's a lost opportunity."[5] According to Kreps, a perceived lack of student engagement had become an area of great concern among GSB administration by the mid-2000s: "In our business model, over 50 percent of our annual budget is met by alumni in the form of endowment income and annual giving. And our model for faculty development depends on students and faculty engaging one another in the MBA classroom. So it is imperative that students leave here satisfied and believing that the school added value to their lives, and it is imperative that they engage faculty members and vice versa."

"Revolutionary Change"

In these challenges, GSB saw an opportunity to respond to changes in the student population's needs, changes that were driven by a shift in the level of preparedness of incoming students, increasing diversity in the student body, and demands for different skills. "Those of us who started MBAs in the late 1980s and early 1990s had prior jobs in which there was a fair bit of manual work, for example, culling annual reports at consulting firms," MBA Program Associate Director Lisa Schwallie (GSB '92) explained. "But now with information being so available, people have a richer and fuller understanding of business and have had more responsibility by the start of their MBAs."

At the same time, business schools had been diversifying their student population. Schwallie added, "The gap between the most prepared and the least prepared was getting larger, and it was becoming hard, by hitting the median, to serve the tails, especially the upper tail. To be one of the best business schools in the world we need to challenge the best students in the world." She continued, "We felt the need to do something not because anything was wrong but because we saw a gap in business education. There had been discussions for years about 'what was' and 'what could be.' At an October 2005 faculty meeting we asked: 'What are we hearing and feeling about business education and our program out there?' Coming out of that meeting we felt that people were open to reassessing."

The Saloner Committee

At this juncture, Saloner was asked to lead a committee to review the state of the MBA program and recommend a set of reforms. He requested the right to bring any final proposal to the faculty for an up-or-down vote. The resulting eleven-person committee represented the school's various faculty areas and included tenured faculty members, two adjunct faculty members, and two alumni; Schwallie headed up staff support. "Most members of the committee were relatively young," Joss noted, "so they were the future of the school." The committee devoted four months to intense study and extensive interviews with faculty as well as hundreds of students and alumni from around the world. Saloner himself spoke to 10 percent of the students in the classes of 2006 and 2007, most of them at private dinners at his house; the committee as a whole met with around one-third of all students.

The group went right back to basics. Saloner recalled: "We said, 'If we were to develop an MBA curriculum from scratch, what would it look like?' At the same time, we knew that we had to build on what we had." The faculty members and alumni discussing curriculum changes considered various options in terms of design and incentives. Some were in favor of grade disclosure and tighter graduation standards. But the committee ultimately chose to use the carrot, Saloner said, not "the whip and chains" approach. Stanford opted to leave grade disclosure up to the students. "In the end, we decided that in order to change student behavior we had to show that we are willing to change ourselves," Joss recalled. "The thought was: let's not change the culture," one professor said, "but give students more challenging things to grapple with."

After four months of investigation and deliberation, the committee recommended a curriculum overhaul with several new features. The new program would begin with a set of "management perspectives" courses, including one focused on the global context, followed by a set of customizable core courses in eleven "management foundation areas." Each of the eleven areas would offer at least three choices, one of which—called the "advanced-applications" option—would "severely challenge" the upper 20 percent or so of the class in terms of preparation. Many areas chose to offer three levels of course; a few areas chose to differentiate based on topic. (See table 12-2 for an overview of the first year and the final capstone seminar.)

The new curriculum would radically change the flow of the MBA program: whereas the old curriculum started with disciplines, then moved to functions, before ending with integration, the new curriculum started with perspectives and then moved to disciplines before focusing on functions. Over the course of the committee's work, Schwallie said, "there was a bit of debate around what specifically should be perspectives and what should be foundations, what could be postponed or not, etc., but the major ideas remained the same." In the second quarter, the new curriculum offered students the option of taking core courses in three different variations in the hope of better fitting their individual level and interest. Other features included the addition of a Critical Analytical Thinking course (described in detail in chapter 6), a build-out of Stanford's prior leadership development program featuring extensive coaching and experiential learning, faculty advising to help students design their MBA plan of study, and a second-year capstone course.

Although the fundamentals—finance, accounting, operations, marketing, strategy, organizational behavior, and economics—were still there, the proposed curriculum capitalized on the school's strategic choice to remain small and encouraged students to think about what was necessary for good management from the first week on campus.[6] "These new ideas do not tweak at the margins; they aim to create a new, more global, and more engaging experience for students," said Saloner.[7] A central goal was to make the transition from work to school more appealing. "Garth recognized that the MBAs had come here to learn business, but in the first quarter they were getting lots of math," Professor Jeffrey Pfeffer explained. "So he said, 'Let's give the MBAs the stuff they came here for at the start, and then later show how the analytical foundations help them address the business problems.' The idea is to give them interesting problems and show their relevance."

TABLE 12-2

The class of 2009 required curriculum

Management Perspectives

First year, Autumn

- Accounting Information
- Critical Analytical Thinking
- Global Context of Management
- Managerial Finance
- Managing Groups & Teams
- Organizational Behavior
- Strategic Leadership (including Strategic Insight, Strategic Implementation, and Leadership and Personal Skills, and Leadership Management Skills)

First year, Winter

- Ethics in Management

Second year, Spring (Capstone Perspectives Course)

- Synthesis Seminar

Management Foundations[a]

First year, Winter/Spring

- Data Analysis & Decision Making
- Finance
- Financial Accounting
- Human Resources
- Information Technology
- Managerial Accounting
- Marketing
- Microeconomics
- Modeling for Optimization & Decision Support (MODS)
- Non-Market Strategy
- Operations

Source: Stanford Graduate School of Business, "Stanford MBA Program: Curriculum First Year," http://www.gsb.stanford.edu/mba/academics/curriculum_year1.html.

a. Some Foundations options could be delayed into the second year.

Making It Happen

On May 17, 2006, Saloner presented his committee's findings and proposals to GSB faculty. No advance materials had been circulated, but there had been intense discussions beforehand within the offices and corridors of Littlefield, the main faculty building, as committee members had shared news of the committee's work and outcomes with colleagues. Following two hours of presentation and one hour of discussion, approximately 85 percent of the faculty approved the changes. "The proposal passed because everyone was unhappy with the existing situation," Pfeffer concluded.

"After the faculty had voted and we walked out of the meeting, a couple of us stared at each other and said 'Whoa,'" Schwallie recalled. "It was then that the scale of the implementation really hit us." A small group of senior administrators and members of the Saloner Committee immediately started working on a to-do list. Joss set up and chaired an oversight committee to guide the implementation. He also tasked a high-level implementation committee, also staffed by Schwallie, to manage and execute the implementation, reporting to the oversight committee.

Getting the vision implemented, Professer Sunil Kumar explained, meant extensive debates on resource allocation and managing the demand on faculty time imposed by some of the new perspective courses. It also meant creating some slack in the curriculum to make sure that students could be placed at the right levels. "We also had to make sure that we would not lapse back into the old core courses," Kumar said. "Because we were no longer using mandatory common courses, we wanted a clear distinction with advanced-applications courses, designed not just to challenge on quantitative skills but also to take the application of these skills seriously."

The New Educational Model

The Stanford MBA program's new educational model was built on four key elements: (1) a highly customized program facilitated by faculty advising; (2) a deeper, more engaging intellectual experience; (3) a more global curriculum; and (4) expanded leadership and communication development.[8] The new curriculum was more personalized than in the past. After a common "perspectives" program in the first quarter, students had no specific required courses, but rather a set of distribution or "foundations" requirements "that give them the breadth of knowledge a general manager requires."[9] The distribution requirements gave students the flexibility to pursue their own interests and also pushed them to think "across disciplines and functions." They varied "by pace, depth, and assumed knowledge to challenge every student regardless of past experience."[10] With their career goals in mind, students could tailor their course choices to reflect their particular interests and potential future business needs. Entrance exemptions, however, were no longer possible.

To give students the time to focus on the perspectives courses and settle in, the administration decreed an "Exclusive Academic Period" for the first six weeks of the quarter. Until the end of their midterms in week 6, in early November, students were not to participate in job-search activities, nor were they to engage in any club or service activities that required them to make future commitments.

The First Quarter: Management Perspectives

The first quarter of the new program was a (largely) lock-step program, intended to provide students with basic management perspectives and personal skills. The quarter was expanded to last eleven weeks (ten weeks is the normal length of a Stanford quarter), and comprised seven courses:

- Managing Groups and Teams

- Accounting Information

- Organizational Behavior

- Managerial Finance

- The Global Context of Management

- Strategic Leadership

- Critical Analytical Thinking (CAT)

During this first quarter, students also formed an advising relationship with a senior member of the faculty, their CAT instructor, who provided the necessary support and depth of knowledge to help students customize their study plans to satisfy the foundations requirements over the remainder of their first year.

Managing Groups and Teams. This course was largely unchanged from the former core curriculum, introducing students to the structures and processes that affected group performance and highlighting some of the common pitfalls associated with working in teams. Topics included team culture, fostering creativity and coordination, making group decisions, and dealing with a variety of personalities. The course also featured a number of group exercises to illustrate principles of teamwork and give students practice not only in diagnosing team problems but also in taking action to improve total team performance. The course was taught the first week of the program for five days in a row, Monday through Friday, in three-hour sessions.

Accounting Information. This very short course, lasting four sessions, covered basic concepts and forms of accounting information. Topics included the structure of financial statements, including balance sheets and income statements; the accrual basis of accounting; the role of accounting numbers in providing information to investors and managers; and the distinction between economic and accounting profitability. "The intent of the course was to bridge the gap between the bookkeeping skills the students acquired via the online assessment tests in the summer, and the needs of the Managerial Finance and Strategy courses in the fall quarter," Professor Madhav Rajan explained. The course provided students with a conceptual understanding of the structure of accounting reports and the manner in which they interacted. The course also provided perspective on the different constituents who used accounting information, and the trade-offs this induced in the content and level of detail of accounting disclosures.

Organizational Behavior. This course, lasting five weeks (meeting twice a week for ninety minutes a session), was also unchanged from the previous core curriculum. Building on the discipline of social psychology, it analyzed the ways in which organizations and their members affected one another, reviewing concepts such as individual motivation and behavior; decision making; interpersonal communication and influence; small-group behavior; and dyadic, individual, and intergroup conflict and cooperation.

Managerial Finance. In choosing courses for the first quarter, the Saloner Committee looked for those in which diverse student backgrounds would be less of an impediment and in which a diversity of experiences would be most important in terms of discussion. This led them to push back most of the more quantitative courses into the foundations requirements. However, the committee included a finance course in the fall for several reasons: financial-market valuation was central to management objectives in for-profit firms, and the committee wished to include at least one quantitative course in the first quarter. In the old program, a required finance course stressed principles of market valuation; most students elected to follow this up with an elective in corporate finance. This new course, coming in the first quarter, was meant to cover the basics, which spawned debate over whether corporate finance or capital markets constituted the basics. The course that emerged trained students to apply the fundamental ideas of financial economics to problems in corporate finance. It provided an overview of valuation and how financial decisions, capital structure, dividend policy, and investments could affect valuation, and helped students learn basic principles of corporate finance from the perspective of a financial manager. Students were also called upon to analyze many of the important financial decisions made within firms and other institutions.

The Global Context of Management. This brand-new course aimed to promote a strong understanding of global management. The course centered on the political, economic, financial, and cultural drivers of the global marketplace. It developed students' understanding of both the global and individual markets that composed the world economy. By focusing on markets, the course provided students with general and specialized knowledge to help them ask necessary questions and take appropriate actions when entering a new market. The course opened with a series of lecture-style classes for the entire incoming class and then broke up into sections of about sixty students; some small-team projects, such as a report on various countries, were also part of the design.

Beyond the course, the school claimed to have committed itself to the continual globalization of its cases and course materials. GSB also committed to facilitating an international studies or internship program for all students in their first year.[11] The Global Experience Requirement (GER), consisting of an international internship, an international service-learning project, or a study trip, was required of each student prior to the start of the second year. This experience had to occur in a country in which the student had not lived or worked before. "The alumni really support this," Kreps noted, "and faculty members enjoy participating in such activities." "Everyone had also been saying that the business world is getting more global. We wanted to create more global awareness and real understanding," Schwallie added. "But we are also attached to the integrity of our experience, so we did not want to break up the class with semesters abroad."

GSB's commitment to exposing its students to an international experience was not new. Since 1997 it had supported the Global Management Immersion Experience (GMIX), encouraging MBA students to gain international work experience by spending part of their summer in corporate, government, or NGO-sponsored internships in areas of the world that were new to them. Since its beginnings in China, GMIX had expanded to include internships in forty-one countries in Asia, Africa, Australia, Europe, Latin America, and the South Pacific. A typical GMIX was structured as a supplement to a student's summer internship. Students usually spent eight to ten weeks with a summer employer and then at least four weeks working on a GMIX internship. Following that internship, students shared their experiences with the GSB community and had the option of completing a research paper on an international business topic related to their internship for two academic credits. In 2007, prior to the rollout of the GER, the GSB supported one hundred GMIX internships.

Strategic Leadership. This course integrated "strategy with leadership development and implementation."[12] Pfeffer explained the philosophy behind the course: "To solve the knowing-doing gap, you need to know the substance of subjects like accounting, but the knowledge alone is not enough. One goal behind Stanford's changes was to build some ways of integrating and applying knowledge. We want to build additional skills, such as leadership, and make them stick through practice. That was a big motivation for the curricular changes. The question is, 'How do we give tools, concepts, *and* practice?'" Strategic Leadership was designed as a partial answer to that question.

Whereas the standard full-quarter course at Stanford met twice a week for approximately ten weeks, Strategic Leadership met three times a week and had four parts, each led by a different faculty member or lecturer: Strategic Insight, Strategic Execution, Leadership Interpersonal Skills, and Leadership Management Skills. Strategic Insight met (on average) once a week in sections of about sixty students and explored the basic concepts of strategic management. Strategic Execution, which also met once a week in sections, was concerned with the implementation of strategy and, in particular, the role of leadership in implementation. Leadership Management Skills, which met a total of four times in sections toward the end of the quarter, focused on a number of common managerial challenges faced by executives in leadership positions. These sessions, culled from the elective course Managing Growing Enterprises, the most popular and sought-after elective at the school, were taught by distinguished practitioners who were members of GSB's adjunct faculty. These segments of the course were fairly traditional, involving (primarily) case studies driven by conceptual readings, although Strategic Execution also used short videos of managers discussing leadership crises that they had faced, and Leadership Management Skills frequently asked students to role-play important conversations between management and other key individuals.

Leadership Interpersonal Skills, which met once a week for the first six weeks of the quarter, in three-hour sessions, was conceived of as a "laboratory" for skills development. The sessions were designed and run by Evelyn Williams, based on a similar program she had run previously at the University of Chicago, in collaboration with other faculty members. Williams noted:

> Leadership Interpersonal Skills are a part of the conceptual Strategic Leadership course. You can take a chemistry class with a lecture, but then you go to the lab to work on the practical application. We are trying to blend those two learning experiences

from a business context. Many tend to think of leadership as a black-and-white entity, either you have it or you don't, but it is very much like playing music. Some are better at some music than others. Some play jazz and others play classical, for example, but even virtuosos have to practice. In Leadership Interpersonal Skills, we are helping students practice that "leadership" music, to improve their insight acquisition skills and their behavioral analysis skills and to create a culture where feedback is thought of as a gift, so they get comfortable with diagnosing, managing, reflecting, and applying new behavior.

Leadership Interpersonal Skills offered coaching and provided selected second-year MBAs with the opportunity to act as Leadership Fellows, coaching first-year students. In fall 2007, Williams and a staff of executive coaches coordinated thirty-two such fellows who had received training the previous spring.

The Wednesday-morning lab sessions usually started with twenty minutes in sections, with students then breaking up into "squads" of six to eight people (two squads formed a CAT group—see the next section) to work on the various simulations staffed by trained protagonists, some of whom were executive alumni. Typically, protagonists were given a set of information that the interlocutor was supposed to tease out, and in doing so, drive the conversation to a better outcome. Over the course of the quarter, students experienced twelve simulations, which concluded with post-mortem discussions and feedback.

Besides the Wednesday-morning lab sessions, squads met weekly with their fellows for further reflection and discussion of what they had learned in the course. The labs also made use of a number of personal assessment tools: A 360-degree tool was completed by students prior to coming to campus and would be redone at the end of their summer internship experience, as well as several years after graduation. Students also completed the Myers-Briggs Personality Inventory and the Thomas-Killman Conflict Mode Instrument to identify their preferred conflict resolution style. "These tools allow us to talk about behaviors that are important to executive action, such as listening and conflict management, among many others," Williams explained.

The climax of the Strategic Leadership course came in December, when the entire first-year class engaged in a daylong "Executive Challenge" simulation with alumni "board members." About 160 senior alumni attended and participated in the session.

Critical Analytical Thinking. To foster a more profound "intellectual exploration of both broad and narrow subjects" throughout their two-year course of study, students were required to take a nine-session CAT course.[13] "Students are taught to think and argue about . . . issues clearly, concisely, and analytically," school materials explained, "setting the tone for the rest of the program."[14] The CAT course was designed to help students think about causal inference, ask the right questions, be more critical, assess the logic behind an argument, and uncover their assumptions. Taught in a seminar format that comprised fourteen to sixteen students, CAT sessions addressed a multitude of business, social, and ethical issues and involved the weekly submission of a three-page essay every Wednesday at 11 p.m. CAT classes met on Fridays. (Chapter 6 discusses the CAT course pedagogy in more detail.)

In the CAT seminar, students were often called upon to present and defend their arguments. "Under the old curriculum," Kumar noted, "Stanford students were not particularly trained or used to arguing with each other and taking on each other's ideas while being entirely objective. This cooperative ethic, which is a good thing, led them to be perceived by some potential employers as not intellectually aggressive enough. CAT is supposed to help with this." CAT was also designed to train students to cut through "a world of jargon and bombast, in which the medium is mistaken for the message. This is hard in the business world. So teaching students to distinguish between a slogan supported by an anecdote and a thoughtful idea supported by solid evidence was seen as important," a faculty member explained. Each student was assigned a writing coach, who reviewed all essays, provided writing advice, and graded the papers on style. CAT instructors also graded papers for logic and argumentation. GSB had recruited a team of twelve writing coaches from a pool of over fifty applicants. Many writing coaches had journalism or English studies backgrounds. To measure the success of the CAT course, Joss planned to rely on the quality of student papers, the quality of the faculty advising, and, "as a real measure, the extent of intellectual engagement of the students in all classes over the two years."

The challenges of implementing this course revolved around finding topics amenable to all twelve instructors, whose disciplinary interests ranged from economic theorists to social psychologists to applied statisticians, and whose contextual interests ranged from human resource management to not-for-profit management to operations to entrepreneurship to e-commerce. In the actual delivery, instructors found that students needed more structure and guidance than was initially provided.

Advising. In fall 2007, twelve senior faculty members each taught two sections of CAT, serving also as academic advisors to students in their two sections. (In some of the sections, the senior faculty member was joined by an adjunct faculty member.) To help faculty members advise students in the design of their second and third quarters, the MBA program office devised an algorithm that took into consideration a student's background, experience, interests, and test scores to make nonbinding recommendations for their course of study. Students were receptive to such input, a faculty member observed: "I ask students 'Tell me what you want.' Some don't want to strain themselves but will change after pushback. Some really want to take hard classes and you talk that through. Most of my pushback has been up. About twenty of my advisees are no problem, and for about five I need to say that I am not signing off on their wishes."

The Second and Third Quarters: Management Foundations

Having completed "perspectives" in the fall quarter of their first year, students moved on to a more tailored set of "management foundations."[15] In each of eleven subject areas, students were required to take one course from a menu of at least three courses. A small number of these subjects could be delayed until the second year, but most had to be completed by the end of the first year. The "required" workload, meaning the combination of lock-step perspectives courses and the menu options of the foundations, increased from forty-nine units in the old curriculum to sixty-three in the new, both out of a total of one hundred. (The fourteen additional units were as follows: four more units of finance, four units of CAT, four units of Global Perspectives, one more unit of ethics, two more units in a capstone Synthesis Seminar, and one fewer unit of modeling.)

Most of the eleven subject areas offered options that were differentiated by three levels. The base-level course was, typically, the former core course. An accelerated version of the base-level course was offered for students with a reasonably strong background in the field; it covered the basic material more quickly before addressing more advanced topics. Those students with very strong backgrounds in the subject matter took an advanced-applications option, which jumped right into application of the core principles. For example, in microeconomics, about 60 percent of the students were expected to take the base-level course, 25 percent the accelerated course, and perhaps 15 percent a course that applied microeconomics to the analysis of organizations. (A second section of the advanced-applications option was offered to second-year students as an elective.)

In some of the eleven subject areas, the options were organized by topics or pedagogical technique. For instance, in the area of marketing, about 55 percent of the students (those with little or no formal knowledge of marketing) took the base-level course, which was the former core course. Another 25 percent (those with some formal knowledge of marketing) chose a base-level course that, for example, emphasized business-to-business marketing and used marketing simulation exercises extensively. A further 20 percent elected the advanced-applications option. The faculty members in each subject area devised the menu of three or more courses that they offered (finance, modeling, and information technology offered four options), subject to approval by the oversight committee. The only fixed requirement was that each subject area had to offer an advanced-applications option.

For 2007–2008, there was only one advanced-applications course per subject, but faculty aimed to expand the number of advanced offerings over time. About 20 percent of the courses did not exist during the previous five years; 80 percent were repackaged or unchanged.

To avoid any gaming by students hoping to get a better grade by enrolling in a basic course when they had the ability for an accelerated or advanced-applications course, the recommended grading curve for sections of these courses was modified to provide a greater number of higher grades. Even so, faculty advisors reported that some students were reluctant to challenge themselves, and a bit of pushing was necessary. But when student preferences were matched to seats in each foundations option, demand generally matched supply. In most cases where there was an imbalance, it involved excess demand for the advanced-applications option.

That said, as the first quarter ended relatively successfully, the administration and faculty were holding their breath about student reactions to the winter quarter. "It gets very quantitative and foundational all of a sudden. But with more perspective given up front," Kreps stated, "we hope that students will understand why they need to learn subjects such as data analysis and microeconomics. And while students have less opportunity to take absolutely unconstrained electives, we hope that the psychological impact of being able to select foundations options will give students the feeling that they have more control over their fate. There is no question, we think, that they will be better matched to the level and pace of the courses they take."

The Second Year: Deep and Tailored

Although most students completed most of their foundations requirements in the winter and spring of year one, many delayed one or more of their foundations courses for their second year. The second year for the majority of students consisted of a free selection of electives.[16] GSB offered over one hundred electives, half of which were new or substantially revised every five years. Two types of electives had somewhat novel pedagogical forms:

- Intensive courses met for three hours every day in a week or for one and a half hours every day in two consecutive weeks. GSB had offered these courses for several years, in the week prior to the start of the regular fall quarter; the new program called for afternoons in the fall quarter to be devoted exclusively to these courses. In a few cases, existing electives such as negotiations and interpersonal dynamics were adapted to this format. In most cases, however, faculty members used the novel format to try out ideas for new courses or to teach courses that introduced students to cutting-edge research. Faculty gave students research papers to read and shared with them the latest insights in a particular area of study. "This is a bit like a PhD class for MBA students. MBA students are very excited and interested in faculty research; faculty love it," Rajan remarked. Past topics included "Trading Strategies Using Accounting Information," "Valuation in Emerging Economies," "Bioterrorism," and "Ethics and Cheating." The school also hoped to use the intensive format of these courses to bring to the classroom interesting visitors, both academic and practitioner.

- Bass seminars were full-quarter courses, with enrollments typically limited to fifteen to thirty students, in which students, with faculty advice and guidance, were principally responsible for the curriculum. The seminars typically started with two to three weeks of lectures by a faculty member, after which students researched (usually in teams) specific topics and organizations of their own choosing. The seminars reconvened late in the term to discuss students' findings in the classic graduate-seminar format. "The objective is for students to learn how to generate intellectual property of their own," Rajan explained. A recent Bass seminar had examined West Papua, Indonesia and its development challenge from the perspective of British Petroleum. Another, "Managing Talent," examined human resource management in organizations in which highly talented and mobile employees were the key to success; students studied in teams the practices of particular organizations that they had selected, bringing their findings back to the class. For 2007–2008, ten Bass seminars were slated to be offered.

These two innovations, quite different in form, shared two fundamental objectives: to increase student engagement in academics and to build stronger ties between students and faculty members. So far, they seemed to be working: "Both students and faculty members say that these courses are among the most enjoyable and engaging classroom experiences they have had," reported Kreps.

MBA students were also able to take up to twelve of the one hundred units required for graduation at courses offered by other schools in the university. Particularly popular were courses offered by Stanford's Schools of Engineering and Education. Courses in environmental studies, offered by the School of Earth Sciences, were developing a following as well. In general, cross-listed electives that mixed students from different schools were on the increase, as were joint-degree programs in which students earned another degree with the MBA.

Near the end of their two years of study, students rejoined their original Leadership Squads and CAT groups for a "Synthesis Seminar" in which they reviewed what they had learned, examined strengths and weaknesses in their personal leadership style, and reflected on how they hoped to achieve their goals as they embarked on their careers.[17]

Synthesis Seminar. The Synthesis Seminar was divided into two distinct parts:

- The General Management Synthesis (weeks 2–6) component consisted of three challenges, each of which simulated corporate executive meetings. With GSB alumni acting as board members and judges, each group of students was tasked with examining a company at critical stages of its development and recommending courses of action. As distinct from cases, which assigned specific questions, these challenges forced students to analyze problems and issues based on raw, partial, and sometimes conflicting information.

- The Professional and Personal Development (weeks 6–9) component provided students with the opportunity to reflect on the values that would guide their personal and professional lives, and to plan for lifelong development and learning. In their original CAT groups, students worked with mentors—often GSB alumni—to consider three important life and career themes: Fulfillment and Meaning, Failure and Resilience, and Transitions and Renewal.

Living Up to the Potential

The new curriculum required adjustments in staffing and facilities, as well as in students' expectations. It also raised a number of questions for the future.

Faculty and Staffing

The dean's office envisioned several major benefits to the new curriculum, including a boost to faculty morale as a result of greater intellectual engagement with their teaching. Kreps noted that "the faculty is really excited about teaching some of the new courses. I've personally seen this in particular in the Critical Analytical Thinking course. I have not seen my colleagues as excited about or engaged in teaching in twenty years."

Although the teaching load would still be three courses a year per professor, the new curriculum was very faculty intensive. Schwallie noted, "A main question concerns sustainability and staffing. Can we sustain this level of faculty energy and intensity?" CAT was particularly time-intensive as a relatively unstructured cross-disciplinary course. "Making this happen in the first place would have been difficult if strong faculty members early on did not say 'Hey, I would be interested in this.' This remains something to keep an eye on going forward, but it is something to which we are very committed," Schwallie added.

To sustain this new model, faculty ranks would have to be increased 10 to 15 percent. In 2007–2008, only two faculty members had been able to take sabbaticals, compared with the usual fourteen or fifteen. Some senior faculty were concerned that the prospect of greater faculty involvement with students would discourage the most research-driven young faculty from joining Stanford GSB. Another concern was that, with fewer "commodity" courses, the time required of faculty for class preparation would increase. Others countered that newer faculty members would be teaching more tailored sections and that the less broad a course, the easier it became to teach, thereby freeing up time for research. New faculty members would continue to be encouraged to teach in foundations menu courses.

Kreps thought that increased academic engagement was key: "Teaching can be fun *and* can contribute to research, if students are engaged. If, and it is a big if, this program enhances student engagement in academics, all segments of the faculty will be winners." Kumar saw other benefits for the faculty as a whole: "We are highly decentralized, and the academic freedom of the instructor is the foundation of any university department. We care deeply about that here at Stanford. So having the perspective courses encourage some amount of integration among faculty members from different areas is great in my opinion."

New Learning Spaces

To support the style of learning promoted by the new curriculum, GSB was planning a set of new buildings to create a new campus. "[A] new campus is essential to enabling our new MBA curriculum and our academic vision for the future," Joss explained. "More multidisciplinary classes that bring engineering, medical, law, education, and business students together to share in creating a project will require flexible classrooms with movable seats where teamwork can take place." The school's amphitheater-style classrooms were not conducive to small class sizes and the intimate learning environment the new curriculum fostered. Further, its emphasis on teamwork required new spatial designs. The old campus had five single-level classrooms with movable chairs, but the new curriculum required fourteen more. The new buildings would have more seminar rooms (expanding the total set from five to nineteen) and fewer tiered classrooms (down from sixteen to ten).

The school also needed to expand its number of study rooms to accommodate group work and leadership coaching. The new campus would offer forty-eight such rooms. A new six-hundred-person auditorium would also be built, large enough to hold an entire MBA class with room to spare. The new facilities, located across the street from the Schwab Residential Center for MBAs and executives, would reflect the flexibility and innovation that characterized the new curriculum. The flexibility worked into the design provided room for adaptation and change as the curriculum and teaching methodologies evolved over time. The campus would also be a leader in green technology.

Student Expectations

The new curriculum offered students a richer understanding of the relationship between deep, functional knowledge and cross-functional, integrated managerial problems. Yet starting with perspectives posed potential challenges. "At worst, a perspective class will be a worship of superficiality," said a faculty member. "Or, if it is too thorough and excellent, students starting foundations might ask 'Why should I learn the details?' But if perspective is right it should be 'I feel unfulfilled but I need to learn more'—guaranteed to pique interest."

In addition, faculty and administrators fretted that the contrast between the faculty teaching the perspective courses and those teaching foundations might be stark. "We hire people out of their disciplines, like other business schools," a faculty member explained, "and they have little or no work experience, yet will be teaching students in larger sections who have been meeting great guest speakers and have all these great ideas. It is going to be quite a transition." "We will have to help functional faculty link into perspectives, and we need to link tenured faculty with what others are teaching," Joss said. "The new curriculum can be seen as an attempt to force interdependence that has previously been lacking," Professor Charles O'Reilly explained. "However, the change is not as big as some might think since many of the core courses are still the same, just with different varieties." It also remained to be seen whether or not faculty advisors had received enough training, were sufficiently engaged to meet students' expectations, and could place students at the right course levels.

The key challenge was whether the required depth of functional knowledge could be achieved while simultaneously reaching the desired level of integration. Students in the MBA class of 2009 were in the process of discovering the answer to this question. Although they were very impressed with faculty commitment to the new curriculum, some questioned the purpose of parts of the program. "We really are the guinea pigs for this new curriculum," a student explained, "and some of the rationale for the changes was not made clear to us."

"With the new curriculum you cannot hide, especially with advisors on an individual level," Pfeffer noted. "Students cannot complain that they already know the material or think they know it because of the customization. The new curriculum is a good step toward solving this fundamental issue of student engagement." Students reported long hours. "Students are a bit overwhelmed by the reading," Joss explained. "In the first quarter some students used to drown but some thought it was easy. Now all have long workweeks, and everyone might be drowning sometimes."

Looking Ahead

To evaluate how well the new curriculum was serving its various stakeholders, Stanford's leadership planned to use a mix of hard and soft measures. Schwallie explained:

> Because we survey students often in both large surveys and smaller groups, we will be getting a lot of feedback. We'll look closely at what they say about the value of their education. The faculty's response will also be important to monitor—do they think the curriculum is giving appropriate emphasis to issues, and that students are learning the requisite concepts? Will they remain committed to delivering the curriculum, with all its intensity? Another important metric will be faculty-student relationships: are both groups having fun and do they agree on what they are having fun about? Are they finding the interaction positive? We will also ask recruiters if our graduates are well prepared for their jobs, more global, and so forth.

"So far our alumni are reacting well, and these are the people who are hiring our students," Kreps said. "But it is too early to see what our graduates will be like in five years." "The concept, I think, is excellent," an alumnus told the press. "That's exactly what's going on on the Web with a much more customized and bite-sized approach to content. Everyone's trying to deliver the right content to the right person at the right time."[18] "If we're successful, I really do think this is something other schools will emulate," said Saloner.[19] He added:

> Twenty years ago, students came to business school to get the fundamentals about doing business and a tool kit for how to do modeling, shadow pricing, strategy frameworks, and the like.

Now students have greater aspirations. They don't always care if they don't have a job lined up after school. They used to exit business school and take a "branded" job with a well-known firm. Nowadays they are more concerned with long-term self-actualization. The MBA is just a platform. Students identify with leaders who have changed the nature of competition in sectors or made a significant difference to a community. They are thoughtful about changing the world. Leading schools of management need to rise to that challenge.

In March 2009, as the economic crisis unfolded, we obtained an update on the Stanford Graduate School of Business's view of its curriculum and courses. The key responses and initiatives included the following:

- Stanford reaffirmed its commitment to recent curricular reforms that increased the time devoted to globalization and leadership development and added customization to functional and foundational courses.

- The Synthesis Seminar was offered for the first time in spring 2009, and served as both a capstone course and an opportunity for students to reflect on their personal and professional goals.

- The school was considering whether and how to provide increased attention to areas, such as macroeconomics and business and society, that had become higher priorities because of the economic crisis.

- In response to the need for a broader, multidisciplinary perspective, the school was considering developing courses with other departments in the university, such as political science, history, and economics.

Conclusion

Business Schools at a Crossroads

F
OR SEVERAL YEARS NOW, business schools have been quietly
rethinking their curricula and course content. The global economic crisis has raised further questions about the changes
needed, while sharpening the rhetoric and publicizing deeply felt concerns. The headlines have been stark. "Business Schools Face Test
of Faith," one article proclaims.[1] Another asks, "Is It Time to Retrain
B-Schools?"[2] To at least some observers, the deepening economic crisis and the growing need to reform MBA education have become two
sides of the same coin.

We believe that although the pressures of the economic crisis may
well abate, the underlying issues facing business schools will not. As
we noted in the introduction, with the exception of our follow-up interviews, virtually all of our research was conducted in 2007 and 2008,
before the economic crisis began. But we believe that subsequent
events have largely confirmed and reinforced our initial findings and
validated many of the changes already under way. In this chapter, we
shift from empirical analysis to presenting our own opinions and recommendations. In the process, we draw on the evidence and conclusions
of earlier chapters to answer the question, Where should business
schools go from here? After charting that path, we identify a number of
practical implementation challenges that must be addressed if MBA

programs are to move in the desired direction. Throughout, our tone is optimistic and hopeful because we have already seen a number of schools experimenting and reinvigorating their programs.

Our argument is built around four broad themes. First is the growing imperative for change. In recent years, there have been any number of calls to rethink MBA education. Most have foundered because the forces of inertia have been strong. At many schools, the unstated assumption has long been "It ain't broke, so don't fix it." But this time, we argue, the need for reform is urgent. If business schools hope to continue to thrive, they must respond far more emphatically than they did in the past. Our analysis shows that the MBA marketplace is changing, as is society's perception of the roles, requirements, and responsibilities of business leaders. Moreover, our interviews, as well as our case studies, highlight the growing consensus among deans, executives, and students about the shortfalls and opportunities facing graduate business education today. A number of schools have already moved to fill these gaps; those that stand pat, we believe, run the risk of losing their standing and student appeal.

A second theme is the need for rebalancing. In response to the Carnegie and Ford reports, business schools wisely and appropriately introduced greater rigor and disciplinary knowledge into their programs. The result was a sharp increase in the analytical capability of graduates, as well as improved academic respectability. But this shift came at a cost. MBA programs devoted less time and attention to developing students' managerial skills, attitudes, and sense of purpose or identity. In the language of earlier chapters, the center of gravity of MBA education shifted strongly toward "knowing" and away from "doing" and "being." We believe that it is now time to rebalance the scales. The vast majority of opportunities and unmet needs described in chapter 4, as well as the underlying concerns about the declining added value of MBA training, are rooted in deficiencies in skills, attitudes, and beliefs. At the same time, there is a need to fill gaps in knowledge in areas such as managing risk, and understanding both the limitations of models and how best to apply them in practice.

A third theme focuses on the redesign of the curriculum. Here, we have four interrelated suggestions. First, we believe that programs must move quickly to address the opportunities and unmet needs identified in chapter 4. As chapters 5 and 6 point out, there are a number of possible approaches, and schools will have to decide on the type and level of commitment in each area. Few will be able to afford to move on all fronts simultaneously, and there are real opportunities for specialization and genuine differentiation. To make these choices wisely, however, schools will have to think clearly about their missions, capabilities, and goals. At the same time, we believe that all schools must move on two fronts: improving their teaching of thinking, reasoning, and creative problem-solving skills; and focusing more attention on issues of accountability, ethics, and social responsibility. Many of the criticisms of MBAs can be traced to deficiencies in these areas. Third, to ensure progress in teaching "doing" and "being," we believe that schools must continue to experiment with and commit to new pedagogies and techniques, especially those that involve action learning, field experiences, and reflective exercises. Even now, we know relatively little about the best way to teach practical managerial skills or the most effective way of instilling a sense of purpose and identity. The wider the array of experiments, the more successful business schools are likely to be in tackling these challenges. Finally, we believe that a significant opportunity for curricular innovation lies in rethinking the second year of MBA programs. As our case studies show, this area has been largely untouched in most of the reforms to date; in fact, as the data in chapter 2 make clear, many European business schools have concluded that a second year is unnecessary. Yet if it is used creatively, the second year offers enormous potential for experimentation and bold ideas. At the moment, most two-year programs treat the year as an unmanaged smorgasbord, a diverse menu of courses driven largely by individual faculty interests rather than as a complementary set of activities, experiences, and courses created by thoughtful design.

Our fourth theme is the challenge of implementation. In the concluding section of this chapter, we assess the barriers that stand in the way of continued changes in MBA education. The most difficult challenges are systemic and economic. They involve questions of how best to secure faculty with the necessary skills despite persistent shortages, limited managerial experience, and spotty clinical training; how best to broaden research approaches used by business school scholars and encourage research in areas such as globalization, leadership, and integration as well as field-based research; how best to change the mix and motives of students so as to attract a new breed of applicants and a more diverse portfolio of recruiters; and how best to overcome the high costs of curricula that accompany extensive small-group experiences, intensive global exposure, and personalized advising and feedback. Although these challenges are deep and pervasive, we believe that they can be overcome, provided business schools think creatively and work in concert. The way forward, we believe, lies in adopting the same spirit that sustained our research from the start—a willingness on the part of members of the business school community to collaborate and share, to come together and jointly solve the problems that we face.

The Imperative for Change

Jack Welch, the former CEO of General Electric, once observed that "change has no constituency."[3] Most people prefer the status quo to a risky, unfamiliar future. That is why organizations are so difficult to move in new directions, and why much of graduate business education has changed so little in the past decade. Dissatisfaction, discomfort, and unease with the current state of affairs must first intensify and become widely shared if significant change is to occur. MBA programs are no exception. Today, we believe, that level of discontent has finally been reached.

Questions are increasingly being raised about the value of the MBA degree. Employers are hiring undergraduates and promoting from within, and then suggesting that their best young people stick around rather than return to school for additional business training. Firms that continue to recruit from leading MBA programs emphasize screening and selection benefits as well as the skills and training schools offer. The more deeply that executives feel that business schools are not providing students with the necessary preparation in knowledge, skills, and attitudes, the more likely it is that they will invest in providing the training themselves. Student enrollments at lower-ranked two-year, full-time, in-residence MBA programs have declined, whereas those at part-time and executive MBA programs and other specialized degrees have increased.

Post-crisis, the opportunity costs for young people still holding secure jobs have risen substantially. Student loans have become more difficult for international students to secure, making one-year degrees look even more desirable.[4] The rise of high-quality business programs in countries such as China has added to these pressures because such schools provide students with a set of credible, lower-cost substitutes. History suggests that these programs are likely to gain in stature as their countries' economies grow stronger. Those who do attend traditional MBA programs now spend even more time networking and securing jobs; many schools report that engagement in the classroom is down while commitment to recruiting activities is up. Meanwhile, criticisms from within the academy have continued to escalate. Initially, the concern was that programs favored rigor over relevance; today, that concern has broadened to a growing recognition that a number of critical management and leadership skills are simply not being taught fully or effectively.

To this mix, the economic crisis has added two additional forces favoring change. The first is the shakeout in the financial sector. Before the crisis, most elite MBA programs sent 40 to 60 percent of their graduates to jobs in financial services. Many students, in fact, enrolled in MBA programs for precisely this opportunity. They were "career switchers," lured back to school by the promise of high-paying jobs in investment banking, private equity, and other financial services. The economic crisis has made this shift far more difficult; in many cases, it is now impossible.[5] Many large investment banks, for example, have sharply reduced their hiring, as a result of downsizing and their absorption by commercial banks. The large pay premiums in the financial sector are predicted to decrease; scholars have noted that wages in this sector were "excessively high" from the mid-1990s until 2006.[6] They are likely to return to more equitable levels once financial services firms have been fully restructured, become more tightly regulated, and institute more prudent approaches to risk management. Faced with this reduction in the availability and pay of financial services jobs, many MBA programs will have to rethink their offerings. Students are unlikely to accept the argument that programs that were designed to send large numbers of graduates into analytical jobs in financial services will, without fundamental changes in perspective and course offerings, be equally effective at preparing students for completely different careers such as managerial positions at large multinationals, entrepreneurial roles at high-tech startups, or leadership of NGOs.

The economic crisis has also unleashed a second, equally powerful force favoring change: societal pressure. Whether this is temporary or indicative of a deeper shift remains to be seen. But there are indications that the wave of populist anger caused by the subprime meltdown, the poorly understood risks of exotic financial instruments such as collateralized debt obligations, the ever-rising cost of bailouts, and the untimely bonuses paid by Merrill Lynch and AIG has been transferred to business leaders and business schools more generally. Both are now blamed for a litany of misdeeds and sins.

These criticisms are surely overstated. The economic crisis, like most complex problems, has many causes. Business schools must shoulder their share of the blame, but so too must regulators, central bankers, lawyers, the designers of incentive systems, and senior financial executives who climbed the ranks without MBAs. At the same time, these criticisms are certain to prompt deeper reflection on the purpose and values of business and business leaders. In fact, we believe that such reflections on purpose—including assessments of the responsibilities of corporations, the accountability of executives, and the at times conflicting demands imposed by a desire to maximize shareholder value while still acting in society's best interests—are essential if business schools are to regain the public trust.

Together, these forces make a compelling case for change. It is indeed time to rethink the MBA and introduce reforms on multiple fronts. But even with this alignment of forces, some may argue that the harsh economic climate demands a more muted response. Difficult economic times, they will claim, call for retrenchment and cutbacks, not bold steps forward. Clearly, resources are tight and budgets are under the microscope; as endowment incomes and gifts fall, many schools have been forced to tighten their belts. Business schools are indeed facing enormous financial pressures today, but a difficult environment offers an important advantage: it "provides the leader with the platform to get things done that were required anyway and the sense of urgency to accelerate implementation."[7] As Benjamin Netanyahu, the prime minister of Israel, put it: "Never waste a good crisis."[8] In the many examples we have described in this book, business schools have already demonstrated their capacity to develop innovative, cost-effective solutions to the challenges they face.

The Need for Rebalancing

Graduate business education is built on an ever-growing base of disciplinary knowledge. Economics, statistics, psychology, and sociology now permeate the curriculum and provide the foundation for many functional courses. Accounting, finance, marketing, and operations have become technical fields in their own right, filled with quantitative analysis and rigorous methodologies. Today's MBA students are expected to master concepts and techniques that are increasingly challenging and complex.

These changes are a vast improvement over the anecdotal, loosely organized courses that predominated fifty years ago, before the reforms launched by the Carnegie and Ford reports. But we, as well as many other members of the business school community, believe that something has been lost—or at least shortchanged—in the process. MBA curricula have indeed become more rigorous. But at the same time, many programs today underemphasize essential professional competencies. Management, after all, is a practical art; it involves getting things implemented and executed through people and organizations. For this reason, it requires more than knowledge alone. Moreover, that knowledge must be grounded in readily applicable frameworks that will help students translate the theories they have learned into practice. As we have argued in several places in this book, students must be provided with critical skills and perspectives; they must be schooled in doing and being as well as knowing.

When the deans and executives that we interviewed identified unmet needs and gaps in the curriculum, they almost invariably pointed to exactly these areas. To them, having a global perspective meant much more than being knowledgeable about other countries' trade policies or regulatory regimes; it also meant skill and sensitivity when working with people whose cultures, norms, and standards of behavior were different from one's own. Understanding organizational realities meant more than simply mastering theories of congruence and strategic alignment; it also meant skill at navigating the difficult terrain of organizational politics, middle-management coalitions, and functional fiefdoms. What we heard in our interviews, and what we found in many of the most innovative curriculum changes, was a desire to devote greater attention to skill building and the development of personal capacities and perspectives. Without a commensurate set of "doing" skills, knowing is of little value. And these "doing" skills are likely to be ineffective and directionless without the self-awareness and reflection on values and beliefs that come from developing "being."

The current economic crisis has intensified this need. On the one hand, ethically questionable actions have been distressingly common, and leaders have at times appeared to have had little interest in the social and organizational repercussions of their decisions. On the other hand, the crisis exposed significant knowledge gaps in our understanding of risk management, the design of incentive systems, regulatory oversight, the degree of interconnectedness of the global economy, and the limitations of mathematical models. As we discussed in chapter 4, there is much work to be done on the "knowing" dimension as it relates to risk, regulation, and restraint.

For all these reasons, we believe that business schools need to rebalance their programs to take a more managerial perspective. They need to value the cultivation of skills and to inspire students to develop a sense of purpose and identity as much as they value the teaching of practical and useful concepts and frameworks.[9] The deficiencies in these areas are clear. A recent study reported that "business school students' confidence in their preparation to manage values conflicts at work fell throughout their time in the program, as did the proportion of people agreeing that they had opportunities to practice ethical and responsible decision making as part of their MBA."[10] As we noted in chapters 5 and 6 as well as in our case studies, remedying these deficiencies will require a substantial shift in pedagogy away from lectures and toward greater use of reflective discussions, practical exercises, personal coaching, and experiential learning.

Many deans supported this change in emphasis. At the same time, however, they shared a deep concern that took the form of a warning: MBA programs should avoid at all costs returning to the "trade school mentality" of earlier eras. The continued success and vitality of graduate business education, they argued, rests on its commitment to high-quality research. We agree completely. Rebalancing the scales by giving greater attention to skills, purpose, values, and identity does not in any way mean a repudiation of scholarship. But it does require, as the recent AACSB report on research suggests, a shift in scholarly attention, with mechanisms "to inform and motivate academic research in areas that are of greatest practical interest" as well as "stronger academic engagement with practice."[11] Only then will the teaching of topics such as leadership development, ethical decision making, the uses and abuses of power, and how best to stimulate creativity rest on a firm foundation.

Reshaping the Curriculum

Now is the time for many business schools to revisit their curricula and introduce new topics, courses, and materials. The unmet needs identified in chapter 4 are even more pressing as a result of the current economic crisis and the associated shifts in the employment of MBA graduates away from jobs with a heavy emphasis on analysis and toward more managerial positions.

Moreover, faculty and deans no longer have the luxury of claiming "It can't be done;" the examples we present in chapters 5 and 6, coupled with the case studies of part II, provide detailed roadmaps of precisely how schools might proceed with changes at both the course and program levels. If MBA degrees are to remain relevant, they must use these examples as springboards for expanding and enriching their offerings in the areas of globalization; leadership development; integration; organizational realities; creativity and innovative thinking; critical thinking; oral and written communication; the role, responsibilities, and purpose of business; and understanding the limits of models and markets.

We do not, however, believe that every MBA program should be moving simultaneously on all of these fronts, nor that every school should be making the same changes or teaching the very same courses. Some degree of specialization is certain to be beneficial. After all, schools differ dramatically in their resources and capabilities, as well as their underlying philosophies. This, in fact, is one of the central lessons of our case studies: there is no single best way to proceed. Diversity is to be encouraged and applauded. As one dean put it, "There is room in this marketplace for multiple different models." To identify their desired direction, another dean suggested, "Schools need to ask, 'What are we really good at? Where can we be distinctive? How can we add value?'" We agree wholeheartedly. Our only caution is that, in the process, schools avoid spending too much time fine-tuning and reengineering their program structures and architectures without changing the substance of their schools' offerings. As we noted in chapter 3, these efforts, although leading to differentiated student experiences, are of unclear educational value.

At the same time that we favor diversity, we believe that all schools would benefit from action on two fronts. First, we suggest that MBA programs devote far more attention to teaching thinking and reasoning skills. These skills all involve cognitive processes of some sort that serve as the input or foundation for reaching better judgments and making more effective decisions. Prominent examples include problem finding, problem framing, project scoping, creative thinking, integrative thinking, and critical thinking. Many of the concerns voiced by executives about the value and effectiveness of MBA training can be traced to deficiencies in one or more of these areas. Our examples and case studies show that a number of schools have already moved aggressively and creatively on these fronts, offering several models to emulate. Their approaches fall into two broad categories: (1) platform courses, positioned at the start of programs, with lessons that are then applied across a multitude of courses that follow (e.g., Stanford's Critical Analytical Thinking course and Rotman's Integrative Thinking course), and (2) individual courses, positioned toward the middle or end of programs, where thinking skills are taught and then immediately applied in an intensive experiential exercise (e.g., Stanford Design School's Creating Infectious Action course and Michigan's Multidisciplinary Action Projects). Whichever approach is taken, we believe that a deeper grounding in thinking and reasoning skills, coupled with opportunities to practice newly acquired techniques and perspectives in the relatively safe, protected environment of the classroom, is essential preparation for executives today.

For similar reasons, we believe that all MBA programs need to focus more attention on issues of accountability, ethics, and social responsibility. These topics are no longer frills or window dressing. They have become essential to effective management—indeed, they always have been. Management decisions are increasingly subject to public inspection and evaluation. As the public's expectations of business leaders have risen, so too have the accompanying calls for broadening the scope of business training. All too many MBA programs are still falling short. One dean observed, "We need to push harder on these issues. Our best students don't think that we're raising their sights enough, not pushing them hard enough to think about their responsibilities to the community and to the wider society, or their global responsibilities."

Once again, MBA programs have choices, and diversity is to be encouraged. Schools can meet this need in a number of different ways: (1) by developing courses that focus exclusively on these topics (e.g., Harvard's Leadership and Corporate Accountability course), (2) by folding these considerations into the reflective portions of leadership development or capstone courses (e.g., Yale's Integrated Leadership Perspectives course and Stanford's Synthesis Seminar), or (3) by incorporating broader discussions of issues such as compensation, ethics, governance, and risk taking into traditional functional courses such as accounting and finance (e.g., INSEAD's approach, which includes summative sessions on these topics led by functional faculty). There are some hopeful signs already. Students in the 2009 graduating MBA class at a number of top-ranked programs have initiated an oath they will take at graduation, similar to the Hippocratic Oath in medicine. Among its elements is a commitment to integrity, ethics, and social responsibility.[12]

Beyond these substantive changes in the curriculum, we recommend that schools continue to experiment with new pedagogies. Many of the most innovative courses today employ some type of experiential or active learning, often involving team projects or group exercises. Leadership development classes rely heavily on these methods, as do courses that teach critical, creative, and integrative thinking. Yet we still know relatively little about the most effective ways to combine classroom learning with real-time experiences, whether they are simulated or in the field. Nor have we fully resolved the staffing challenges imposed by a proliferation of small-group activities. A number of schools are experimenting with combinations of faculty, adjuncts, alumni, and second-year students to oversee these projects; others are considering partnerships with organizations such as IDEO and the Center for Creative Leadership (CCL) that specialize in these activities. Meanwhile, CCL itself is revisiting its high-touch approach in hopes of finding more cost-effective ways of combining intensive one-on-one coaching and small-group facilitation with broad-based, multipurpose, online tools and support.

Here, one possible staffing model for business schools to emulate is that of medical schools. In 2008–2009, Harvard Medical School, with an entering class of 165 students, had a total faculty of 10,884.[13] The latter figure is astonishing, but relatively easy to explain. It includes those doctors who work in Harvard's seventeen affiliated hospitals who also serve as faculty because they lead an occasional clerkship, clinical rotation, or small-group tutorial. The core faculty, based on "the Quad" where most classes and laboratory sessions take place, was 668, a far smaller number. Business schools might consider adopting a similar model, supplementing their core faculty with a diverse collection of alumni and practitioners drawn from affiliated companies or service organizations. An example would be the Creating Infectious Action course at Stanford's Design School, which is heavily staffed by executives from the nearby office of IDEO. Such an approach could easily be expanded. New York–based MBA programs might draw additional faculty from nearby banks and financial firms, California-based MBA programs might draw faculty from nearby Internet and high-technology start-ups, and Chicago-based MBA programs might draw faculty from nearby consumer and industrial goods companies.

Long-term, continuing associations would ensure the availability of a stable set of skilled instructors, who would then assume responsibility for coaching individual students, guiding field projects, and facilitating small-group discussions. Many schools, in fact, have already recruited distinguished executives to fill full-time senior lecturer and professor of management practice positions. Faculty members from practice bring a wealth of business experience that enriches both faculty research and classroom learning. Given the current shortage of business school faculty, we expect these trends to intensify, particularly because clinical faculty have the talent and experience to help students develop "doing" and "being" skills.

A related question facing MBA programs is how best to restructure their curricula so that these experiential, skill-based courses have maximum impact. Most of the innovations we described in chapters 5 and 6 were implemented in the first year of their respective programs. Thinking skills, such as those represented by the Critical Analytical Thinking and Global Context of Management courses at Stanford, the Problem Framing course at Yale, and the Integrative Thinking course at the Rotman School, are offered early in the first year so that students can benefit from repeatedly applying these skills in the functional courses that follow. In marketing courses, for example, students practice the new forms of reasoning they have learned when developing marketing plans, considering how marketing might differ in various geographic, cultural, and institutional contexts, and integrating manufacturing considerations into marketing decision making. One way to characterize the intention of the required curricula at these schools is that they start with thinking skills, move to disciplines and functions, and conclude with synthesis in the form of strategy or general management. As a result, students develop insights into both "knowing" and "doing" early in their programs. For similar reasons, schools such as Michigan require students to take a seven-week experiential learning course before the end of the first year. Michigan argues that learning by doing enriches the concepts and frameworks students will absorb in their second-year electives. "Being" courses, such as the leadership development laboratories at Stanford, Yale, and Chicago Booth and the Leadership and Corporate Accountability course at Harvard, are also offered in the first year. In all of these cases, students come to view knowing, doing, and being as holistic components in their development.

But curriculum changes cannot be limited to the first year. At most business schools today, the second year of the program, if it exists at all, is less designed than assembled. The typical second year consists of a potpourri of electives, driven largely by the academic interests of individual faculty or departments, from which students choose as if they were facing a smorgasbord or a buffet table. This is hardly a prescription for effective design or an approach that maximizes learning or educational impact. The year could be vastly improved by thinking of it as an integrated whole, with a unifying purpose and the goal of addressing one or more of the unmet needs identified in chapter 4. In fact, we believe that the second year affords a great opportunity to supplement the "knowing" that dominates first-year classes with even more exposure to "doing" and "being." Schools might, for example, focus on improving students' leadership skills by combining coursework and reflective exercises with job shadowing and real-time observation, develop more global mind-sets in students by coupling international work experiences with the opportunity to take classes on partners' overseas campuses, or acquaint students with implementation challenges by linking development projects aimed at commercializing cutting-edge technologies with class discussions that teased out differing perspectives from each team's MBAs, scientists, lawyers, and designers.

To make these shifts, most schools will probably have to experiment with more flexible program structures and course formats, eliminating the rigidity of semesters and quarters while embracing more modular approaches that allow for both brief, intense exposure to topics as well as extended immersions and experiences. In fact, we can imagine a wide range of schools using their second year to develop collections of courses, activities, and projects that focus on distinct themes and offer specialized expertise and skills. Examples of such themes might be creativity and innovation, leading nonprofits and NGOs, global management, and sustainability and clean-tech industries.

At this point, some readers may be wondering, "Who will or should make these changes?" We remain agnostic on this point, but can suggest a number of possibilities. In some cases, change will be driven from the top, by a forceful dean or university president. In other cases, reform will be bottom up. Individual faculty, on their own or collectively, will propose and develop innovative courses or projects. In still other cases, change will come through a collective response of the business school community, orchestrated perhaps by the AACSB or a foundation, as it was during the Ford and Carnegie eras.

The Challenges Ahead

These changes will not come easily. As we noted in chapters 5 and 6, the barriers to implementation facing schools wishing to progress in each of the eight areas of unmet needs are large and substantial. Collectively, these challenges can be grouped into three broad categories: expanding and diversifying the faculty, attracting new students and recruiters, and revising the business model.

To succeed with the changes described in this book, business schools will have to develop new competencies within their faculties, targeting both individuals and groups. They will, for example, have to improve the linkages, cooperation, and amount of integration between those who specialize in scholarship and those who are experts in practice. Put simply, they will have to overcome the "two cultures" problem described in chapter 4. Because it reflects a deep philosophical divide, this is a long-standing problem that will not be solved overnight. Herbert Simon, the prize-winning economist, political scientist, and organizational theorist, described the challenge succinctly over forty years ago: "Organizing a professional school . . . is very much like mixing oil [disciplinary experts] with water [experienced practitioners] . . . Left to themselves, the oil and water will separate again."[14]

Still, we can imagine a number of strategies for moving business schools in the desired direction. One approach would be to develop a critical mass of faculty who are comfortable with and skilled at melding the worlds of theory and practice. This might be accomplished in a number of ways: by subtly changing the incentives facing faculty, including the policies of academic journals, so that there were greater rewards for applied, managerially oriented research; offering a range of internships or industry immersion experiences for doctoral students and young faculty so that they had direct exposure to the challenges and realities of business practice; and insisting on joint teaching assignments coupling academics with practitioners so that the involved faculty produced courses that forced them to integrate the best thinking of both worlds.

A second approach would be for business schools to give higher standing to clinically oriented faculty, as a number of medical schools have done.[15] Full-time clinical faculty would have the opportunity for long-term appointments, but would be subject to different standards and criteria. At the same time, MBA programs might expand their efforts to equip clinical faculty with more of an academic mind-set. One way to do so, a dean suggested, would be for business schools to work together to train and develop clinical professors, for example, by insisting that the large numbers of successful, experienced executives wishing to switch careers and enter academia first participate in a new, three-part program. That program would combine training in selected disciplines to familiarize potential faculty with the knowledge base in their fields, training in basic research methods to ensure that their future work met at least minimal scholarly standards, and training in teaching and pedagogical skills to prepare new instructors for the demands of the classroom. The established faculty of leading MBA programs would assume responsibility for one or more parts of the program based on their areas of expertise, and candidates would rotate from school to school to receive the full complement of training. For example, before assuming a teaching post, a recently retired executive might spend two weeks at a quantitatively oriented school taking classes on finance, two weeks at a research-oriented program taking classes on research methods, and two weeks at a teaching-oriented school taking classes to improve pedagogical skills.

An equally powerful approach to expanding the pool of faculty and diversifying course offerings would be for business schools to draw more heavily on the resources of the wider university. As one dean put it, "Do we really have the right faculty for teaching our students about responsibilities to the community or society? Probably not. But we could integrate with other parts of the university, such as political science and history. This subject matter lends itself to cross-school interaction. Besides, it's good to invite the critics under our tent. We need more two-way exposure. We don't necessarily have to be completely self-contained as a school." Other deans echoed this view, citing the importance of expanded partnerships with law schools, public policy programs, and arts and sciences departments as vehicles for broadening the base of faculty teaching business students and expanding the range of disciplinary perspectives. But even with these collaborations, we believe that business schools will have to find ways of growing and deepening their own faculties, because other parts of the university are unlikely to be willing to teach large numbers of MBA students without some commitments from business schools that balance the scales and open up MBA courses to cross-registrants.

In much the same spirit, a related challenge facing MBA programs is the profile and preferences of today's business school students. Despite the current economic crisis, the majority of graduates, especially from elite programs, still prefer jobs in financial services and consulting. Many have come from these settings and wish to return to them for further seasoning; others wish to shift into these sectors because of their advantages in pay, prestige, and opportunities to work with fellow MBAs. Students continue to express far less interest in entrepreneurship, managerial positions, or jobs at corporations, not-for-profits, and NGOs. Yet those are precisely the types of organizations that placement officers are seeking to attract to their campuses in the face of the falloff in demand from more traditional recruiters. Unless this mismatch is addressed by changes in the desired profile of incoming students, the disparity of interests is likely to persist in the future.

How, and in what ways, to change the mix of students remains an open question. Because of the global economic crisis, business executives (and, by association, MBA programs) are now regarded with some suspicion. Resentment and populist anger are on the upswing.[16] At least a few undergraduates who are undecided about their careers—especially those who are wavering among business, law, and public policy or who "want to change the world"—may be less likely to apply to MBA programs at this time. Yet these are precisely the kinds of students that business schools need most if they are to alter the image of MBA graduates, become more managerial, and shift their portfolios toward courses focused on doing and being.

This, of course, is a classic chicken-and-egg problem. To attract a different mix of students, schools will first need to offer a different mix of courses, but that mix of courses will only be forthcoming if faculty believe that the student mix has changed sufficiently to ensure adequate demand for their courses. Although a single business school working on its own can make some headway, a collective process is likely to be far more effective. The pressure for such change is likely to come from prospective students shying away from management careers and from current faculty and students sensing unmet needs and opportunities. Such an effort, designed to rethink and reposition MBA education, might also be associated with greater outreach to undergraduates in the humanities, sciences, and social sciences, who are underrepresented in business schools. Of course, to be effective these efforts must be more than simply public relations. They must be accompanied by real shifts in the mix of courses offered by business schools and reinforced by significant changes in the set of recruiters invited to campus and offering jobs.

The final challenge facing business schools is how to retain viable business models in the face of these changes. Small-group activities, personal coaching, team-taught classes, and global immersions are all expensive innovations that add to the already high cost of two-year, full-time MBA degrees. Yale's curriculum reforms, for example, cost the school an additional $2 million to $5 million, and Stanford's reforms necessitate a 10 to 15 percent increase in the size of the faculty for sustainability. Few schools can afford these extra expenses without commensurate cutbacks in costs or increases in revenues. However, it is hard to imagine business school tuitions rising much further without an accompanying falloff in demand. The opportunity costs are too great, and the alternatives, such as ten- and twelve-month programs, are too appealing. Business schools will therefore have to become more creative in their approaches to faculty staffing, pursuing lower-cost alternatives such as the medical school model discussed earlier in this chapter. They will also have to develop more compelling mixes of part-time and executive programs to complement their full-time MBA degrees. Opportunities for lifelong learning are one possibility, with short bursts of education for all MBA graduates spaced every five to ten years and linked to the stages of their careers. Another option would be annual industry-based programs aimed at executives from a single sector, such as advertising, agribusiness, biotechnology, or venture capital, and devoted to collective reflection on the latest developments in the field.

The economic crisis may also prove to be a blessing in disguise. Many institutions have already been forced to trim their budgets substantially; most have become far leaner in the process. Because of persistent financial pressures, faculty and deans have had to think hard about where they can safely and wisely cut back. This same logic, we hope, will continue to infuse curricular planning when the economy begins to turn around. MBA programs must learn to subtract. Whenever they add courses, activities, and experiences, schools must simultaneously phase out or reduce the time devoted to other subjects. A number of organizations and governments have "sunset rules" that require unsuccessful or declining programs to be phased out or at least carefully reevaluated after a certain period of time has elapsed; the same logic might be applied to business schools. This is certain to be a difficult, divisive set of discussions that will require firm leadership. But if undertaken by the business school community as a whole, the resulting recommendations are far more likely to gain acceptance and legitimacy.

In many ways, we end as we began—on an optimistic note. Business schools are indeed at a crossroads. Their role, purpose, and functioning are now subject to increased scrutiny and debate. They no longer provide guaranteed access to secure, well-paying jobs in fields like finance. Deans and executives believe that programs are falling short in key areas and that curricula are underdeveloped. Overall, the situation facing business schools is well captured by the words of Paul Valéry, a French symbolist poet, who long ago noted, "The trouble with our times is that the future is not what it used to be." A recent article on MBA programs put it more harshly: "Goodbye, yellow brick road."[17]

But business schools have been down this road before. They have outlasted many earlier crises, including the Great Depression, and have shown themselves to be extraordinarily flexible, adaptive institutions. Their collective response to the Carnegie and Ford reports proved their capacity to respond boldly and thoughtfully to well-framed critiques. Moreover, our evidence suggests that many of the necessary adaptations, innovations, and reforms have already been pioneered by one or more schools. These institutions have identified some of the sources of dissatisfaction with the status quo and responded with creative courses and curricular reforms.

The leading edge of change is already visible and under way, and is well documented in our book. For all these reasons, we are hopeful about the future of the MBA and believe it will continue to be a degree in transition.

Notes

Chapter 1: Introduction: A Degree in Transition

1. Roger Thompson, "Building a Better MBA," *HBS Alumni Bulletin*, September 2008, 25.

2. Frank C. Pierson, *The Education of American Businessmen* (New York: McGraw-Hill, 1959); Robert A. Gordon and James E. Howell, *Higher Education for Business* (New York: Columbia University Press, 1959); and Lyman W. Porter and Lawrence E. McKibbin, *Management Education and Development* (New York: McGraw-Hill, 1988).

3. For ease of exposition, we use the word *industry* to represent all business schools delivering graduate business education.

4. Anjali Athavaley, "Escape Route: Seeking Refuge in an M.B.A. Program," *Wall Street Journal*, October 14, 2008, D1, D4; and Alison Damast, "B-Schools and the Financial Bust," *BusinessWeek*, November 24, 2008, 41–45.

5. "It's a Good Time to Go to a B-Level B-School," February 10, 2009, http://www.forbes.com/2009/02/10/b-level-business-school-leadership_0211_mba_print.html.

6. William J. Holstein, "Helping 240,000 Find a Future After Wall Street," *New York Times*, January 17, 2009, B2.

7. Robert Weisman, "The Dark Night of the Part-Time MBA Program," *Boston Globe*, January 18, 2009, G1, G4.

8. Damast, "B-Schools and the Financial Bust," 41.

Chapter 2: The Changing MBA Marketplace

1. U.S. Department of Education, National Center for Educational Statistics, Higher Education General Information Survey, "Degrees and Other Formal Awards Conferred," 1970–1971 through 1985–1986, and 1990–1991 through 2006–2007.

2. Personal communication, Rachel Edgington, Director, Market Research & Analysis, Graduate Management Admissions Council, October 16, 2008.

3. Alison Damast, "U.S. Business Schools: Why Foreign MBAs Are Disappearing," *BusinessWeek*, August 3, 2009.

4. Personal communication, Jessica Brown, Manager, Knowledge Services, AACSB International, September 4, 2009.

5. The approaches of European business schools are considerably more diverse than those of American schools. Some European schools are competing internationally and have adopted the American model, whereas others are applying more idiosyncratic national approaches. See Don Antunes and Howard Thomas, "The Competitive (Dis)Advantage of European Business Schools," *Long Range Planning* 40 (2007): 382–404.

6. Della Bradshaw, "The Must-Have Degree," *Financial Times*, June 18, 2007, 46.

7. Personal communication, Rachel Edgington, October 16, 2008.

8. Some state schools favor part-time and executive MBA programs because tuition revenues from these programs can be retained fully by the schools, unlike tuition revenues from full-time MBA programs, which must be shared with the university.

9. "Business School Rankings and Profiles," *BusinessWeek*, http://www.businessweek.com/bschools/rankings, accessed August 26, 2009.

10. Ibid.

11. We observed a similar pattern to figure 2-6 when we examined full-time enrollment at the next twenty-five ranked business schools. A handful showed increases, but more than half showed substantial declines.

12. Some schools argued that business school rankings contributed to declining enrollments. If a school filled its classes with students whose GMAT scores were lower than the school's current median GMAT, the school would fall in the rankings, leading to fewer applications in the future. To avoid this problem, a number of schools preferred to cut their class sizes to maintain or increase their place in the rankings.

13. All data on job placements have been drawn from the case studies that appear later in this book.

14. Louise Story, "Bye, Bye B-School," *New York Times*, Sunday Business Section, September 16, 2007, 1, 9.

Chapter 3: A Close Look at the Curriculum

1. Harry R. Lewis, *Excellence Without a Soul* (New York: Public Affairs, 2006), 22.

2. David Damrosch, *We Scholars* (Cambridge, MA: Harvard University Press, 1995), 123.

3. Derek Bok, *Our Underachieving Colleges* (Princeton, NJ: Princeton University Press, 2006), 16.

4. Robert A. Gordon and James E. Howell, *Higher Education for Business* (New York: Columbia University Press, 1959), 273–279; and Frank C. Pierson, *The Education of American Businessmen* (New York: McGraw-Hill, 1959), 249–267.

5. Lyman W. Porter and Lawrence E. McKibbin, *Management Education and Development* (New York: McGraw-Hill, 1988), 314–315.

6. Tricia Bisoux, "The Extreme MBA Makeover," *BizEd*, May/June 2005, 27; and Lindsey Gerdes, "B-Schools with a Niche," *BusinessWeek*, September 5, 2005, 70.

7. Henry Mintzberg, *Managers Not MBAs* (San Francisco: Berrett-Koehler, 2004), 162–165.

8. Eli Segev, Adi Raveh, and Moshe Farjoun, "Conceptual Maps of the Leading MBA Programs in the United States: Core Courses, Concentration Areas, and the Ranking of the School," *Strategic Management Journal* 20 (1999): 549–565.

9. Peter Navarro, "The MBA Core Curricula of Top-Ranked U.S. Business Schools: A Study in Failure?" *Academy of Management Learning and Education* 7 (2008): 108–123.

10. To ensure accuracy, we recontacted each of the participating schools in 2009 to confirm our data. Many, but not all, schools responded. In most cases, we incorporated their suggestions because they reflected differences in interpretation of our 2006–2007 data. In a few cases, however, respondents provided us with updated 2008–2009 data. We did not include this data because we wanted to ensure that all tables were based on information from the same time period.

11. The six schools that divide the year into semesters are Carnegie Mellon, Harvard, MIT, NYU, Wharton, and Yale. Some schools, such as Carnegie Mellon and Yale, further divide each semester in half. The four schools that divide the year into quarters are Chicago, Dartmouth, Northwestern, and Stanford. Even though they call their terms *quarters*, students only take classes for three quarters per year.

12. To calculate total course weeks—the total amount of class time over an entire program—we assumed that students take the equivalent of four courses per semester. If each semester is 20 weeks, students take 80 course weeks per semester. Over two years of four semesters, students have 320 course weeks in which to take courses. We did a similar calculation for INSEAD's ten-month program to arrive at a figure of 200 total course weeks.

13. Chicago is a bit of an exception here in that students are not told which specific courses to take or when to take them. They must, however, take nine courses in certain broad topic areas. Some of these areas (e.g., financial accounting) are required, but students are allowed their choice of level. Others areas (e.g., marketing management) are part of a larger menu from which students must select a subset of areas and courses.

14. Columbia Business School is a recent convert to this approach. In December 2007 it announced that the following fall it would alter its core curriculum, giving students additional flexibility in the first year by reducing the number of required core courses from nine full-semester courses to six and a half, while adding eight new electives to the program that could be taken through a new distribution requirement. Like so many other schools, this shift was driven largely by recruiting pressures. According to a member of Columbia's curriculum-review committee, "One of their [students'] concerns in the first year is getting prepared for a summer internship. For many of them that's very important. That's one of the reasons why they look for flexibility. Being able to take more electives in the first year allows them to tailor some of the foundational knowledge to what they plan to do during the summer." See "Columbia Revamps Its Core," *The MBA Life*, December 20, 2007.

15. At least one study argues that this shift toward specialization within MBA programs, which is even more pronounced among midtier schools, does not offer employment advantages. After reviewing over 750 job advertisements, both in newspapers and on the Web, in which an MBA degree was specified as a preference or a requirement, the study concluded that most employers preferred or required only a general

MBA degree. To the extent that specialization was requested, it took the form of an undergraduate major. See Pola B. Gupta, Paula M. Saunders, and Jeremy Smith, "Traditional Master of Business Administration (MBA) Versus the MBA with Specialization: A Disconnection Between What Business Schools Offer and What Employers Seek," *Journal of Education for Business* 82, no. 6 (2007): 307–312.

16. It is important to emphasize that many of the courses that schools exclude from their core are still offered as electives and are taken by large numbers of students. The presence of a course in the core is partly a statement of educational philosophy and partly a function of department size and faculty mix.

17. The coding of topics is clearly a judgment call, and one that requires training and experience in the field. HBS professors Srikant Datar (financial accounting), Jan Rivkin and Jordan Siegel (strategy), and Tom Delong (leadership/organizational behavior) helped determine the categories in their respective areas. We are extremely grateful for their assistance.

18. The textbooks are, respectively, Clyde P. Stickney and Roman L. Weil, *Financial Accounting*, 12th ed. (Mason, OH: South-Western College Publishing, 2006), and Charles T. Horngren et al., *Introduction to Financial Accounting*, 9th ed. (Englewood Cliffs, NJ: Prentice-Hall, 2005).

19. The textbook is David Besanko et al., *Economics of Strategy*, 3rd ed. (New York: Wiley, 2003), which is used at three schools.

20. Our findings are broadly consistent with earlier work showing that strategy offerings have evolved from integrative business policy courses, often offered late in the program as capstone courses with a strong managerial emphasis, to first-year required courses with "an almost exclusive emphasis on theory and analysis, slanted toward industrial economics." See Larry E. Greiner, Arvind Bhambri, and Thomas G. Cummings, "Searching for a Strategy to Teach Strategy," *Academy of Management Learning and Education* 2 (2003): 405.

21. Figures are approximate because many courses were difficult to classify and the number of sessions was not always clear from the syllabus. We also made a number of judgment calls when classifying courses in the domain of leadership and organizational behavior. For example, we excluded HBS's Leadership and Corporate Accountability course, discussed in chapter 10, because it is more about ethical and legal behavior than leadership per se, but included Yale's Careers and Employee courses, discussed in chapter 11, because of their organizational and human resource management emphasis.

22. Kent L. Womack, "Core Finance Courses in the Top MBA Programs in 2001," November 2001, Tuck School of Business working paper 01-07, http://ssrn.com/abstract=291973; and Kent L. Womack and Ying Zhang, "Core Finance Course Trends in the Top MBA Programs in 2005," http://ssrn.com/abstract=760604.

Chapter 4: A Rising Chorus of Concerns

1. Earl F. Cheit, "Business Schools and Their Critics," *California Management Review* 27 (1985): 43.

2. This argument draws heavily from Rakesh Khurana, *From Higher Aims to Hired Hands* (Princeton, NJ: Princeton University Press, 2007). It is worth emphasizing that

the challenge of establishing legitimacy continues to the present day and is faced by many professional schools, not just schools of business. Harold Shapiro, former president of Princeton and the University of Michigan, captured the issue neatly when he asked, "Why are the faculty of so many professional schools, particularly those at research universities, anxious or uneasy about their status within the university? Another way of posing the question is: Why have the arts and sciences faculties come to believe that they are the sole definers and defenders of the soul of the university?" See Harold T. Shapiro, *A Larger Sense of Purpose* (Princeton, NJ: Princeton University Press, 2005), 113–114.

3. James G. March and Robert I. Sutton, "Organizational Performance as a Dependent Variable," *Organization Science* 8 (1997): 703.

4. Robert A. Gordon and James E. Howell, *Higher Education for Business* (New York: Columbia University Press, 1959); and Frank C. Pierson, *The Education of American Businessmen* (New York: McGraw-Hill, 1959).

5. Khurana, *From Higher Aims to Hired Hands*, 158.

6. Gordon and Howell, *Higher Education for Business*, 100.

7. Mark De Rond and Alan M. Miller, "Publish or Perish: Bane or Boon of Academic Life?" *Journal of Management Inquiry* 14 (2005): 321–329.

8. Khurana, *From Higher Aims to Hired Hands*, 311; and Jeffrey Pfeffer and Christina T. Fong, "The End of Business Schools? Less Success Than Meets the Eye," *Academy of Management Learning and Education* 1 (2002): 78–96.

9. Warren G. Bennis and James O'Toole, "How Business Schools Lost Their Way," *Harvard Business Review*, May 2005, 96, 98.

10. This discussion draws from several of the leading critiques of business schools, including those cited above as well as Stephen R. Barley, Gordon W. Meyer, and Debra C. Gash, "Cultures of Culture: Academics, Practitioners, and the Pragmatics of Normative Control," *Administrative Science Quarterly* 33 (1988): 24–60; Harold J. Leavitt, "Educating Our MBAs: On Teaching What We Haven't Taught," *California Management Review* 31 (1989): 38-50; Henry Mintzberg, *Managers Not MBAs* (San Francisco: Berrett-Koehler, 2004); Jeffrey Pfeffer, "A Modest Proposal: How We Might Change the Process and Product of Managerial Research," *Academy of Management Journal* 50 (2007): 1334–1345; Jeffrey Pfeffer and Christina T. Fong, "The Business School 'Business': Some Lessons from the U.S. Experience," *Journal of Management Studies* 41 (2004): 1501–1520; and Lyman W. Porter and Lawrence E. McKibbin, *Management Education and Development* (New York: McGraw-Hill, 1988).

11. Michael Mol and Julian Birkenshaw, *Giant Steps in Management* (London: Financial Times/Prentice Hall, 2008). Cited in Pfeffer, "A Modest Proposal."

12. Patrick G. Cullen, "Living with Conflicting Institutional Logics: The Case of U.K. and U.S. Research-Led Business Schools" (unpublished doctoral thesis, University of Cambridge, 2007).

13. Andrew H. Van de Ven and Paul E. Johnson, "Knowledge for Theory and Practice," *Academy of Management Review* 31 (2006): 802.

14. James Bailey and Cameron Ford, "Management as Science Versus Management as Practice in Postgraduate Business Education," *Business Strategy Review* 7 (1996): 8.

15. De Rond and Miller, "Publish or Perish," 325.

16. In their eyes, the problem is largely one of perception and poor communication. As one of them put it, "I don't think the MBA is broken. But we have allowed the perception to get away from us. We are not communicating why MBA training is necessary and why what we are doing is essential."

17. Some deans pointed to a recent article (Nicholas Bloom and John Van Reenen, "Measuring and Explaining Management Practices Across Firms and Countries," *Quarterly Journal of Economics* 122, no.4 [November 2007]: 1351–1408) that concluded that U.S. firms are, on average, better managed than European firms as evidence of the value-added of the MBA (given the greater prevalence of business school–trained managers in the United States in comparison with Europe). However, many of the management practices described in the article, such as process improvements, performance dialogues, target setting, and follow-through refer to skills that are currently not emphasized in most MBA curricula. In fact, they are the kinds of "doing" skills that we believe need much greater development in MBA programs.

18. *Final Report of the AACSB International Impact of Research* (Tampa: AACSB International, 2008).

19. This is the core of Henry Mintzberg's critique of MBA programs. See Mintzberg, *Managers Not MBAs*, especially pp. 33–42. Also see Leonard Sayles, "Whatever Happened to Management? Or Why the Dull Stepchild?" *Business Horizons* 13 (1970): 25–34.

20. James Howell, one of the coauthors of the Ford Foundation study, anticipated this problem decades ago. In a 1984 interview he was asked, "Has the increased popularity of business education in the seventies made its leaders complacent?" Howell responded, "Sure, they've become complacent. They've become successful and respectable—very respectable. That's made them smug, and it's a serious problem. Business is a young academic field, and I think it could slide back into being nearly as irrelevant in the nineties as it was in the fifties." See James W. Schmotter, "An Interview with Professor James E. Howell," *Selections*, Spring 1984, 9–13.

21. Harry DeAngelo, Linda DeAngelo, and Jerold L. Zimmerman, "What's Really Wrong with U.S. Business Schools?" unpublished working paper, University of Rochester, July 2005; Joel M. Podolny, "The Buck Stops (and Starts) at Business School," *Harvard Business Review*, June 2009, 64–66; Khurana, *From Higher Aims to Hired Hands*, 335–345; Andrew J. Policano, "What Price Rankings?" *BizEd*, September–October 2005, 28; Pfeffer and Fong, "The Business School 'Business,'" 1506–1508; and Jeff Wuorio, "The Impact of the Rankings: Multiple Perspectives," *Selections* 1 (2001): 26–37.

22. This concern is not new. Twenty years ago, in their sweeping review of management education, Porter and McKibbin observed, "It is our impression from extensive interviewing that business schools, collectively, have not yet become really serious about the international dimension of management." See Porter and McKibbin, *Management Education and Development*, 319. As a later chapter will show, business schools, by most accounts, appear to have finally become serious about the topic. Most, however, have not yet succeeded in addressing it fully.

23. P. Christopher Earley and Elaine Mosakowski, "Cultural Intelligence," *Harvard Business Review*, October 2004, 139–146.

24. Pankaj Ghemawat, for example, has argued that the degree of global interconnectedness is vastly overstated—for many communication and trade flows, he notes, the international component is only about 10 percent of the total—and that we actually live in "a semi-globalized world, in which neither the bridges nor the barriers between countries can be ignored." See Pankaj Ghemawat, "Why the World Isn't Flat," *Foreign Policy*, March–April 2007, 57.

25. These activities have long been staples of leadership training programs aimed at practicing managers. For an early discussion, see Jay A. Conger, *Learning to Lead* (San Francisco: Jossey-Bass, 1992).

26. Scott Snook, "Leader(ship) Development," Case 9-408-064 (Boston: Harvard Business School, 2007), 5.

27. Podolny, "The Buck Stops (and Starts) at Business School," 66.

28. Herminia Ibarra, Scott Snook, and Laura Guillen Ramo, "Identity-Based Leadership Development," paper prepared for the Colloquium on Leadership: Advancing an Intellectual Discipline, Harvard Business School, April 30, 2008, 2.

29. Vartan Gregorian, "Colleges Must Reconstruct the Unity of Knowledge," *Chronicle of Higher Education*, June 4, 2004, B12.

30. The same might be said of research. It too requires a "scholarship of integration . . . making connections across the disciplines, placing the specialties in larger context, illuminating data in a revealing way . . . serious, disciplined work that seeks to interpret, draw together, and bring new insight to bear on original research." See Ernest L. Boyer, *Scholarship Reconsidered* (Princeton: Carnegie Foundation for the Advancement of Teaching, 1990), 18–19. For a discussion of the link between this kind of research and business school teaching, see Karl E. Weick, "Speaking to Practice: The Scholarship of Integration," *Journal of Management Inquiry* 5 (1996): 251–258.

31. Howard Gardner, *Five Minds for the Future* (Boston: Harvard Business School Press, 2006), 46.

32. Jan Rivkin, "The Strategic Importance of Integrative Skills," *Rotman Magazine*, Winter 2005, 42.

33. Howard Gardner has termed this approach "multiperspectivalism" and distinguishes it from a truly interdisciplinary perspective. He notes, "A multiperspectival approach recognizes that different analytical perspectives can contribute to the elucidation of an issue or problem. While full-fledged disciplinary mastery may be an unattainable goal, individuals of most any age can reasonably be expected to appreciate the complementary strengths of different perspectives." See Gardner, *Five Minds for the Future*, 71–72.

34. Louis B. Barnes, C. Roland Christensen, and Abby J. Hansen, *Teaching and the Case Method*, 3rd ed. (Boston: Harvard Business School Press, 1994), 50.

35. Jeffrey Pfeffer, *Managing with Power* (Boston: Harvard Business School Press, 1992), 8. For two classic academic introductions to this perspective, see James G. March, "The Business Firm as a Political Coalition," *Journal of Politics* 24 (1962): 662–678, and Michael L. Tushman, "A Political Approach to Organizations: A Review and Rationale," *Academy of Management Review* 2 (1977): 206–216.

36. According to research by Daniel Isenberg, senior executives are extremely attuned to these political and organizational realities: "The primary focus of on-line

managerial thinking is organizational and interpersonal process. By 'process' I mean the ways managers bring people and groups together to handle problems and take action . . . 'Who are the key players here, and how can I get their support? Whom should I talk to first? Should I start by getting the production group's input? What kind of signal will that send to the marketing people? I can't afford to lose their commitment in the upcoming discussions on our market strategy.'" See Daniel J. Isenberg, "How Senior Managers Think," *Harvard Business Review*, November–December 1984, 82–83.

37. We thank our colleagues Mark Moore and Dutch Leonard for this distinction.

38. For a detailed look at managerial behavior within large, hierarchical corporations, including approaches to conflict and decision making, see Robert Jackall, *Moral Mazes* (Oxford: Oxford University Press, 1988).

39. For more on the importance of negotiation, discussion, and indirect influence, see Allan R. Cohen and David L. Bradford, *Influence Without Authority* (New York: John Wiley & Sons, 1990).

40. For discussions of the rise of social critics, shareholder activists, and NGOs and the pressures they bring to bear on corporations, see David Vogel, *The Market for Virtue: The Potential and Limits of Corporate Social Responsibility* (Washington, DC: Brookings Institution, 2005), and Michael E. Porter and Mark R. Kramer, "Strategy and Society," *Harvard Business Review*, December 2006, 78–92.

41. For a detailed discussion of the challenges posed by ambiguous, rapidly changing environments and the repertoire of skills required to respond effectively, see Paul J. H. Schoemaker, "The Future Challenges of Business: Rethinking Management Education and Research," *California Management Review* 50 (2008): 119–139.

42. For a definition of ambiguity and how it differs from uncertainty, see Karl E. Weick, *Sensemaking in Organizations* (Thousand Oaks, CA: Sage Publications, 1995), 91–100.

43. William F. Pounds, "The Process of Problem Finding," *Industrial Management Review* 11 (1969): 1. Italics in original.

44. David A. Garvin and Lynne C. Levesque, "Emerging Business Opportunities at IBM (A)," Case 9-304-075 (Boston: Harvard Business School, rev. February 28, 2005), 11.

45. Leonard R. Sayles, *Leadership: Managing in Real Organizations*, 2nd ed. (New York: McGraw-Hill, 1989), 16.

46. The problem is not confined to business school students, but is true of many college graduates. Colleges and universities have been largely unsuccessful in teaching writing and oral communication. See Derek Bok, *Our Underachieving Colleges* (Princeton, NJ: Princeton University Press, 2006), chapter 4.

47. Henry Mintzberg, *The Nature of Managerial Work* (New York: Harper & Row, 1973), 38.

48. For a thoughtful comparison of these two views, see William T. Allen, "Our Schizophrenic Conception of the Business Corporation," *Cardozo Law Review* 14 (1992): 261. For a classic statement of the shareholder perspective, see Milton Friedman, "The Social Responsibility of Business Is to Increase Its Profits," *New York Times Magazine*, September 13, 1970, 32–33, 122, 124, and 126. For an overview of the stakeholder perspective, see Thomas Donaldson and Lee E. Preston, "The Stakeholder Theory of the Corporation: Concepts, Evidence, and Implications," *Academy of Management Review* 20 (1995): 65–91.

49. For a comprehensive introduction to this topic as well as a summary of the empirical evidence, see Vogel, *The Market for Virtue*.

50. Friedrich August von Hayek, "The Pretense of Knowledge," http://nobelprize.org/nobel_prizes/economics/laureats/1974/hayek-lecture.html.

51. See *Be-Know-Do: Leadership the Army Way* (San Francisco: Jossey-Bass, 2004); Scott Snook, "Be, Know, Do: Forming Character the West Point Way," *Compass: A Journal of Leadership* 1 (2004): 16–19, 38; and Scott A. Snook and Rakesh Khurana, "Developing 'Leaders of Character': Lessons from West Point," in R. Gandossy and J. Sonnenfeld, eds., *Leadership and Governance from the Inside Out* (Hoboken, NJ: John Wiley, 2004), 213–232.

52. We have altered the usual sequence of the three components. The Army puts "be" or "being" first because it believes that "leadership starts . . . with the character of the leader . . . with the values and attributes that shape . . . the kind of person you are." See *Be-Know-Do*, 8–9. Although we agree with this view, we have changed the order to better frame the current strengths and weaknesses of graduate business programs.

53. Jeffrey Pfeffer and Robert I. Sutton, *The Knowing-Doing Gap* (Boston: Harvard Business School Press, 2000).

54. David A. Garvin, "Teaching Executives and Teaching MBAs: Reflections on the Case Method," *Academy of Management Learning and Education* 6, no. 3 (2007): 364.

55. This point is well made by Donald A. Schon in his book *Educating the Reflective Practitioner* (San Francisco: Jossey-Bass, 1987).

Chapter 5: Meeting the Challenges of Globalization, Leadership, and Integration

1. Pankaj Ghemawat, "The Globalization of Business Education: Through the Lens of Semiglobalization," *Journal of Management Development* 27 (2008): 402.

2. The good news here is that the current generation of students appears to be more comfortable working with people from different ethnicities and cultures. See Sylvia Ann Hewlett, Laura Sherbin, and Karen Sumberg, "How Gen Y and Boomers will Reshape Your Agenda," *Harvard Business Review*, July–August 2009, 71–76.

3. "Global MBA Rankings 2009," *Financial Times*, http://rankings.ft.com/businessschoolrankings/global-mba-rankings, accessed August 10, 2009. For an earlier set of data on the internationalization of students and faculty in U.S. and European business schools, see Gabriel Hawawini, *Management Education for the 21st Century and the Future of Business Schools* (forthcoming).

4. Ibid.

5. Ghemawat, "The Globalization of Business Education," 392; see also Tarun Khanna and Krishna G. Palepu, *Winning in Emerging Markets* (Boston, MA: Harvard Business Press, 2010).

6. The "Globalization of Business Enterprise" course was developed by Pankaj Ghemawat for use at IESE. For more information on this course, see Pankaj Ghemawat, "Bridging the 'Globalization Gap' at Top Business Schools," working paper, 2009.

7. Ghemawat, "The Globalization of Business Education," 392.

8. Hawawini, *Management Education for the 21st Century and the Future of Business Schools* (forthcoming).

9. Scott Snook, "Leader(ship) Development," Case 9-408-064 (Boston: Harvard Business School, 2007), 1.

10. Benjamin C. Esty, "The Harvard Business School MBA Degree: Educating Leaders, General Managers, or Tradespeople?" working paper, 2007.

11. Rakesh Khurana, *From Higher Aims to Hired Hands* (Princeton, NJ: Princeton University Press, 2007), 357.

12. Ross School of Business, University of Michigan, *Multidisciplinary Action Projects Handbook*, 2008.

13. In a global world, leadership has become increasingly virtual—those in charge of organizations and teams must often lead and influence from a distance. Simulations offer an interesting new opportunity to teach leadership by focusing on the leadership environment, speed, sensemaking in ambiguous environments, and managing virtual teams. Simulations also dovetail well with the learning styles of the current generation of students. For further discussion, see Byron Reeves, Thomas Malone, and Tony O'Driscoll, "Leadership's Online Labs," *Harvard Business Review*, May 2008, 59–65; and Clark Aldrich, *Simulations and the Future of Learning* (San Francisco: Pfeiffer, 2004).

14. Web site of the Rotman School of Management, University of Toronto, http://www.rotman.utoronto.ca/integrativethinking/definition.htm. We are grateful to Mihnea Moldoveanu, Director, Marcel Desautels Center for Integrative Thinking, Rotman School of Management, for generously giving of his time in several conversations about integrative thinking and for sharing his work in this area.

15. Mihnea Moldoveanu and Roger Martin, *The Future of the MBA: Designing the Thinker of the Future* (New York: Oxford University Press, 2008) argues that model building is a key capability that business school academics should aim to transfer to their students.

16. Roger Martin, *The Opposable Mind* (Boston: Harvard Business School Press, 2007) shows many other cases in which abductive reasoning, as it was defined by the American philosopher Charles Sanders Peirce, is significantly more helpful than deductive or inductive reasoning in complex business situations.

17. Ibid.

18. Ibid.

19. Milton Friedman, "The Social Responsibility of Business Is to Increase Its Profits," *New York Times Magazine*, September 13, 1970, 32–33, 122, 124, 126; and Sumantra Ghoshal, "Bad Management Theories Are Destroying Good Management Practices," *Academy of Management Learning and Education* 4, no. 1 (2005): 75–91.

Chapter 6: Innovations in Pedagogy and Course Design

1. Arnold B. Arons, "Critical Thinking and the Baccalaureate Curriculum," *Liberal Education* 1, no. 2 (1985): 142; and Richard Paul and Linda Elder, *Critical Thinking: Tools for Taking Charge of Your Learning and Your Life* (Upper Saddle River, NJ: Pearson/Prentice Hall, 2005). Italics in original.

2. The Critical Analytical Thinking course is very much a work in progress, and what we describe here is the course as it existed in its second incarnation.

3. Arnold B. Arons, "Critical Thinking and the Baccalaureate Curriculum," 142.

4. Tava Olson, "A Critical Look at Critical Thinking," *Operations Research Management Science Today*, April 2008.

5. For example, Design Thinking (Tim Brown, "Design Thinking," *Harvard Business Review*, June 2008, 85–92), a customer-centric innovation process using brainstorming and rapid experimentation; and Systematic Inventive Thinking (Jacob Goldenberg, Roni Horowitz, Amnon Levav, and David Mazursky, "Finding Your Innovation Sweet Spot," *Harvard Business Review*, March 2003, 121–129), a complementary product-centric innovation model based on removing product components (such as buttons on a DVD player), adding more copies of a component with a different function (for example, Gillette's multiblade razor), dividing products into component parts (for instance, modularizing computers and music systems to allow for customization), unifying two tasks in a single component (for example, a suitcase with wheels), and changing the relationship between a product and its environment (such as a sprinkler kit for indoor gardeners).

6. Based on material created by Diego Rodriguez and Alex Kazaks (Institute of Design course instructors) for the Future of MBA Education Colloquium, Harvard Business School, March 6–7, 2008.

7. Brown, "Design Thinking," 88.

8. Interview with Diego Rodriguez (CIA course instructor), February 11, 2008.

9. Brown, "Design Thinking," 88.

10. Ibid., 87.

11. Ibid., 89.

12. Interview with Diego Rodriguez, February 11, 2008.

13. Ross School of Business, University of Michigan, *Multidisciplinary Action Projects Course Handbook*, 2009.

14. Alice Y. Kolb and David A. Kolb, "Learning Styles and Learning Spaces: Enhancing Experiential Learning in Higher Education," *Academy of Management Learning and Education* 4 (2005): 193–212.

15. David A. Kolb, *Experiential Learning: Experience as the Source of Learning and Development* (Englewood Cliffs, NJ: Prentice Hall, 1984); and D. Christopher Kayes, "Experiential Learning and Its Critics: Preserving the Role of Experience in Management Learning and Education," *Academy of Management Learning and Education* 1 (2002): 137–149.

16. Kolb, *Experiential Learning*, 41.

17. Morris T. Keeton and Pamela J. Tate, eds., *Learning by Experience: What, Why, How: New Directions for Experiential Learning* (San Francisco: Jossey Bass, 1978), 2.

18. Joseph A. Raelin, *Work-Based Learning: The New Frontier of Management Development* (Upper Saddle River, NJ: Prentice Hall, 2000), 57.

19. David A. Kolb, "On Management and the Learning Process," in David A. Kolb, Irwin M. Rubin, and James M. McIntyre, eds., *Organizational Psychology: A Book of Readings* (Englewood Cliffs, NJ: Prentice Hall, 1974), 28.

20. Ibid., 30.

21. Ibid.

22. Ibid.

23. Ibid.

24. Ross School of Business, *Multidisciplinary Action Projects Course Handbook*.

25. Some schools are assigning students to practicing managers, who serve as their mentors. For example, a student interested in entrepreneurship may have a venture capital partner as his mentor, with the explicit goal of having the student develop a business plan that will be incubated during the program and implemented upon graduation.

26. Michael Barbaro, "Wal-Mart: The New Washington," *New York Times*, Week in Review, February 3, 2008, 3.

27. Robert J. Shiller, "How Wall Street Learns to Look the Other Way," *New York Times*, February 8, 2005, A25.

28. For a broad overview of the LCA course, see John S. Rosenberg, "An Education in Ethics: Teaching Business Students Life Lessons in Leadership," *Harvard Magazine*, September–October 2006, 42–49, 102–103.

29. For example, The Financial Crisis of 2007–09: Causes and Remedies, taught by several faculty at New York University's Stern School of Business.

30. Jon Elster, "Excessive Ambition," *Capitalism and Society* (forthcoming).

31. Harvard Business School's Designing Organizations for Performance, to be taught by Robert Simons during the 2009–2010 academic year.

32. For example, Chicago Booth's Economic Analysis of Major Policy Issues, taught by Gary Becker, Kevin Murphy, and Edward Snyder; and Harvard Business School's Creating the Modern Financial System, taught by David Moss, and Economic Strategies of Nations: Capitalism, Democracy, and Development, taught by Bruce Scott.

33. For example, Analysis for General Managers, taught by Paul Argenti and Sydney Finkelstein at Dartmouth's Tuck School of Business.

Part II: Institutional Responses

1. The original case studies have been edited and condensed for this book. The longer versions, which remain available as freestanding cases, are Srikant M. Datar, David A. Garvin, and James Weber, "University of Chicago Graduate School of Business," Case 9-308-014 (Boston: Harvard Business School, 2008); Srikant M. Datar, David A. Garvin, and Carin-Isabel Knoop, "INSEAD," Case 9-308-009 (Boston: Harvard Business School, 2008); Srikant M. Datar, David A. Garvin, and Carin-Isabel Knoop, "Center for Creative Leadership," Case 9-308-013 (Boston: Harvard Business School, 2008); Srikant M. Datar, David A. Garvin, and Carin-Isabel Knoop, "Harvard Business School," Case 9-308-012 (Boston: Harvard Business School, 2008); Srikant M. Datar, David A. Garvin, and James Weber, "Yale School of Management," Case 9-308-011 (Boston: Harvard Business School, 2008); and Srikant M. Datar, David A. Garvin, and Carin-Isabel Knoop, "Stanford Graduate School of Business," Case 9-308-010 (Boston: Harvard Business School, 2008).

Chapter 7: University of Chicago Booth School of Business: Flexibility and the Discipline-Based Approach

1. For detailed information on the Chicago Booth class profile and employment placement, see Srikant M. Datar, David A. Garvin, and James Weber, "University of

Chicago Graduate School of Business," Case 9-308-014 (Boston: Harvard Business School, 2008), and the accompanying teaching note, 5-309-016.

2. "The Best B-Schools of 2006," *BusinessWeek*, October 23, 2006.

Chapter 8: INSEAD: The Credo of Globalization

1. INSEAD was founded in 1957 as "Institut Européen d'Administration des Affaires" (European Institute for Business Administration), hence the original acronym that became its trademark name.

2. INSEAD, "Discover INSEAD: Quick Facts," http://www.INSEAD.edu/discover%5FINSEAD/quick_facts.htm, accessed July 3, 2007.

3. "INSEAD Appoints J. Frank Brown as New Dean," Business and Advanced Technology Center, May 19, 2007, http://batc.iuplog.com/default.asp? Item=172356.

4. For further information about class demographics, see Srikant M. Datar, David A. Garvin, and Carin-Isabel Knoop, "INSEAD," Case 9-308-009 (Boston: Harvard Business School, 2008) and the accompanying teaching note, 5-308-119.

5. Sumathi Bala, "The City-State Makes Its Point as a Regional Hub," *Financial Times*, January 26, 2004, http://search.ft.com/nonFtArticle?id=040126001431.

6. Sumathi Bala, "INSEAD's Foothold in the Region," *Financial Times*, December 15, 2003, http://search.ft.com/nonFtArticle?id=031215008794.

7. INSEAD, "Asia Campus," http://www.INSEAD.edu/campuses/asia_campus/index.htm, accessed October 9, 2007.

8. For more details on the exchange programs, see INSEAD, "MBA Programme: Campus Exchange," http://www.INSEAD.edu/mba/life/exchange.htm, accessed July 3, 2007.

9. The school also organized trips to Silicon Valley, China, India, and South Africa, among other destinations. Although these trips were very popular with students, Fatás thought they were of limited value compared with being on-site in Singapore.

10. These included Sino-Taiwanese relations, Asian regional integration, the two Koreas, 9/11 and the politics of Islam and South East Asia, and Indonesia and the overthrow of the Suharto regime.

11. For more details please see INSEAD, "FAQS," http://www.INSEAD.edu/discover%5FINSEAD/faqs.htm, accessed July 3, 2007.

12. The Wharton School of the University of Pennsylvania, "Playing Across Three Continents: MBA Students Participate in Simulation Through the Wharton/INSEAD Alliance," http://www.wharton.upenn.edu/whartonfacts/news_and_events/features/2007/f_2007_10_684.html, accessed December 16, 2007.

13. Ibid.

14. "Alliance Between Wharton and INSEAD: Globalization," *Almanac*, April 3, 2001, http://www.upenn.edu/almanac/v47/n28/Wharton-INSEAD.html.

15. Sixteen Centers of Excellence focused on topics such as corporate social responsibility, strategy, health care, and leadership-supported faculty research. The faculty also engaged in case writing, capturing eight of the top ten European Case Clearing House Awards in 2006.

16. "INSEAD Appoints J. Frank Brown as New Dean."

Chapter 9: The Center for Creative Leadership:
Leadership Development at the Core

1. "Center for Creative Leadership Names New President; John R. Ryan, Chancellor of State University of New York, to Assume Helm at global Leadership Development and Research Institution," *PR Newswire*, March 7, 2007.

2. For more details, please see the Center for Creative Leadership's Web site, http://www.ccl.org/leadership.

3. Center for Creative Leadership, "Quick Facts," http://www.ccl.org/leadership/about/glance.aspx, accessed July 8, 2007.

4. Center for Creative Leadership, http://www.ccl.org/leadership/index.aspx, accessed July 18, 2007.

5. Cynthia D. McCauley et al., "Our View of Leadership Development," in Ellen Van Velsor et. al., eds., *Handbook of Leadership Development* (San Francisco: John Wiley & Sons, 2004).

6. Ibid.

7. Linda Anderson, "Essential Step for Making the Most of a Course—Preparation," *Financial Times*, May 14, 2007.

8. McCauley et al., "Our View of Leadership Development."

9. Ibid.

10. Center for Creative Leadership, "About CCL: Recognition and Honors," http://www.ccl.org/leadership/about/recognition.aspx?pageID=27, accessed June 29, 2007.

11. "Center for Creative Leadership Ranks Seventh in Executive Education," *Financial Times*, May 18, 2007.

12. Center for Creative Leadership, "CCL Network Associates," http://www.ccl.org/leadership/capabilities/networkAssociates.aspx?pageId=102, accessed July 8, 2007.

13. "Center for Creative Leadership Names New President."

14. Center for Creative Leadership, "CCL at a Glance," http://www.ccl.org/leadership/about/glance.aspx, accessed July 8, 2007.

15. Center for Creative Leadership, *Annual Report 2006–2007*, http://www.ccl.org/leadership/pdf/aboutCCL/CCL2007AnnualReport.pdf.

16. Center for Creative Leadership, "CCL at a Glance."

17. Center for Creative Leadership, *Annual Report 2006–2007*.

18. Anderson, "Essential Step for Making the Most of a Course."

19. Center for Creative Leadership Web site, http://www.ccl.org/leadership, accessed June 29, 2007.

20. Sarah Glover and Meena Wilson, *Unconventional Wisdom: A Brief History of CCL's Pioneering Research and Innovation* (Center for Creative Leadership, 2006), 7. Available at http://www.ccl.org/leadership/pdf/research/UnconventionalWisdom.pdf.

21. Cynthia D. McCauley et al., "360-Degree Feedback," in Van Velsor et. al., eds., *Handbook of Leadership Development*.

22. Ibid.

23. Ibid.

24. Most psychometric assessment data tended to be collected on individuals being treated for psychological problems. See Glover and Wilson, *Unconventional Wisdom*, 9.

25. For more details, see Owen C. Gadeken, "Through the Looking Glass: A New Way to Learn Program Management," *Defense AT&L*, September 1, 2004, http://www.thefreelibrary.com/Through+the+looking+glass:+a+new+way+to+learn+program+management-a0140409615.

26. Ibid.

27. Ibid.

28. MIT Sloan School of Management, "Sloan Innovation Period," http://mitsloan.mit.edu/mba/academics/sip.php, accessed November 12, 2007.

Chapter 10: Harvard Business School: General Management and the Focus on Practice

1. C. Roland Christensen, "Teaching with Cases at the Harvard Business School," in Louis B. Barnes, C. Roland Christensen, and Abby Hansen, *Teaching and the Case Method* (Watertown, MA: Harvard Business School Press, 1994), 34.

2. "Harvard Has Plan to Aid Shoe Trade," *New York Times*, May 17, 1913, http://query.nytimes.com/mem/archive-free/pdf?res=9D06E7DE143FE633A2575ACIA9639C946296D6CF.

3. David A. Garvin, "Making the Case: Professional Education for the World of Practice," *Harvard Magazine* (September–October 2003), 60.

4. Ibid.

5. For further details on class demographics and placement, as well as faculty composition, see Srikant M. Datar, David A. Garvin, and Carin-Isabel Knoop, "Harvard Business School," Case 9-308-012 (Boston: Harvard Business School, 2008) and the accompanying teaching note, 5-309-014.

6. Harvard Business School Web site, http://www.hbs.edu/mba, accessed February 7, 2008.

7. Harvard Business School, "Entrepreneurship: It Can Be Taught," http://www.hbs.edu/entrepreneurship/newbusiness/2002spring_3.html, accessed October 23, 2007.

8. Harvard Business School, "Academics: Term II Courses," http://www.hbs.edu/mba/academics/term2.html, accessed October 23, 2007.

9. Harvard Business School, "Entrepreneurship: It Can Be Taught."

10. "Harvard Business School Offers New Course in Ethics," June 21, 2004, http://www.hbs.edu/news/releases/062104_ethics.html.

11. Harvard Business School Web site, http://www.hbs.edu/mba, accessed February 7, 2008.

12. Sean Silverthorne, "What Great American Leaders Teach Us," *HBS Working Knowledge*, April 12, 2004, http://hbswk.hbs.edu/item/4053.html.

13. Manda Salls, "HBS Celebrates Social Enterprise Initiative," *HBS Working Knowledge*, March 29, 2004, http://hbswk.hbs.edu/item/4021.html.

14. "Featured Research," http://www.hbs.edu/global/research-larc.html, accessed February 13, 2008.

Chapter 11: Yale School of Management:
Integration and Large-Scale Change

1. For further details on class composition and placement, as well as extensive course descriptions and transition cost data, see Srikant M. Datar, David A. Garvin, and James Weber, "Yale School of Management," Case 9-308-011 (Boston: Harvard Business School, 2008) and the accompanying teaching note, 5-109-017.

2. James Baron, Joel Podolny, and Heidi Brooks, "Leadership and Commitment," Case 07-028 (New Haven, CT: Yale School of Management, rev. August 31, 2007).

3. Joel M. Podolny, "Curriculum Reform at the Yale School of Management: Making the MBA More Relevant," draft.

Chapter 12: Stanford Graduate School of Business:
Customization and Large-Scale Change

1. Stanford Graduate School of Business, "Curriculum—A Bold New Vision," http://www.gsb.stanford.edu/mba/academics/curriculum.html, accessed July 11, 2007.

2. Stanford Graduate School of Business, "Distinguished History," http://www.gsb.stanford.edu/history/, accessed July 11, 2007.

3. Stanford Graduate School of Business, "Facts and Figures," http://www.gsb.stanford.edu/about/facts.html, accessed July 11, 2007.

4. For further details on class demographics, placement, and faculty background, see Srikant M. Datar, David A. Garvin, and Carin-Isabel Knoop, "Stanford Graduate School of Business," Case 9-308-010 (Boston: Harvard Business School, 2008) and the accompanying teaching note, 5-309-015.

5. Della Bradshaw, "Stanford to Opt for the Personal Approach. Curriculum Revamp: The School Is to Move Away from the 'One Size Fits All' MBA in Favour of Tutorials and Mentoring," *Financial Times*, June 12, 2006.

6. Stanford Graduate School of Business, "New Curriculum," http://www.gsb.stanford.edu/about/how_we_teach.html, accessed July 11, 2007.

7. Ibid.

8. Ibid.

9. Ibid.

10. Ibid.

11. Robert Weisman, "Stanford to Let Students Tailor MBA Studies," *Boston Globe*, June 6, 2006.

12. Ibid.

13. Ibid.

14. Ibid.

15. One perspectives course, Ethics and Management, was taken in the second half of the winter quarter; a final perspectives course, Synthesis Seminar, was taken in the spring quarter of the second year.

16. Electives were available in the following areas: Accounting, Entrepreneurship, Finance, Global Management, Human Resources, Information Technology, Leadership, Managerial Economics, Marketing, Operations, Organizational Behavior, Political Economics, Public Management, and Strategic Management.

17. Weisman, "Stanford to Let Students Tailor MBA Studies."

18. Ibid.

19. Ibid.

Chapter 13: Conclusion: Business Schools at a Crossroads

1. Kabir Chibber, "Business Schools Face Test of Faith," BBC News, http://news.bbc.co.uk/2/hi/business/7941385.stm, accessed March 18, 2009.

2. Kelley Holland, "Is It Time to Retrain B-Schools?" *New York Times*, Sunday Business, March 15, 2009, 1–2.

3. "Jack Welch's Lessons for Success," *Fortune*, January 25, 1993, 88.

4. Alison Damast, "Loan Crisis Hits the MBA World," *BusinessWeek*, January 22, 2009.

5. In 2009, anecdotal reports from both students and business school placement officers suggested that many financial services firms were making prior experience in finance a prerequisite for hiring. Such a requirement further raises the barrier to career switching.

6. Thomas Philippon and Ariell Reshef, "Wages and Human Capital in the U.S. Financial Industry: 1909-2006," NBER working paper no. 14644, National Bureau of Economic Research, Cambridge, MA, January 2009.

7. Bill George, "Seven Lessons for Leading in a Crisis," *Wall Street Journal*, March 5, 2009, http://online.wsj.com/article/SB123551729786163925.html.

8. Ibid. This quotation has been attributed to several sources. For further discussion see Jack Rosenthal, "A Terrible Thing to Waste," *New York Times*, August 2, 2009, http://www.nytimes.com/2009/08/02/magazine/02FOB-onlanguage-t.html.

9. Some readers may be concerned that efforts to shape students' values could easily become a form of indoctrination. This is a legitimate concern, and one that should not be taken lightly. For a discussion of this tension, as well as arguments supporting the conclusion that "it is perfectly possible to teach moral reasoning or prepare students to be enlightened citizens without having instructors impose their personal ideologies or policy views on their students," see Derek Bok, *Our Underachieving Colleges* (Princeton, NJ: Princeton University Press, 2006), 58–66. The quotation is from page 65.

10. Aspen Institute, *Where Will They Lead? 2008 MBA Student Attitudes About Business and Society* (New York: Aspen Institute, Center for Business Education, 2008), cited in Jeffrey Pfeffer, "Leadership Development in Business Schools: An Agenda for Change," research paper no. 2016, Stanford Graduate School of Business, February 2009, 11.

11. *Final Report of the AACSB International Impact of Research* (Tampa: AACSB International, 2008), 39.

12. Leslie Wayne, "A Promise to Be Ethical in an Era of Immorality," *New York Times*, May 30, 2009, B1, B4.

13. Harvard Medical School, "Facts and Figures 2008–2009," http://hms.harvard.edu/hms/facts.asp; and Harvard Medical School, "Harvard Medical School Admissions," http://hms.harvard.edu/admissions/default.asp, accessed April 2, 2009.

14. Herbert A. Simon, "The Business School: A Problem in Organization Design," *Journal of Management Studies* 4, no. 1 (1967): 16.

15. For a discussion of this approach, used by Harvard Medical School as part of a broader reform of the curriculum, see Daniel C. Tosteson, S. James Adelstein, and Susan T. Carver, eds., *New Pathways to Medical Education* (Cambridge, MA: Harvard University Press, 1994), 96–98.

16. For three diverse sources that describe this discontent, see "Making Sense of Populist Rage," *BusinessWeek*, March 30, 2009, 22–31; Gerald F. Seib, "Taming Populist Anger Is Big Test," *Wall Street Journal*, April 3, 2009, A2; and many of the entries in the blog How to Fix Business Schools, http://blogs.harvardbusiness.org/how-to-fix-business-schools/2009/03/are-business-schools-to-blame.html.

17. Robert Weisman, "Degree of Uncertainty," *Boston Globe Magazine*, March 29, 2009, 24.

Index

About the Authors

Srikant M. Datar is the Arthur Lowes Dickinson Professor of Accounting at Harvard Business School. He has taught in the MBA, General Management, and Advanced Management programs and served as Senior Associate Dean for Executive Education, Faculty Recruiting and Development, and Research. He also teaches in executive programs and consults with organizations worldwide.

Datar researches management control and strategy implementation. He is coauthor of the *Cost Accounting: A Managerial Emphasis*, and author or coauthor of over forty articles and over thirty HBS case studies and technical notes. He has served on several journals' editorial boards.

Datar graduated with distinction from the University of Bombay and with gold medals from the Indian Institute of Management Ahmedabad and the Institute of Cost and Works Accountants of India. He also qualified as a chartered accountant in India. He received his MS in statistics, AM in economics, and PhD in business from Stanford University. Before joining the School, he was a faculty member at Carnegie Mellon's Graduate School of Industrial Administration and at the Graduate School of Business at Stanford University, where he received the George Leland Bach Teaching Award and the Distinguished Teaching Award, respectively. He serves on the boards of Novartis AG, ICF International, KPIT Cummins Info Systems Ltd., Stryker Corporation, and Harvard Business Publishing.

David A. Garvin is the C. Roland Christensen Professor of Business Administration at Harvard Business School. He has taught in the MBA and Advanced Management programs, and served as chair of the Elective Curriculum and faculty chair of the Teaching and Learning Center. He also teaches in executive programs and has consulted for over fifty organizations globally.

Garvin's research interests are in general management and strategic change. He is the author or coauthor of ten books, including *General Management: Processes and Action*, *Learning in Action*, and *Education for Judgment*; over thirty articles; and over fifty HBS case studies, multimedia exercises, and technical notes. He is a three-time winner of the McKinsey Award, and has won the *Sloan Management Review*'s Beckhard Prize as well as *Harvard Magazine*'s Smith-Weld Prize.

Garvin received an AB summa cum laude from Harvard and a PhD in economics from MIT, where he held a National Science Foundation Graduate Fellowship and a Sloan Foundation Fellowship. Before joining the School, he was an economist for the Federal Trade Commission and the Sloan Commission on Government and Higher Education. He has served on the Board of Overseers of the Malcolm Baldrige National Quality Award, the Manufacturing Studies Board of the National Research Council, and the board of directors of Emerson Hospital.

Patrick G. Cullen is a research associate at Harvard Business School. His current research explores the relationship between professional schools and their constituencies, in particular the evolution of business schools.

Cullen received a PhD in management from the Judge Business School, University of Cambridge, an EdM from the Harvard Graduate School of Education, and a BA from the University of Nottingham. Before joining the School, he was an Assistant Vice President for Research at The Association to Advance Collegiate Schools of Business and worked for Princeton University Press and the University of California Press.